M J

MUHAMMAD IN THE QUR'AN

THE TASK AND THE TEXT

MUHAMMAD IN THE QUR'AN

THE TASK AND THE TEXT

Kenneth Cragg

MELISENDE
LONDON

Muhammad in the Qur'an
by Kenneth Cragg

First published 2001
by
Melisende
39 Chelmsford Road
London E18 2PW
Tel. +44 (0) 20 8498 9768
Fax +44 (0) 20 8504 2558
E mail: melisende@cwcom.net
www.melisende.cwc.net

ISBN 1 901764 13 3

Edited by Leonard Harrow
Printed in England by the St Edmundsbury Press

CONTENTS

'Recite in the Name of thy Lord who created.'
(Surah 96. 1)

'Your sole liability is the thing preached.'
(Surahs 5.99, 13.40, 24.53, 29.18, 36.17
and 42.48)

'You have in hand a great undertaking.'
(Surah 68.4)

'Have We not made you to be open of heart? Have We not lifted from
you the burden that was breaking down your back and have We not
established your reputation?'
(Surah 94.1-4)

'Comparably no previous messenger ever came to those in earlier times
of whom they did not say: "He is either a sorcerer or he is mad." Is this
a habit they have passed down to each other?'
(Surah 51.51-53)

'Is it that you are distressing your very soul with grief over the way
they are—so unbelieving of the message?'
(Surah 18.6)

'The apostle said: "Lord, my people have been altogether dismissive of
this Qur'an." It has been Our way in the case of every prophet to have
him experience enmity from those who are evil bent. But in your Lord
there is all you need to guide and sustain you.'
(Surah 25.30-31)

'Say: "God is all the witness I need between me and you."'
(Surah 29.52)

'Await with patience what your Lord determines.'
(Surah 76. 24)

[See also page 211]

INTRODUCTION

How sacred Scriptures, in all religions, came about and how thereafter, they came to be the deeply venerated possessions they are among their faithful, are two closely related perplexities for those who stand outside them. 'My doctrine shall drop as the rain, my speech shall distil as the dew,' sings the famous 'Song of Moses', the exordium in the biblical Book of Deuteronomy. The lilt even of the English translation is beautifully poetical but did ever Scriptures come that way 'like dew on the grass' or 'the gentle rain from heaven'?

Moreover, in this case—as so often—the 'my' is not 'his'. A nameless author is devising to be Moses. Again what is there is not, in any normal sense, 'doctrine'. The Hebrew might better be: 'What is to be received,' the poetic muse that kindles into eloquence and so bequeaths an ever open text, for which 'dew on grass' makes very slender analogy.

How then did it truly eventuate in its first origin? Why did it find perpetuation to be the hallowed repository of a community of faith persisting by virtue of the status it enjoyed—a status with which they endowed it? 'Distil' is at once an apt and tantalising word, telling what is gradual, sequential, cumulative, what 'lets fall and grows,' 'exudes and imparts itself minutely.' Thus 'instil' comes to mind and what we are seeking moves out from natural into mental process, away from weeping clouds and herbal arts and into the psyche of the yearning prophet.

Nowhere is this double question of the whence of prophethood through inspiration, and the age-long sacredness of the Scripture that ensued, more intriguing than in the story of the Qur'an of Islam. It is a Scripture that sees itself finalising all others insofar as these are consistent with itself. Inside it, Muhammad's prophethood is severely singular since, in Quranic terms, Allah spoke through none other. Its incidence is through twenty-three years of his adult life and during these, according to the persistent view of his fiercely possessive community, his receiving of it came to pass in the necessary abeyance of authorial powers, so that it might, thereby, be more assuredly, and aptly Allah's word alone. No sacred word then is more literally 'divine' than the text of Islam's Qur'an. Yet

1

throughout, in every Surah or Chapter, on every page, the persona of Muhammad is paramount. He is the perpetual addressee in the reiterated command: 'Say ...' by which the reactions of his hearers in Mecca are countered and reproved. Though his personal name occurs only four times—itself an index to how far he is fused into his office as 'envoy of Allah'—he is everywhere the immediate agency whereby the text supervenes on the situation in which everywhere he is crucial to its incidence.

The entire event by which the Qur'an arrives to be the Arabic revelation in which its heavenly bestowal transpires, Muhammad is the personal crux whereby it is believed to happen. The sequences of the Qur'an correspond with the years of his 'inspiration', the *wahy* by which it was received and uttered to become, by inscription, the Book of Allah. Those years, with their antecedent preparation in his biography, are known in Islam as the *Sirah*, the 'career' he underwent, the 'course' of his story as the concomitant of the Qur'an in his reception of its divine 'sending'.

The purpose and hope of these chapters is to study what might be described as 'the soul of the *Sirah*'. How might we think our way into the psyche of Muhammad in the incidence of a sacred text to which he was the unique party, the decisively solitary and entirely crucial 'apostle'? The study is made the more difficult, even dubious, by the fact that, traditionally, Islam disallows that he was a 'party' at all in the Qur'an. It cherishes the theme of his complete authorial absence from the text. The notion that it was 'his Book' would deny its being Allah's. That age-long insistence needs respect. Believing communities have to be allowed their own believing versions about what they have in trust. Authorship anyway, even in human secular texts, is always a teasing and troubling notion.

Even so, and with due regard for the susceptibilities of Muslim orthodoxy, what is beyond contention is that Muhammad is steadily addressed in the Qur'an in insistently individual terms. He is denominated as 'enmantled', 'designated', 'of a noble rank', 'bent to a mighty task'. He is the theme of divine 'celebration' in which angels and men are enjoined to share. All these deep valuations of his own being and identity are given to fall from his own lips. The pronoun 'thou' is everywhere. It reverberates through the text. While normally Hebrew prophets had the formula: 'Thus says the Lord,' Muhammad has the direct imperative: 'Say ...' He has to be the very voice of God.

It seems fair, then, to seek to study how this superb destiny had place inside the psyche of the personal Muhammad. It is a study which has rarely been ventured—rarely from within Islam because of the ideology about the Qur'an which disallows it as being both unnecessary and deplorable, as lacking both in devout scruple and sincere commitment. It has sometimes and sadly been ventured by outsiders to Islam whose ends in view were calumny and false accusation. Muhammad was an adventurer, a cheat, an impostor, a self-pretentious dupe—or duper. His deliverances were a self-serving alibi for the overweening pride of ambition.

Such hostile malign animadversions, totally repudiated here, do not begin to measure the genuine issues. They ride roughshod over Muslim integrity and disqualify themselves from the real onus of a task they distort and despise. We only begin to explore 'the soul in the *Sirah*' when we recognise both the reality of Islamic faith-keeping and of the life-story that gave it being. Scriptures underlying faith-communities are never appreciated in studied rejection of the communities they have in their possession. Or, as T S Eliot has it in another context in words we will cite in Chapter 3:

> ... the words sufficed
> To compel the recognition they preceded.

It is their sufficiency to compel the recognition that shapes the study they must undergo. Salient to that study in respect of the Qur'an must be the role of the personal psyche in the entire experience of prophethood, the discharge of the obligations it imposed in the there and then of revelation received and mediated.

What must it have meant within that psyche for Muhammad to be—as Islam understands—'upon a mighty task', one upon whom 'is cast a weighty word,' 'of a high creating'? And these affirmations about him also coming from him as their voicing? When, in due course, Muhammad believed he could no longer remain only an ethical teacher and the Hijrah to Medina happened, what must it have meant, within himself, to find himself saying, on several occasions: 'Obey God and obey the apostle'? In that Medinan context there were many other situations where the text inevitably impinged on episodes in which vital personal interests were at stake. It could not have been otherwise, so closely was the *Sirah* occasion to the text, the Qur'an committed to the *Sirah*.

And through all, once it had been enunciated in Surah 33, there was the aura of the *Tasliyah*, studied in Chapter 6, where—via Muhammad's own lips—the Qur'an enjoins the 'calling down of blessing' on him, an injunction Muslims fulfil at every mention of his name. There is,

3

throughout, this strange first party/third party dimension with the Prophet, the 'I' speaking and also the 'he' the theme. That there is a profound meaning both latent in, and told by, the one soul, the identified psyche, cannot be in doubt.

But why a study, surely valid in its purport, to be proposed and ventured from outside Islam? The question certainly presses, in that Islamic auspices would be more readily expected, more naturally assumed. The answer must partly be because the task has been so widely omitted inside Islam. Maybe an alien venture can stimulate a domestic one, the better to read its way.

That what is at issue is essentially a religious problem all faiths incur is evident enough and sufficient warrant for what otherwise might seem intrusion. Indeed, in our contemporary world, no faiths have any utterly private duties. A Christian mind, addressing the phenomenon of Muhammad as the Qur'an's sole addressee, might seem, at first glance, to be at special disadvantage, thanks to the long antipathies the two faiths have harboured. On the contrary, there are intriguing aspects, to be explored here in Chapters 7 and 8, of differing 'solutions' to a common burden, namely the inter-relation of what is divine and what is human in the incidence of sacred Scriptures. That both dimensions are present and crucial is implicit in their being such. A potentially mediating concept of 'agency' or 'on-behalf-ness' may be discerned in both which may help to moderate, if not resolve, long centuries of incomprehension and self-frustrated controversy.

In any event, it may serve well to bring together that way 'God via Muhammad Qur'an-wise' and 'God in Christ', as Christian faith holds it to have been. Latent in any such venture must be the hope of a Christian appreciation of Islam and of an Islamic appreciation of why Christians believe as they do in Incarnation and the Cross. For this may follow, however tentatively, from genuine depth of mind and sympathy, whether in the prophetology explicit in Islam or in the Christology that makes Christianity the faith it is.

These inter-faith hopes aside, there is the interior self-duty of Islam which circumspect study may serve. What transpired existentially in the soul of Muhammad ibn 'Abdallah in the crowded, burdened, distilling sequences of the *Sirah*? Without the Qur'an's incidence it would not have been what it was: via the Qur'an's incidence it became the personal saga of the sole prophet-envoy of Allah. Can the classic view well persist which holds that Muhammad had no part in what the Qur'an contains, receiving it rather word by word by a celestial mediation so that it might be the more infallibly God's? Need it be assumed that to be incontrovertibly from Allah it must be free of all fallible human factors? For then how could we take the manifestly entailed persona as 'party' to it?

The concern for authenticity is entirely scrupulous and only so could it be aptly religious. But is the scruple rightly placed if it fails to do justice to the participatory agency present in the actuality? The *Sirah* and the eventuation of the Book are one history. What Muslim scholars know as *asbab al-nuzul*, 'the occasions of revelation', are the time-places of Muhammad's individual career.

Could he, then, have been at their psychic centre without being acutely alerted to his own identity? Was that identity, from the summons of Surah 96.1, not always a dual one—that of Muhammad Rasul Allah and Muhammad ibn 'Abdallah? What he was given to say so far turned on the significance of his own self.

The present study, accordingly, hopes to develop the several aspects of this significance of 'Muhammad in the Qur'an'. That he was indeed 'party to it' in the terms of Chapter 1 here, needs to be carefully circumscribed so that it does not violate what Muslims intend about its being 'God's speech' in their traditional account of Muhammad's 'neutrality' inside its contents. For it is precisely that conviction about its revelatory status as *Qawl Allah* or 'what Allah said' that must turn on the person of Muhammad as its human *sine qua non*. For to none other was the Qur'an committed.

Readers aware of earlier studies on my part in Quranic themes may wonder about the concern of this one. The focus here on 'the soul in the *Sirah*' was not in hand elsewhere. *The Event of the Qur'an* (1973, 2nd ed. 1994) overlaps only partially in that it had to do with the phenomenon of the Book in its time and place and only incidentally with the inner psyche in its incidence. *Readings in the Qur'an* (1988, new ed. 1999) aimed to facilitate the approach to it of new readers, exploring the problems of translation, of Surah-sequence, and contemporary relevance. The last was also the emphasis in *Returning to Mount Hira'* (1994). This did study the locale of Muhammad's meditation prior to the summons to the prophetic task and some of the factors that induced it. But 'returning' there was directed towards 'a theology worthy of God', 'a polity worthy of humanity' and 'relationships worthy of faith'—all in the contemporary scene that is ours today. There was then what was meant to be 'a final quest of Muhammad' bearing on the present study but differently pursued.

A recent *Islam among the Spires* (2000) takes up in a very specific context the issue of how 'God's word' has been, and might be seen, as bearing on the temper of religious authority *vis-à-vis* a secularity stemming from technology or agnosticism. That theme is only latent here, though *Islam among the Spires* proved, in retrospect, something of a seedbed for what is ventured here.

These nine chapters are also something of a foray into comparative theology but only in the hope of servicing an Islamics as any lively orientalism might. Dogmatics have far too long precluded the kind of quest for an inter-religious mind that could circumvent, and then rightly undertake, the confusions and enmities of the past, in some will to mutual interpretation. So much of what goes for 'dialogue' seems first to evacuate meaning in order to achieve meeting, so when meeting happens we are not authentically there with what we should be bringing. It is as if we so fear to seem subversive of the other that we fail to be openly conversant. The sound way surely is to identify all we can for community across disparity and let what remains honestly at odds draw from, and speak into, what unites.

Arabic terms are used here with only the minimal pointing that indicates the *'ain* and *hamza* breathings, as in 'Abd, Qur'an and *I'jaz*. There is a degree of necessary overlap between chapters, seeing that titles and epithets relating to the Prophet have their distinctive accents in a common territory.

There is one further point. It has been customary for long years in the West to ask whether Muhammad was truly 'a prophet', 'the final Prophet', as if Christians would have to give a negative answer if they were to hold fast their Christian faith. For these chapters it is not the question to ask. Rather it is a duty to move from the undoubted fact (irrespective of the other question) that Islam has a confident and altogether positive answer. That is a fact of the situation with which all intelligent relation must begin.

We do so here without prejudice either way. In the courteous and open desire not to start with negation (which forecloses all issues), we can better seek the positive themes that bear upon what 'prophethood' from and for Allah can rightly be. They will locate what questions matter. If, for example, all we humans need from God is guidance, good advice, exhortation and reminder, then it will mean that ignorance and forgetfulness are our only problem. A more radical view of humanity will conclude that we are in need, from God, of more than 'education' and 'information'.

These we can deny and defy. Thus maybe the more than prophethood we need will constrain us to look to God for 'the Saviour'. That larger question absorbs and transcends the other.

Chapter 1
PARTNER TO THE QUR'AN

i

'Partner to' or 'Party to'—either term will do if we are caring for an understanding of the role of Muhammad in reception of the Qur'an. It has long been an insistence of Muslims that the Prophet was in no sense the 'author' of the Book. On any orthodox view of the nature of the Islamic Scripture he could in no way have been its devisor nor its designer. There is not only the matter of his assumed 'illiteracy', his state of being *ummi*—explored later. There is the larger 'illiteracy', or self-abeyance required in prophetic receiving of any divine Scripture when understood in Quranic terms.

Yet, resolute as this Islamic perception is as to what being 'God's language' entails, there is no doubt of a human 'party to' its coming to be in earth-borne time and place. The very inspiration that grants it on human lips must find these in the personal order of things. They will occupy some biography and employ it in terms of whose it is, where it transpires and how it belongs within and beyond its own particular locale. Even centuries may come to date themselves from it.

It is this situation of prophethood and capacity finding each other, and their mutuality, which are here our study. Muhammad-in-the-Qur'an could equally well be the-Qur'an-in-Muhammad. The inter-fusion could be stated either way. The sequences of the Book belong closely with those of the *Sirah*, or prophetic career (through the years 610-632) of Muhammad ibn 'Abdallah. They divide, for either, at the watershed of the Hijrah in 622. The event that was pivotal in the life-story of the Prophet also serves to date revelations as being either Meccan or Medinan, i.e. precedent or subsequent to that defining event. Thus every Surah (save the ninth) has its calendar place—however composite the contents may be—either side that crisis of transition and as the clue to exegesis.

There is throughout the Qur'an a steady alternation of the personal pronoun singular and personal pronouns plural, with verbs likewise, the former addressing Muhammad, the latter Muhammad addressing his hearers, all in the second person. Many times the hearers are in the third person, in verdicts about them and their response to his pleas and meanings. This steady drama of addressing and addressed, being the core of the Quranic situation, thoroughly engages Muhammad as 'party' to the Qur'an, the Qur'an as 'partnered' by Muhammad. The Scripture in its entirety belongs with a historical and biographical incidence as its very *raison d'être*.[1] Reciprocally, it has its being such by the prior *raison d'être* in the divine will that there should be the Qur'an in Arabic on Arab earth. What is prior fulfils itself in what is given, Muhammad being, in instrumental terms, the partner in the whole.

Thought on this 'partner' status of Muhammad is at the very centre of Islamic possession of the Qur'an. It lies at the heart of the classic conviction about his being entirely passive in respect of its contents, albeit crucial to its utterance. That long-standing belief needs to be taken out of all crude polemic and sensitively weighed for all that it involves of due concern for right possession.

It is is with due deference to it that Qur'an readership might venture implicit study into the living dimensions of the Book itself. If, as will be argued in Chapter 2, there can be a historical geography of the Qur'an, can there also be—with proper reverence—a biographical psychology? When revelation addresses its messenger in urgently personal terms: 'Did We not find thee destitute and enrich thee?' gathering past vicissitudes into a present mission, is it not fair to ask what, inwardly, the tidings meant? There is inescapably an ego present at the heart of all personhood—not first or, hopefully at all, in any kindling selfish sense, but actually in the evident sense of what cannot both be, and not be, in what the meaning is. There is no 'being sent' that happens in the world that is not known within the soul.

It will not, therefore, be unduly bold or religiously irreverent to study the inwardness of Muhammad's mission in its coming to him and his going with it. There could be no divorcing awareness of sentness from an awareness of self. The more miraculously external to him—as classic thesis holds—the more startlingly internal to his soul. Those who deplore inquiry into the psyche interior to that mystery hardly do justice to the integrity of their conviction.

---

[1] *Raison d'être* here in the sense of how it fulfils the need that it should be. In Islamic faith the ultimate reason why the Qur'an 'exists' eternally and in earthly Arabic is the divine will to reveal. See further Chapter 7 and 'the preserved Tablet.'

Iqra' b-ismi Rabbika, 'Recite in the Name of thy Lord,' could be in no way an anonymous experience, the less so when promptly confronted by the 'Nay! Not so!' of a hostile society (Surah 96.1-15), and three times summoning Muhammad to 'consider', i.e., 'form thy view concerning' the encounter in its meaning. Such frequent calls on the Prophet to weigh inwardly the sequel to his words argue a duty of ours to study his part in their contents, unless we assume some strangely bifurcated world of revelation.

Or, in the complex world of Medinan power, what might have been the significance within the psyche of being coupled uniquely with Allah in the precept to Muslims: 'Obey God and the Apostle'? Being then 'wrapped in a mantle' was more than a verbal mission and had become a supreme status in political terms. Indeed, the whole saga of prophethood had been from the outset an encounter about status, about an advocacy of God's unity inseparably associated—as in the *Shahadah*—with its final mentor in Muhammad himself.[2] To hold that such sustained crises of emotional and personal intensity belonged to Muhammad's inner self, and—as such—deserve to be pondered means no suspicion as to sincerity. Rather it has to be the way in which that sincerity is acknowledged. For, otherwise, the very task to which sincerity belonged would stay unprobed.

Nor would any such study be a mere academic exercise, still less an intention to provoke controversy. To enquire about the element of inwardness in the recipience of a Qur'an 'sent down upon thy heart' (Surahs 2.97, 26.194 and 42.24), said to Muhammad as for ever and only the sole recipient of such a tiding, is to care rightly about 'God's speech' objectively conveyed there. We are not then attributing the 'genesis' of the Qur'an to Muhammad, nor—in any final sense—its 'composition'. We are seeking to understand how these, with wholly divine initiative, engaged the Prophet's 'heart and mind', staying, that is, inside Islam's own premises.

It is noteworthy that the personal name 'Muhammad' occurs a mere four times in the Qur'an (Surah 3.144, 33.40, 47.2 and 48.29). All assert that he is *Rasul-Allah* while 33.40 notes that he has no surviving male and heir,[3] and identifying him also as 'the seal of the prophets'. That

---

[2] 'Mentor' seems the right word here, meaning that he 'presides over what must ever be had in mind by others,' be the active 'referent' and so 'counsellor' for believers. The word chimes well with the term *dhikr* as a title of the Qur'an and as the action of Muhammad, i.e., 'Reminder of the Reminder'.

[3] 'Muhammad is not the father of any man among you.' This absence of male heirs was not only a deep human grief, but a significant political fact.

the name figures so rarely surely means that the apostolate masters his identity. Yet in doing so it makes his life-span crucial (3.144) and he deserving of unswerving loyalty (48.29).

Is it not then precisely in his person being taken comprehensively into the prophetic office that the inner selfhood of the man belongs, with the Qur'an in every realm of its becoming the Book it is? The Islamic faith that can only rightly acknowledge such 'becoming' as the earthly side of divine *Tanzil*—and so doing recognise an open 'mystery'[4]—is thereby more deeply committed than any agnostic to the human agency central to it.

At every point in that divine *Tanzil* we find a measure of dialogue using the 'thou' pronoun and elucidating what is everywhere biographical. The serial occasions of revelation are throughout rendezvous after rendezvous with inner thought and open decision, with experience in the preaching arena and soliloquy in the soul. Allah's initiative in the first *Iqra'* followed the Prophet's practice of repairing to Mount Hira' which, it would seem, was itself prefaced by the impulse it could well have drawn from the example, or the prompting, of the *hunafa'*—'the monotheists' in the tradition of Abraham. These, too, for their part, were factors in the divine economy. There is divine aegis in the continuity traceable backward and forward round the incidence of the Qur'an and there can be no doubting how it constantly turns on factors involving the persona of Muhammad. Thus, since things prophetical were fused into things personal, each could only have been complementary to the other. The centrality of the Prophet would in no way depreciate the divine initiative. It would be the necessary shape revelatory purpose took.

This 'partnering of the Qur'an' to be traced here in succeeding chapters, aiming to care for all its aspects, had striking external register after Muhammad's death. There were those who had 'submitted' on the false impression that their 'surrender' had been to a man and that his death freed them from a kind of half-converted allegiance. Hence the *Riddah*, or 'revolt', which Abu Bakr, as first caliph, had promptly to crush,

---

[4] It is broadly conceded in Muslim thought that the Qur'an's being 'the direct speech of God verbally conveyed to Muhammad in the Arabic tongue', constitutes a religious mystery. It is a mystery which *Tanzil*, as a concept, must be allowed to contain, not explain. When 'eternal' and 'temporal' are being related, as in revelation, it has to be this way. The issue, in respect of Scripture to Islam, is analogous to that, for Christianity, in Christology or 'God in Christ', which also has to be 'contained' in a theism held to be revelatory. See, further, Chapter 8 below.

refusing to concede that there was any distinction between what was 'political' to a leader and what was religious in a faith. There is a clear mirror earlier, of that situation, in Surah 49.14-16 around just that ambiguity in the very verb *aslamna* ('We have submitted') which such adherents had used. It had to be distinguished—in that context[5]—from *amanna* ('We have believed') seeing that 'Faith had not entered their hearts.' The plain correction, there and then, and in 632-33, of any differentiation between Muhammad and *Rasul-Allah* as totally inadmissible is a truth about the Qur'an that forbids any neutralising of his role throughout. The living, thinking, observing, reflecting Muhammad may not be 'thought out' of the Qur'an by any emphasis on divine *Tanzil* that circumscribes what this could have been in a zeal for divine prerogative. For then prerogative itself would be misread.

Moreover, this 'personal equation' in the Qur'an's historic incidence in time and place, issued into the community's formulation of the *Sunnah* in the centuries after his death. Citing the second (Hijri) century aphorism: 'The *Sunnah* decides upon the Qur'an: the Qur'an does not decide upon the *Sunnah*,' a modern scholar adds:

> 'Strictly situational as its revelations are, it would be irrational
> to suppose that the Qur'an was taught without involving in
> fact the activity of the Prophet as the central background
> activity which included policy, commands, decisions etc.'

Receiving the Qur'an entailed 'a heavy responsibility of which Muhammad was always conscious.'[6] That 'partnering' of text and

---

5   The ambiguity, of course, carries over into the very word *islam* as a verbal noun from the same root. It holds within itself both the holding of a faith and the acceptance of a regime. So it had to be among Arabs here in Surah 49, acceding to Muhammad's power-cause: so it was in the expansion of Islam when new Muslims both received an empire and learned a faith. The point is ironically reinforced when Muhammad is told to ask these 'Arabs': 'Do you want to teach God about your religious practices?', as if holding on to these when Allah had revealed the truth could make any sense. The unity of rule and faith could not be plainer.

6   Fazlur Rahman: *Islamic Methodology in History*, Karachi, 1965, pp. 19 and 9. His argument is that in the early period the mind of the Muslim community freely shaped the *Sunnah* of the Prophet so that it was, in effect, the *Sunnah* of the community, through genuine *Ijtihad* and *Ijma'*. The sense that in this way 'possessed' him, by lights consistent with both, serves to sustain the case for a Muhammad likewise alert and liable in possessing the Qur'an in the first place. It was 'later centuries' that made Islam stolid or stagnant in the way it 'had' both the Qur'an and the *Sunnah*.

'messenger' was the later warrant by which the *Sunnah* took the personality and example as due source for guidance the Book itself did not afford. To be sure, such guidance derived from his behaviour and his dicta when apart from the Quranic state of *wahy*, or text-recipience. Even so it was clear witness to how inseparable his personhood had been from the entire phenomenon of divine text.[7] Our duty, then, is to have the full measure of the cumulative nature of the Surahs of the Qur'an in close step with Muhammad's unfolding place in its sequences.

ii

Thus its coming to be 'the Book on earth' had to be—as Surah 17.106 describes it—*'ala mukthin*, 'at intervals', or 'after interludes', so that this 'in-between' timing might participate in what the text said and, in turn, in how it would be understood. According to 25.32 the pagans themselves seem to have appreciated this when, seeking to disconcert and ridicule Muhammad, they demanded why they could not have it 'in one fell swoop'.

> 'Those who asserted it was false said: "How come the Qur'an was not sent down upon him as one whole?" It is as it is with a view to Our re-assuring your (s.) heart. We have recited it in due order.'

The fact of its being woven into an episodic character was crucial to its intelligibility and to the *bona fides* of Muhammad as truly immersed in a mission, not engaging in fantasy. The sense of things that emerges from his being 'free in the land' and—there—'a native son', as explored here in Chapter 2 and 4, belongs squarely with this steadily accumulating nature of the revelation.

Most pivotal of all in this interplay of received message and

---

[7] Fazlur Rahman's sense of a Prophet 'responsible with the Qur'an' finds Muhammad to be 'a moral reformer and a non-legist'. It was 'nonsensical to make Muhammad almost like a record in relation to revelation.' He asks: 'Did they (contemporaries) never ask themselves the question, even implicitly: "Why did God chose this person as the vehicle of His message?"' *Ibid.* p. 9. He adds: 'God speaks and the Prophet acts *in*, although certainly not merely *for*, a given historical context.' (p. 10)

receiving messenger must be the initiating vocation itself and, with it, the entire word-form of the Qur'an with Muhammad as its 'reciter'. 'Thou who art enmantled' is the clearest rubric under which to comprise that theme. We defer it here to Chapter 3 following, with more theological aspects remitted later still to Chapter 7.

Deferring it may seem counter to the chronology to which the whole case appeals. How can we follow the whither of Muhammad's preaching without the whence of his initiation? Either way, whence and whither must inter-depend and inter-define. There may be point, then, in tracing Muhammad's vicissitudes 'on the way' as useful expository approach to where, in his Mount Hira' experience, they had inauguration. The Prophet *in situ* can well bring us to the Prophet *in via meditationis*.[8]

The Qur'an in fact allows us few glimpses of Muhammad as a preacher in the suqs of Mecca or the markets of the merchants. Two isolated incidents capture a news-bringer's frustration. 'Blind eyes and deaf ears' made his hearers 'like people being called to from a long way off,' (41.44) while on another occasion his audience, 'seeing a chance for trading or amusement went off after these' leaving him standing and dwindling into loneliness (62.11). Such were the hazards of unwanted tidings, unwelcome warnings, unheeded biddings.

More disconcertingly still were the multiplying occasions of controversy. For these inevitably queried his status in disputing his words. It was always this way in prophetic experience, whether Biblical or non-Biblical. Interest, then apprehension about cultural or economic implications, moved from words to warrant. What is he saying? felt the urge to ask: Who is he anyway? Interrogation *about* the messenger was the only way to react to his message, the more so when they sensed a threat to their familiar world. The best defence against all spoken import was to discredit, even vilify, the speaker and so nullify his impact. For just as credentials were vital for the one, so their rubbishing was urgent for the other.

From this situation so much in the content and character of the Qur'an derives. Nor is it intelligible to think that Muhammad in himself was oblivious of his own stake in the very theme of the replies the revealed

---

[8] This *tahannuth*, or 'muse of soul' on Mount Hira' to which Muhammad withdrew prior to his 'being enmantled'—apart from Chapter 3 here—was explored in my *Returning to Mount Hira'*, London, 1994. One might apply to that experience the Vulgate of Psalm 39.3: *In meditatione mea exardescet ignis*, 'while I was thus musing the fire kindled.'

text gave him by which to refute the charges made against him, the calumnies alleged about him. These covered almost every angle of his—indeed of each and every—prophetic mission. The accusations varied as they proceeded. Each rebuttal, given the obduracy unminded to yield, occasioned a new variant of the pseudo reasons why.

Muhammad was disturbing old and culture-protective traditions on which depended the prestige of the Meccan *haram*, on which prestige, in turn, depended the sanctity—and range—of the months of truce, on which months of truce, in turn, depended the material prosperity of Mecca. In that same vein of communal awareness, they alleged that Muhammad had drawn his meanings from 'some stranger', by whom he had been misled. Such sources tainted what 'the ancestors' had always revered. Paganism recruited, and was recruited by, a strong tribalism. Both could tolerate a concept of a single, remotely supreme Allah, but not His sole sovereignty intolerant of all their pious idolatries. Muhammad needed to be silenced for the comfort of their own rites and reliances, though pagan and plural they might be.

Or, that mystery of his eloquence, the very language power he claimed attested his apostolate—these must be attributed to emulation of those Arab rhymers, seers, and reciters who were so fond a feature of their cult of poetry. He was one of those *kuhhan*, but his prowess—though it might superlatively exemplify the art—was quite subversive, given the tenor of what it availed to tell. It was an impressive power of rhetoric faulted by the cause it served. The Meccans were in no mood to be beguiled into new perceptions of Allah and themselves by a power of words they might otherwise have had a disposition to admire.

Or that sense of communal solidarity fortified itself by noting how few of the worthy-great among them had succumbed to Muhammad's preaching. For the long, harried years before the Hijrah, accessions to his cause did little socially to commend it. It would be left to visitors from Yathrib to bring a crucial turn in Muhammad's outward fortunes, while the 'establishment' in Mecca re-assured itself in his rejection by the very firmness of its ranks. That fact in turn was further grist to the mill of their antagonism. Or, when altercation moved from what concerned the person of Muhammad, there were issues aplenty to mingle with Meccan disavowal of him in their incredulity, for example, about corpses raised from dust and ashes and the grand assize at length to judge their deeds.

So, throughout those stressful years, the Prophet lived through the situation described in Surah 15.96-99:

'On your behalf We will take good care of the scoffers …
We know well how your heart is distressed by all they are
saying. Celebrate your praise of your Lord and be one with
other worshippers in prostration. Serve the Lord until the
one sure thing comes to you.'

The periodic character of the Qur'an's mediation to Muhammad, already
noted, only heightened the inner tension in the very experience of awaiting
it. Not least in the early times of his vocation suspense as to the next onset
of inspiration was acute and taxing—hence the several re-assurances that
'he was not forsaken.' These interludes, in turn, left ample occasion for
ridicule to make its scornful mark. What was external in his locale married
closely with the themes—if not the origins—of his deliverances. The very
texture of the Qur'an thus went step by step and hand in hand with what
had to be endured within his psyche.

Some ninety times the word *yaquluna*, 'they are saying,' occurs
in the Book, while, twice that number of times the directive to
Muhammad, *faqul,* ' Say!'—the imperative singular of the verb. The latter
is more frequent, since it prefaces so much of Quranic utterance, all
hostile diatribe apart. But that a half of Muhammad's 'occasions' of being
commanded to 'Say!' were response to such spoken antagonism is fair
measure of how firmly located its contents were in that deeply personal
Sitz im Leben.

iii

The Qur'an gives us no reason to assume that this prolonged experience
of a serial preaching, as also an extended awareness of public malevolence,
did not engross Muhammad's inner self and confront him with its
oppressiveness as both privilege and perplexity. Indeed, it gives us every
reason to the contrary, so that much of the Qur'an's accent on the
sovereignty of Allah springs from re-assuring him, that, beyond all liability
of his, Allah has all things in hand. Consider Surah 42.6:

'As for those who adopt patron deities to the exclusion of
God, well God has them under watch. It is not your job to
be responsible for them.'

Such divine presiding over all things, calling on 'messengers' only for verbal fidelity with the 'message', had been the vital solace of all earlier prophets.

> 'The apostle said: "Lord, my people have been altogether dismissive of this Qur'an." It has been Our way in the case of every prophet to have him experience enmity from these who are evil-bent.' (25.30-31)

In many places, that undergoing of wilful denigration and scorn is linked with the machinations of that 'great accuser,' 'the accursed *Shaitan*', or Satan, finding allies in obdurate humans in malign conspiracy. To think and feel oneself a prey to such Satanic disruption both of speech and soul certainly precludes any *absence d'ésprit* on any messenger's part. For it entails an exacting vigilance both of audition and utterance which tax the self remorselessly.

Is it not out of this pressure that Muhammad asks: 'Shall I desire any Judge but God?' in sequence to the reminder that:

> 'To every prophet We have assigned an enemy—satans, men and jinn, who inspire in one another fair-sounding talk intended to delude ... Be quit of them and their devising to deceive ...' (6.113-15.)

Such mischief (in the old sense of the word)[9] could take sundry forms, some turning on the human susceptibilities that afflict our mortal world. For, in several places, the Qur'an lays stress on Muhammad's mortality. In 25.7 his detractors ask: 'What sort of messenger is this who takes food and walks about in the suqs? Why was no angel sent down to keep him company in his warnings?' Or again in Surah 41.6: 'Say, I am a mortal man as you are.'

Accordingly, it is clear from many passages that a human quality of grief, distress and potential despair characterised those intermittent waitings for the Qur'an in the Meccan time and the many animosities which tauntingly greeted them. These personal misgivings are often noted in the text. 'A Book sent down to you. Let there be no anxiety in your

---

[9] 'Evil doing and the injury so wrought, intending evil consequences.'

heart because of it' (7.2); 'Their aversion to you ... so on your part on no account fail to understand' (6.35); 'We well know how your heart is distressed by all they are saying' (15.97); 'Do not let what they are saying grieve you. All might is wholly God's' (10.66); 'Be patient. Your patient endurance derives only from God. Do not grieve over them or be distressed by their devices' (16.127).

In all these encounters with vexing hostility the comforting fact had to be that it was only coming to him as being meant for the words he brought. Thus 66.33:

> 'We know well that what they are saying grieves you. It is not you whom they are making out a liar. It is the very revelations of God that wrongdoers repudiate ...'

as all earlier messengers discovered. So, in a rare glimpse of such encounter:

> 'When you have named your Lord's Name in the Qur'an—and His alone—they promptly turn their backs in distaste. We know well what they are listening for from it when they give you hearing, and how they go aside to put their heads together with the evil-doers, saying: "You are following a man who is nothing but a victim of sorcery." See what images of you they have coined, going far wrong, in total incomprehension of the true way.' (Surah 17.47-48)

'Bear patiently then with what they say' (20.130) had to be the directive so frequently renewed even when (as in 25.41) they 'take you for a joke,' or 'when they hear the revelation, those who reject the faith look daggers at you and say: "He is surely demented."' (68.51).

This quality of impasse in the burden of Muhammad's mission in the context of pagan obduracy not only explains the sternness of his denunciation, but also the necessary uncoerciveness of the message in the Meccan times. Thus Surah 50.45: 'you have no power of compulsion over them. So by the Qur'an admonish any who will hear My warning.' It was a note to be more formally promulgated in the oft-cited words of Surah 2.256: 'There is no compulsion in religion.'[10]

---

[10] The sentence is a nominal one, i.e., with no 'is', and with the *la* of absolute negation. The positive: 'There is no compulsion ...' has to be read as imperative: 'There ought to be no

It is surely this shape of things in the Meccan Qur'an that requires the strongly uncompromising quality of Muhammad's verbal encounters with the Quraish and their entrenched, pagan traditionalism. Urged, on his part, to be 'on no account a doubter' (6.115) and 'desiring no arbiter but God', he learns to be decisive in his rejection of what disavows the sent word.

> 'People, if you are in doubt about my religion, well—I do not worship what you worship, to the exclusion of God. But I worship God alone, God who determines your mortal span. I am commanded to be among those who believe.' (Surah 10.105)

In Surah 109, at perhaps an even earlier point, comes an equally resolute repudiation of the repudiators.

> 'Say: You who reject faith, I do not worship what you worship, nor do you worship what I worship. Never shall I be a worshipper of what you have worshipped, nor will you be worshippers of what I worship. To you your religion and to me mine.'[11]

Perhaps in Surah 70 we have some portrayal of the sort of scenario on occasions of such confrontation:

> 'What possesses the unbelievers, jostling about in front of you, all agog and crowding in from left to right? ... Let

---

compulsion.' By the law of apostasy a 'compulsion' exists, in the form of a dire threat to any abandoning of Islam. What one is menaced not to leave becomes a prison if and as one wishes to rethink it.

[11] It surely gross misreading to cite these verses as commending mutual tolerance of diverse religions en route to gracious 'dialogue'. This has lately been the habit of some Muslim advocates of inter-faith tolerance. They have sound grounds for doing so, e.g. in 49.13 and 5.48. Surahs 109 and 10.105 are addressed to pagans, 'unbelievers', and firmly differentiate the true from the false. 'To you yours, to me mine' is not conciliatory—how could it be, given Muhammad's mission? On such misuse, see, for example, Mohammad Abu-Hamdiyyah: *The Qur'an, An Introduction*, London, 2000, pp. 53 and 107. Surah 109 recurs significantly in Chapter 3, below.

them chatter and amuse themselves until they reach that
promised Day of theirs.' (70.36, 37 and 42)

The evident intensity of such multiplied occasions in the Qur'an surely
confirms how deeply his inspiration with the text quite radically
incorporated his personality. Just as there was no neutrality in his
message, so there could be no neutralising of his emotions or his mind
in conveying it.

So to realise is to appreciate the occasional references to a
temptation to let the pressure slacken or even to think to be ingratiating
towards his hearers. This would only be confirmation of how strenuous
the loyalty was and how human—as the Qur'an always insisted—was the
urgency. Thus Surah 68.8-9 warns against 'obeying those who call it lies'
and adds: 'Were you to be ingratiating with them they would like it well
and be the same with you.' Surah 17.73 goes further:

'They had almost beguiled you away from what We had
revealed to you with the temptation to invent something
else against Us. On that score they would have taken you
up as a friend. Had We not rallied you, you had almost
conceded to them a little.

How clear it becomes, in the light of these passages that however we
understand *Tanzil*, the mediation to Muhammad of the heavenly Book, it
combines with reactions and factors in his own private mind and spirit.
The frequent references to some ensnaring Satanism present, even if it
consists only in trying to induce 'slips of the tongue', could hardly be
some machination of which mental processes in the self were not aware.
Temptation to be 'ingratiating' cannot happen unawares.

Whatever the precise circumstances to which Surahs 68 and 17
refer they certainly fit the Meccan *mise-en-scène* with its psychic pressures,
its pitting of a lone preacher against the aggressive vested interests of a
sacred shrine and its lucrative prestige. That Muhammad could well feel
overborne in such a conflict would be part of that human quality on
which the Qur'an laid steady emphasis. According to tradition it was
only his status within the Quraishi clan and the protection of his uncle,
Abu Talib, that ensured his survival through the immediate pre-Hijrah
years after his implications against the *status quo* had become all too

apparent and he steadfast in them.

Those hints as to his 'temptation' in some measure to accommodate with Meccan paganism take us to the vexed question of the now famous, so-called 'Satanic verses'. It may be well to preface them with some measure of the sort of animated controversy that occurred and which, for example, Surah 52.29-38 takes up from Muhammad's side with the rhetoric of irony.

> 'Give them to know that you are no soothsayer, no crazy fellow. Or are they saying: "He is a poet. We expect some chance of fate will see to him!" Tell them: Wait as you may: I have my anticipations no less than yours!
> 'Is it their sagacity that constrains them this way or are they pernicious people? Are they putting it around that he has concocted it—this Qur'an? They are not minded to believe. If they mean what they say, let them come out with a discourse like it!
> 'Were they created out of the empty air? Or are they self-creators? Did they bring into being the heavens and the earth? Strangers they are to any sure convictions! Are they in possession of your Lord's treasuries? Or custodians in charge of them? Or have they some ladder from which to eavesdrop in heaven? If so, let some listener of theirs promulgate clearly!'

'They and 'theirs' here are the third party. Only once (v. 31) are they directly addressed. It is almost as if the Qur'an is coming to Muhammad in the guise of his own rumination about what is in contention between him and them. Later he protests that he is not 'asking any fee from them' as if that could be any kind of grudge against him. He queries: 'Do they have some unseen realm within their purview' whereby they can produce the script of it (v. 41-42)? For then they would be matching the Qur'an as heaven-written.

Such overtones of Meccan controversy emerge in Chapter 3 following, in the context of Muhammad's self-consciousness of his prophethood coming into potential temptation. As will be there apparent, at least an arguable tendency towards accommodation with the Meccans on the basis of some mutual co-existence between their plural worships and his witness to divine *Tawhid*, even if never agreed, is witness enough to how deeply he was party to the issue in itself.[12] For only so, could it figure in the text and in tradition around the text in the Surah 53.19-23 passage.

All is evidence that the encounter with Meccan superstition and pagan vested interest could never have been a salient theme of the Book without being, concurrently, an existential experience in the soul living through that piece of the *Sirah*. Indeed, it would be fair to say that a 'passage' of the Qur'an was a 'passage' in the incidence of inspiration. To that extent *wahy* and *Sirah*, what came *into* speech and *on* to the page came with a psychic awareness without which it could have had neither setting nor relevance.

That psychic situation, in its strenuous interior crisis, has to be taken fully into the revelatory status of the Qur'an. As such, it need in no way disconcert the age-long Islamic doctrine of the Book's being 'divine' both in its origin and in its authority. It would only be a matter of comprehending that divine status intelligently. The only concern, in present context, is to leave incontestable the fact of the party Muhammad was to the incidence of the entire Qur'an.

Whatever the final truth of the incident in Surah 53, both its presence and the ultimate issue only serve further to indicate what the very early Surah 94 described—addressing Muhammad directly —as 'the burden that was breaking down your back.' Only in that context of stressful engagement could what follows (v. 4) about 'establishing (his) reputation' find significance. For it was only in the maelstrom of encounter that who Muhammad was, or what the Qur'an, could emerge into clarity and repute.

This frequent form of direct address—or indirect with obvious direct intent—to Muhammad, in being so central to the Qur'an's incidence, is also eloquent testimony to his being the constant 'human factor' in its *Tanzil*. Crucial meanings are often conveyed in straight interrogation of him, turning on the content of his claims and his occasions. Thus in what

---

[12] The long and tedious controversy on this issue need not detain us here. For it does not bear on the course of the argument. That 'names are only names', i.e., 'figments in the mind', might contrive a bridging form of words between those who believed 'the named ones' existed and those who meant by the same words to dismiss them as non-entities. In any event, if Muhammad had meant to find a 'bridging' formula that would allow the Quraish to concede 'Allah' to him as supreme but not solitary and he their sub-deities to them, he rapidly reverted to his *la ilaha illa-Allah* formula and the never real, or only tentative, *modus vivendi* between the parties ended.

is usually understood as the very inaugural Surah 96, where the command to recite is followed by human ridicule on the part of some local notable, Muhammad is asked as to his reaction.

> 'Have you taken account of him who puts a ban on a praying servant in his devotions? Do you see him as rightly guided or as enjoining the fear of God? Is he not rather in your sight repudiating truth and acting perversely? Does he not realise that God is all-Seeing?'[13]

The verbs are all singular. In Surah 53, at the outset, one audience for the text is given assurance about its mouthpiece. 'Your kinsman has not been led astray, nor is he under delusion. He does not speak by some whim of his own' (v. 2-3) Those are the grounds by which it can be known as 'nothing else than a revelation imparted to him' (v.4). The integrity of the man and the veracity of the Book are mutual and inseparable. Muhammad is not, nor could ever be, an anonymous messenger.

He finds himself interrogated by his listeners as to the meaning of what he utters, so that the very content of *Tanzil* brings the answer he must give them. Thus the revelation passes through his intelligence in a conscious process, alerted by questioners and relayed into their curiosity. Nothing transpires as if in some uncomprehending void of human neutrality where no living, reacting Muhammad belongs.

> 'If my servants question you (s.) concerning Me, in truth I am near. I answer the call of the suppliant who cries to Me. So let them harken to Me, let them believe in Me that they may be rightly led.' (2.186)

Here, as often elsewhere, Muhammad is the human sphere of exchange between the asking that addresses him and the answering from God that it can receive.[14]

---

[13] It is unclear whether Surah 96 belongs to one single occasion or whether the section quoted here (from v. 6 on) belongs to a later time. The latter would seem to be suggested if a pattern of prayer was already in being. Either way, the point in question is the same, namely an inviting of Muhammad's musing about the theme into the shaping of the text itself.

[14] It is noteworthy from 'questioning' (i.e. interrogation about God) the response speaks of 'praying'—'let the asker in the one sense become the asker in the other', from, query to supplication. The sequel is not to be about curiosity satisfied but petition heeded with a view to 'right guidance'. Piety is more precious than curiosity.

That obtains also where his persona is the fulcrum on which some lesson turns. 'He frowned'—the title of Surah 80—is one such occasion:

> 'He (Muhammad) frowned and turned away when the blind man approached him. For all you (s.) knew he might have been bringing alms for cleansing. Or he had taken the Reminder to heart and was bent on putting it to use. To anyone who has all he needs you pay attention readily, even though you neglect responsibility for his not being purified by alms. But one who comes to you eagerly in godly fear, him you disregard. This is a revelation, a calling to mind. Let him who will keep it in mind. It is there on hallowed pages, pages that are extolled and purified by the hands of noble and virtuous scribes.' (v.1-16)

There could hardly be a clearer inter-association between a chance biographical incident and 'a preserved tablet' in heaven. The Prophet's demeanour—or on this occasion a misdemeanour—enters, with refreshing honesty, into the sacred text. It is well to read in Surah 80 a paradigm of what is true throughout, namely a human 'party' to divine imparting. Chapter 5, on 'War and Its Burdens' affords many other examples of this fact of the Qur'an when it moved beyond the Meccan origins and into the Medinan régime.

An example, linking the two spheres of the Qur'an might be had from the opening of Surah 48 where the text hinges entirely on a significant event, namely Muhammad's negotiation with the Quraish of the Pact of Al-Hudaibiyyah which paved the way for his final acquisition of Mecca in 630.[15]

> 'It is an evident triumph We have achieved for you, God's purpose being to forgive what has been wrong in you in

---

[15] This is the general 'siting' of the passage. Muhammad who would have come armed with pilgrims, was not allowed to perform the ritual or enter Mecca. The 'Pact' approved an unarmed coming the year following with an agreed number admitted to a Mecca the Quraish vacated for the purpose. What may explain the reassuringly celebratory note in Surah 48 is that to his followers' dismay, Muhammad signed—as the Meccans demanded—not as *Rasul-Allah* but as Ibn 'Abdallah. Some adherents feared this concession unwise but several advantages accrued, not least the equal status the deal suggested, and these soon fructified in what ensued.

the pact and what may yet be, thus making good His grace upon you and guiding you into a straight path. God aids you strongly towards victory. It is He who caused the *Sakinah* to come down into the hearts of the believers so that, out of faith's experience, they might grow in faith.'

Always in line with faith's experience progressed the granting of faith's Scripture. We will encounter many more such coincidings of the Prophet's *Sirah* with the Book's inauguration into earth-dwelling, human recital and possession. Those of the Medinan sphere are different from those of the Meccan—a distinction which the Qur'an itself has always been concerned to identify.

Meanwhile the care of this chapter was to clarify how central to the Scripture's *Tanzil* was a partnering factor in the persona of Muhammad. Deep issues remain concerning the nature of revelation and the place of prophetology (i.e. the nature of divine 'agency') and the theology it pre-supposes.

Those tasks can well be broached by some study of the titles or attributions given to the Prophet, his being 'freeman in the land', 'the mantled-wrapped' in mysterious summons, 'the *ummi* for the *ummiyyun*', 'the war-burdened messenger'. Through and beyond all these is that *Tasliyah*, pregnant of a far-reaching aura in his persona. What could it have meant to be party to the injunction that called upon believers to 'call down blessing upon him' in concert with 'Allah and His angels' in the same employ of salutation? For in that formula of Surah 33.56 the 'party' Muhammad was to the Qur'an finds its deepest greeting—a greeting which integrates all else in the devotion that lies beyond scholarship, yet a posture that scholarship has every duty to explore.

Chapter 2
FREEMAN IN THE LAND

i

Surah 90 ranks among the earliest Meccan Surahs of the Qur'an. It opens with the familiar form of invocation: 'Nay! I swear by this land,' and then—addressing Muhammad, as most readings assume—the parenthesis: '... and in this land thou art *hillun*.' Several meanings are ascribed to the term, so varied indeed that, on reflection, they can be seen to comprise many of the issues that gather around the persona of the Prophet. They therefore serve admirably to initiate us further into the whole enquiry afoot in these chapters, namely the intimate relation between being Muhammad ibn 'Abdallah and being *Rasul-Allah*. At once the singular verb points to the singularity of the singular addressee, unless we assume— as few commentators do—that some collective 'human', mankind in general, is meant.[1]

It is important for readers of the Qur'an to note when singular verbs and pronouns are used and when plural, the more so if the language of translation does not indicate. Immediately here the sanctity of Mecca is pointedly joined, in divine pledge-making, with the fact that Muhammad 'dwells there.' 'Being resident', 'as an inhabitant', or 'as a lodger' are frequent renderings of *hillun*, with *balad* as either 'land', or 'ground,' or—by inference—'city'. The preposition that precedes may be 'in' or 'of'—which tend towards the reading of 'free' in relation to, with sundry, even contrasted, implications. For its open potential, and for containing these variants, 'You (sing.) are a freeman in this land' is the satisfactory English.

The ways in which its import can be read are many and reach proleptically into the whole future, while they situate the potential

---

[1] As, for example, does Muhammad Asad: *The Message of the Qur'an*, Gibraltar, 1980, p. 952 There may be support in the following words: 'By father and fathered—Surely We have created man in trouble' and the stern portrayal of human obduracy in the sequel and of the demands on the moral will. An inclusive 'humanity' meaning, however, seems at odds with the evident locality of 'this city' or even 'this (Arab) land'.

prophethood in the antecedents of its locale. Mecca was Muhammad's birthplace, the home of his youth, the very navel of the earth whose messenger he would become. It was the springboard of his first commerce, the haven of his marriage to Khadijah, its merchant-lady, the nursing ground of his meditative visits to its Mount Hira'.[2] Moreover, his clan, the Quraish, were the chief people in its pilgrim status and its far-ranging trade, the overseers of those 'months of truce' for due pilgrim access when would-be pilgrims to the sacred shrine, the Ka'bah, were 'free of the land'.

'The soil on which thou dost dwell' might suffice to convey all this but the significance that deserves to be taken up into parenthesis of divine 'swearing' is surely some larger thing than mere sojourn. There is the added sense of 'security', of being 'uninhibited' as a resident, of having something of that *parrhesia* on which the Greeks prided themselves, as both a 'freedom with a meaning', so that they were fully articulate, and 'freedom in the public domain' to speak their mind without intimidation.[3]

In that event, it would seem that 'freeman thou art in this place' was more of promise than of fact, of a future rather than a present— uncertain as we must be of the exact timing of the Surah. For at the outset of his mission Muhammad came under severe duress. His initial years were harassed by persistent ridicule and Meccan contradiction and he was denied all honour in his own territory. Were the words then, like others in the first months and years, intended to encourage and sustain, bearing a reassurance as to what would supervene?

If he was hardly 'at liberty' in Mecca as a preacher, did the assurance mean that he was 'at liberty' by divine commission, warranted with the *balagh*, the preached message, as something no human surveillance could preclude, that there was a mandate from heaven in that obdurate place to which he was 'the native prophet'? That sense of *ummi*, to which we must come elsewhere as describing Muhammad,[4] is quite central to

---

[2] The mountain in the Meccan vicinity with the 'cave' to which Muhammad repaired for *tahannuth*, or 'meditation', in the times preceding his first-experience of the Qur'an. Its significance was explored in my *Returning to Mount Hira'*, London, 1994.

[3] The word covered the right of the citizen to speak in the assembly. It also came into the usage of the New Testament Letters—variously translated as, 'plainness', 'boldness', 'confidence'—all that a man thinks and as he pleases. The term, however, would only be apt for Muhammad in the Qur'an in the sense of 'confidence', since the message is far from being his thought or his mind. It is understood as Allah's alone, set upon his lips.

[4] See below, Chap. 4 and *The Event of the Qur'an*, London, 1971, 2nd ed. Oxford, 1994, pp. 56-61.

our entire study of the public role and the private self. It was precisely because the antipathy became strong that the Quranic *parrhesia*, the 'word made ready for lips made ready', came with reassurance for a speaker using the Hijazi Arabic as spoken by his own Quraish. Was 'You are a freeman in this city' telling him, near its outset, the whole phenomenon of the Qur'an as feasibly delivered in the earthly scene from the heavenly source?

There have, however, been readings of the passage that take the meaning of 'free in this land' into the distant, Medinan future after the 'establishment' of Islam in that other city centre. By these lights the 'liberty' would not relate to speech and a message, but to the authority that would come with success in having Mecca (if 'city' be understood), or 'the land' as a whole, under physical control. Such ultimate meaning involves seeing the verse as somehow interpolated here.[5] This seems unlikely in such close adjacence as a parenthesis and with the rhyme in *balad* as a link. Yet the future situation in that shape of unconstrained and unrestricted 'freedom' fits well if *hillun* is read—as it may well be—as the antonym of *haram*, something 'banned' or 'forbidden'.

Mecca, in any event, was a *haram*, a sacred territory, surrounding a holy shrine, intended to be immune from desecration, whose trees could not be felled, where game should not be killed, and to which pilgrim access could be had only under due reverence for its status. Much of the prestige of the Quraish depended on their exercise of such control and the purpose of months of truce was only served as their prestige held. Thus the pledge of Surah 90 might well resonate with those associations concerning the city.

There would be a point in the later post-Hijrah story when the Prophet was not 'free of Mecca', but could only negotiate an access there by the pact of Al-Hudaibiyyah made with the Meccans whereby, the following year, he and his pilgrims would come unarmed—and unmolested—to perform the sacred ritual. To the astonishment of his followers, he signed the pact with his personal name as Ibn 'Abdallah.[6]

---

[5] See Richard Bell: *A Commentary on the Qur'an*, ed. C E Bosworth and M E J Richardson, 1991, Vol. 2, p. 541. Bell was given to much textual replacings. Here he suggests that the second *balad* 'raises the suspicion that an insertion has been made,' presumably to cover the situation as it became in Medina. Otherwise, it seems clear that the Surah is very early and deeply Meccan.

[6] The story figures in the early historians and the form of signature appears to have been demanded by the Quraish—to the deep chagrin of the faithful. See the account based on

Could the pledge in the early Surah have come to mind on that occasion, the concession secured from enemies, by treating with them for what they would concede, being such as the 'non-prophet'—as they still regarded him—could only obtain in that still 'private' capacity?

It would be only a little further time, and partly thanks to the prestige of that pilgrimage, before Muhammad as 'the Prophet' would be entirely 'free of the city', by its full submission to his authority in both kinds, physical and prophetic in one. Then the writ of his faith in the rule of his will would be 'in charge' of Meccan society, of law and order.

In the meantime—and certainly during his sojourn prior to the Hijrah—Muhammad and his cause were in a sort of *haram* in the other sense of 'forbidden' or 'banned'. The Quraish were under no obligation to protect him, he being a sort of 'outlaw' from their regime as inherently pagan and devoted to false idols. This 'bannedness' started almost from the outset in the form of explicit rejection of his words as inimical to all their vested interest. Yet he was of their blood and kin and, for a longer time, they contented themselves with threats and harassment. It was the finally desperate, well-nigh fatal, logic of these that prompted the decision for the emigration to Yathrib (which would become Medina as 'the city of the Prophet') where some Yathribites, drawn by his teaching, were ready to provide the very 'sanctuary' that Mecca denied him.

In due course, by the consolidation of his initially precarious tenure, he became *hillun* in Medina—'free' to proclaim and pursue his mission with gathering impunity. At length the *haram*-state of 'deniedness to him' with respect to Mecca was triumphantly reversed into a 'liberty' there to fulfil Islam in entire vindication of its meaning. Was that then also the proleptic meaning of Surah 94.3 (assuming its early date): 'Have We not lifted from you the burden that was breaking your back and have We not established your reputation?' The term here, variously translated: 'Raised high your esteem,' 'exalted thy fame,' 'given you high renown,' more likely refers to the inclusive prophetic role, to issues of the spirit rather than external factors, such as his marriage with Khadijah.[7]

the sources in William Muir: *Life of Muhammad*, London, 1923, Chapter xix. pp. 352-65. The Quraish intended to disown the 'Prophet of God' claim since, had he truly been such, they would not have been at war with him. Muhammad's conceding the point was purely tactical in anticipation of that to which the truce could well lead.

[7] The marriage is among the suggestions that explains to what his *dhikra* is owed. Important as the marriage was, it can hardly suffice for what is meant in the whole context.

However 94.3 is read, the 'reputation' sanctioned and envisioned in the terms of Surah 90.2, takes our thought to the very heart of the theme of 'Muhammad-in-the-Qur'an', namely the inner experience of the high dignity through which he steadily passed from call to climax. What, in its several aspects, must have been the sense of a destiny possessing mind and conscience as it unfolded both around and within the Muhammad that he was, the *Rasul-Allah* he was experientially becoming? Deep inside the psyche, this core question—though at the heart of all else—has seldom been explored in the terms it deserves. How did the vocational assume the personal? How was the individual taken into the destiny?

ii

Surah 90.2's 'Freeman in the Land' has an immediate ring of paradox in that it at once serves notice on the perversity of humankind in that humans, despite the rich equipment of sense and awareness, baulk at the stern demands of the moral life, 'the steep ascent' of compassionate living. In this it resembles the inaugural 'call to recite', of Surah 96, where the 'Recite—*Iqra'* command' is promptly followed by the *kalla* of aggressive veto by an answering:'Nay, not so!' from the human enmity.The 'freeman' in the Prophet could only be so against the odds of a disavowing public.

Beyond this irony of how the way of prophets is hard, lies another aspect of the 'free of the land' situation. It has to do with the notable role of geography in the fabric of the Qur'an. Muhammad was remarkably conversant with territory as the arena of his preaching.The Qur'an draws heavily on the topography of hill and desert, the panorama of his travels.[8] A register of local history runs through the pages of the Qur'an in the appeals to hearers and readers to read in ruined habitations the index to divine requital of evil deeds. There stood Mada'in Salih, named for one of the Book's 'minor' messengers, rebuking in its desolation the disdain that had disowned his message. The devastating collapse of the Marib Dam, crucial to the irrigation of ancient Arabia Felix, had become a symbol of retribution on the unalert to God.The day-to-day phenomena

---

[8] See, for example, *Journal of Quranic Studies*, Vol. 1, No. 1, London, 1999, 'The Historical Geography of the Qur'an: A Study in *Asbab al-Nuzul*,' pp. 81-92. The following article: 'Rethinking "Revelation": as a pre-condition for reinterpreting the Qur'an: A Quranic Perspective', by Abdullah Saeed, pp. 93-114, is relevant also. See below.

of a harsh and rigorous natural scene told the fleetingness of life in the transient greens in the wake of sudden showers, the shifting dunes of wayward sand, the vagaries of human fortune. Appeal to the natural order rhymed with the poetic ethos of the Quranic speech.

Even as a 'sojourner'—if we limit Surah 90.2 to that bare sense— the Muhammad of the Qur'an is seen to move through the land with a lively perceptiveness of its contours and scenes as disclosing divine ways. There is a theology of nature and of judgement that is legible in the scars and vesture of the ancient earth. Its moods and mysteries yield parables of religious warning and reminder, from the deceiving mirage that misleads the unwary traveller, to the crumbling precipices that tent-dweller ones must take due note of when pitching camp, where craters lie across the lava where volcanoes once erupted. In such admonitory terms, 'the signs of God' are everywhere and the voice of prophethood heralds their abiding import for a heedless folk.

It is in this perception of the 'land' by a Muhammad thus 'free' in it that best gave the lie to the superstitions which had too long populated the earthly scene with a multiplicity of deities and powers and the fears they evoked. The displacement of this pluralism of worship and invocation was not achieved simply by assertion that 'Allah is One,' but by the summons, audible from nature itself, to gratitude and wonder when nature is truly read in these Quranic terms.

There is a striking phrase in Surah 77, with its almost untranslatable quality of Arabic, that captures this aspect of the Prophet's 'freedom with the land'. Without a certain careful 'freedom' on a translator's part it might well remain characteristically enigmatic. With its title *Al-Mursalat*, variously rendered 'The Emissaries', 'Messengers in the Sending', 'The Loosed ones' and 'Those sent forth', it may intend the winds, the angels, human heralds—all gathered into a divine invocation as to the truth of 'the Day of Judgement'. A rendering might be:

> 'By the chartered winds in their familiar courses
> And tempests in their stormy pride,
> By the dispersing, fructifying rain-clouds,
> By all that deciphers and discerns
> And brings home a reminder as plea and as warning—
> All that you are promised will assuredly happen.'[9]

---

[9] Cited from my *Readings in the Qur'an*, London, 1988, pp. 58 and 337.

Lines 4 and 5 (verses 4.5 and 6 of the Surah) are the present concern, having in mind the 'winds, tempests and rain-clouds' first invoked. 'All that deciphers and discerns' uses two English verbs to convey *fa-l-fariqat farqan*, (lit. 'the separators a separating') 'the severally severing' and 'the casting asunder' are other turns of phrase—which in wild terms is what tempests are liable to do. However, in view of the phrase following about 'throwing, hurling, casting' a 'reminder' that is both 'warning' and 'hinting', it seems right to read the human attentiveness that can discriminate more tellingly than the random passion of nature. Yet it is a discrimination that moves from and with phenomena that are so arresting in our experience of the world, whether tumultuous, as here, or more quiet and subtle in a harsh or deceptive landscape as men daily fare forth across it.

Read in this way, the poetic eloquence of Surah 77, as of many other passages, confirms a sacred text 'free in the land'—free of delusion, free for comprehension and certainly freed from ignorance and apathy. All spelled a monotheism deep in the emotions of the soul as well as told in the witness of a creed. The nature that constitutes the hinterland of the text is also the homeland of the Prophet who utters it.

Moreover, it is well to note that frequently when we have divine 'swearing' in the Qur'an Allah's 'invocation' of winds, storms, tempests, seasons and stars, it is to enforce moral claims on human living and to reinforce these by an eschatology of crisis. Divine sovereignty in an order of things that is not itself volitional drives home the realm where human wills belong. Nature in this way is called to witness against all human waywardness, to interrogate the heedless habits of human negligent indifference and lack of gratitude. In this feature of Muhammad's mission to echo the rebuke of nature to the perversity of humankind there is a clear kinship with the Biblical: 'Have they not heard, have they not understood ...? (Isaiah 40.28) and sundry other passages through the whole prophetic tradition. Muhammad's 'freedom in the land' was this capacity to give voice to the theological significance of all human habitation, all territorial nomadism.

It is fair to conclude that the incidence to him of the words we now read in the Qur'an are

'the record of an exceptional responsiveness or of an
ordinary responsiveness exceptionally remembered (in) ...
moments of sensory apprehension ...'

in what, elsewhere, Wordsworth called 'high instincts … obstinate questionings of sense and outward things.' If so what that poet adds of 'moving about in worlds not realized' would exactly apply to Meccans wilfully dismissive of Muhammad's mission.[10] Whether thinking so necessarily contravenes the classic Muslim reading of Muhammad's receiving of the Qur'an is an issue it is agreed to defer to Chapter 4. The text as we have it is witness enough to the role of the land, of nature as known to its sojourners, and of both in the deliverances of the Prophet.

iii

The keen and ample observation of nature which the Qur'an contains constitutes a deep and reverent theology closely akin in its doxologies to the Biblical Psalms. We find ourselves invited to read external nature as the purposive handiwork of God. Moreover, it is a handiwork slanted towards the autonomy of humankind. Whether or not it was the observer Muhammad, it was assuredly the preacher Muhammad who read the creation as intended, intrinsically, for the cultivation and the culture of humanity. Meant for creaturehood, it yielded itself into human creativity, fulfilled in the peasant and the plough, the herdsman in the pasture, the cameleer with his beasts, even the seaman on his vessel harnessing the winds.

Creation has a glory, a legibility, awaiting both recognition in praise and gratitude and in the desires and the devices by which we enlist its powers and patiently explore the enabling means it affords. Among the striking instances of this truth are the four questions of Surah 56.57-73:

> 'It is We who have created you. How is it you do not recognise that truth? Have you considered what you do in intercourse? Is it you who do the creating or is it We? … Have you considered the soil you till? Is it you who bring the crop or are We the real agent of growth? … Have you considered the water you drink? Was it you who made it fall from the rain-clouds or are We the rain-maker? Had We so willed

[10] Stephen Gill, *William Wordsworth. A Life*, Oxford 1989, p. 32. The Wordsworth lines: *Poetical Works*, ed. Thomas Hutchinson, London, 1905, 'Intimations of Immortality …', Stanza ix, line 149, p. 589.

bitter water had We sent! How is it that you have no gratitude? Have you considered the fire you kindle? Was it you who made the tree to grow or are We the source of its being? We devised it to be a point of recollection and to provide solace for those who pass through desert ways. Praise, then, each of you the Name of your great Lord.'

It was this double truth of divine munificence destined into human utility which idolatry distorted. For the making of idols and the shaping of taboos dissipated the central truth and sanctioned endless fragmented fears. They invoked pseudo-protection and ascribed to half chaotic factors the feasible order and discipline of a cosmos. The central message of the divine unity was rooted firmly in the perspective of a land, of a terrain that for all its harsh unpredictability summoned its people to Allah in worship.

It was also the complete emotional disavowal of the *Jahiliyyah*, the state of uncouth 'ignorance' with which the Qur'an characterises its people before its own advent. As the complement of plural worships, that condition of wayward mentality depreciated the natural phenomena as these truly were when appreciated as 'under God' and, thereby, a realm of ordered human management within their ordained limits. The Quraish, the tribes of the desert, were all doubtless expert cameleers, canny merchants and subtle negotiators around feuds and protection profits, the pattern of their world. But, lacking the clue within the *Tawhid* of Islam, their society lived 'ignorantly' of its own meaning so that, faith-wise, they were 'unfree of the land'. So the *Jahiliyyah* concept meant to say.

This territorial dimension in Muhammad's preaching tied into what would now be known as 'the anthropic principle',[11] was present immediately in—as general consent holds—the inaugurating words of the Qur'an: 'Recite in the Name of thy Lord'—at once the intense force of the personal pronoun making the summons a deep soul-engaging thing; then 'thy Lord who created,' and, for that cosmos, 'created man from a sperm-cell' seeing how 'altogether gracious is thy Lord.' At once with that world in being, that humankind in place, there follows the capacity,

---

[11] Defined in the *New OE Dict.* as 'the cosmological principle that theories of the universe are constrained by the necessity to allow human existence'—which is a 'let there be' about all that is, and its intention the human meaning, i.e. the Biblical/Quranic faith as to creation—not the question how but the question why.

the intelligence, whereby 'taught by the pen', the human custodian enters a responsible 'enlandisement' wherein to accomplish a 'highly favoured' vocation (Surah 96.1-5). 'The pen'—words, writing—are the highways of the mind.

It is not merely that here are striking rhymed word—*khalaqa*, *'alaq, 'allama, qalam*,[12] with telling assonance and rhythm. These only celebrate the human meaning as they gather into its origins the whole enterprise of its destiny. Humanity, for Muhammad, for the Qur'an, is not the 'mistake of creation'.[13] 'Land', that first and last commodity, that habitat, workshop and theatre of history, the good earth, the benign planet, is for the Qur'an the domain and dominion of the whole race, the human denizens of the world. It is as though 'thy Lord who created' said to all humankind: *Anta hillun bi-hadhihi-l-dunya*, 'You are freemen of this world,' as so commissioned by the only Lord. Only so could there be a sphere for their due *islam*.

This human freedom as tenants of the good earth, its managers, responsive to its potentialities and responsible for their entrustedness, is enshrined in the Quranic concept of 'the cosmic oath', in Surah 7.172. Unlike the covenant of Sinai in sequel to a tribal exodus and anticipating a tribal entry into a given land, the 'pledge' of 7.172 is the answer of all humankind to the divine question: 'Am I not your Lord?' to which all humans in the womb of the future answer: 'Yes! We so acknowledge.' Such awareness of divine sovereignty, explicitly registered and freely recognised, was in order that it could never be said, to the end of time: 'We did not know.' The consciousness of Allah as Lord is thus seen as implicit in human experience, the reality pertaining to all moral, social and intellectual life, the fact of a humankind meant for the divine relatedness. Yet these—the awareness, the reality, the fact—have been the theme of an interrogation to which assent has been made.[14]

What this measure of the human situation means for the Qur'an's theology is clear enough. The *Allahu akbar* omnipotence has posed the question in the negative, implying—but nevertheless awaiting—the positive

---

[12] With their *lams* and *'ains* and *qafs*. ('He created,' 'a sperm-clot', 'He taught', 'the pen'.)

[13] The opinion a character in D H Lawrence expressed, musing on how the landscape might be without the human presence. See his: *Women in Love*, London, 1921, p. 102, 'There would be no absolute loss if every human being perished tomorrow ... a world empty of people, just uninterrupted grass ...' On human entrustment, see further pp. 146-48 below.

[14] Questions in the negative are so phrased to anticipate assent but only hint at, not induce, the answer. Such—the verse implies—is the forbearance of the Almighty.

response, a would-be persuasive, not an implacably coercive, sovereignty. Its seeking human assent does not make it less majestic, less ultimate, less 'our Lord', only more deliberately so. Such is our 'freedom' in the land, designed to sober, discipline, constrain and regulate our celebration of it in culture, in the manifold 'wealth of nations'.

The divinely offered, humanly accepted, charter of Surah 7.172, is entirely in line with the creation theology of Surah 2.30. The passage has long been familiar as the heart of Quranic humanism. Allah announces to the angels in conclave the appointment of humans as 'deputy in the earth'. The angelic reaction is one of dismay and disbelief. How can the good earth be wisely entrusted to a charge and care so volatile, so frail and fickle, so obviously liable to 'corrupt' it? Enigmatically the Lord tells them: 'I know what you know not.' There is a purpose and a wisdom which concede, but override, the grounds of angelic anxiety. The command is renewed: 'Prostrate to Adam!' In the meaning of this supreme myth about all human history, the dignity of humankind as *khulafa'*, 'dominion-holders', in the world is the stake-holder for the wise sovereignty of Allah. In their recognition of the creaturely dignity the angels are acknowledging, if scarcely approving, the plan—and risk—divinely present in our human creaturehood.

The arch-Satan, Iblis, remains adamant and refuses the prostration to the humans he despises and deplores. So doing, he is 'the accuser', 'the disputer', 'the enemy'. As such, he intrigues against the creature, he plots by subtlety and guile, so to ensnare and embroil their creaturely frailties and lusts as, in due course, to demonstrate to God, the folly and futility of the whole divine/human design. So doing, he thinks to avenge himself on God.

The theme is familiar enough in the Biblical story. Milton made it memorable in his epic of a 'Paradise lost'. It constitutes a profound Quranic philosophy of history. For it follows that, 'warned', 'advised' and 'alerted' about the Satanic scheme of evil (the words all tell the prophets' task), we humans must give the lie to the liar, repudiate the repudiator who repudiates us, defy his wiles, and so vindicate the great Creator and 'justify' His risk. The Qur'an is to be seen as the revelatory crux of exactly such a result via the knowledge, the law, the exhortation that, with the example of the Prophet, it means to bring to pass.

Our creaturehood, then, as 'freedom in the land', is a sustained crisis, a drama over which judgement hangs. In no way are we 'beyond good and evil' in any Nietzschean sense. Good and evil, the right and the wrong, the allowed and the forbidden, are in Muhammad's preaching real polarities, final antinomies. The Qur'an will not allow us to sing with the Welsh poet:

> 'All your deeds and words,
> Each truth, each lie,
> Die in unjudging love.'[15]

Moral issues are at the heart of the cosmic arena of the human meaning. To have it so is the very core of our being 'freemen in the earth'.

iv

All the foregoing is illustrated by the many doxologies of the Qur'an. For it is with doxology that all right theology begins and ends. 'Praise be to Allah, Lord of the heavens and the earth, Lord of the worlds,' was the refrain of Muhammad's 'freedom in the land', the hymn in his prophethood. The range of the celebrations of nature is as wide as their fervour is deep, taking the dawn and the dark, the face of the sky and the mood of the earth in their awesomeness as setting for the human experiment which is their *raison d'être*. That the human habitat is so extraordinarily impressive to the senses tells the truth of its being more than a market for economic forces, more than a theatre of aesthetic pleasure but—with these—a realm, a 'mosque' even, of moral and spiritual *taqwa*, or inclusive *pietas*.[16]

Hence the reiterated call in Muhammad's preaching for gratitude and the unhappy verdict on the Meccan scene: 'Most of them give no thanks,' (10.60 *et. al.*) or '... do not comprehend' (28.57). The frequency of the phrase *aktharuhum la* ... 'most of them do not ...' with verbs about apprehending or realising tells how far Muhammad registered the minority status of his following in Mecca, how uphill the labour of his mission. That sense of things only made more urgent the perception of 'humans in nature', of 'nature for humans', the land and its folk, as a struggle against

---

[15] Dylan Thomas: *Collected Poems, 1934-52*, London, 1952, 'This of the Truth', p. 99.

[16] *Taqwa* and derivatives are a full key to the ethics of the Qur'an as rooted in steady, awed awareness of Allah. See: FazIur-Rahman: *Major Themes of the Qur'an*, Minneapolis, 1980. *Pietas* would be potentially the approximate Latin term.

wilful 'ignorance'. The economic liberty to occupy, possess and exploit the land was divinely meant for due exercise only in the freedom that had learned to pray. There was no place for the secular in the Qur'an's world if the secular was all. The legitimacy of everything material and sensuous lay always in its enfolding into a spiritual worship, the antithesis of which was living—as the recurring phrase has it—*min duni-Llahi*, 'to the exclusion of God'.

Thus the doxologies of the Qur'an and their prescript for 'freedom in the land' were more than the high psalmody of a religious praise: they are also the celebration of a moral universe. The point is perhaps well caught in Surah 89 with its mysterious first four verses, if read in the following context of pagan depravity. In one light they are clear doxology:

> 'By the dawn and the ten nights, by the multiple and the individuated, by the night on its way—are not these what may be sworn to by a man of sense ?'

The words could be understood as of the dawn *(fajr)* in its rising drama and the night like a wayfarer taking its leave *(yasri)*. But why 'ten nights' and what of 'even and odd'? There are things 'double' or 'paired' in nature but all are 'individuated' when they occur. Or does 'the single' *(watr)* intend us to understand 'the singular' as the utter unity of Allah who has 'none like to Him'?[17] All might still be a cryptic way of hymning the Creator.

But what of the suggestion that here is—remotely perhaps—a parody of those pagan soothsayers from whose bizarre ways Muhammad insistently distanced himself as the bearer of authentic revelation? Or, more likely, can the adjuration of 89.1-5 be read as recalling the 'ten nights' of the sacred month of pilgrimage when in the *Jahiliyyah* there was gambling and dicing (the 'even' and the 'odd') when the long night wore away in games of chance and vulgarity?[18]

---

[17] These are familiar and standard readings that stay with nature under God and do not reckon with verses three and four otherwise nor carry the allusions further into the Surah.

[18] The suggestion is made by H Amir 'Ali: *A Student's Qur'an*, Hyderabad, 1952, p. 137. Its reference to Islamic Hajj goes back to the classic commentators in their reading of the 'ten nights', as does the association with the 'ten nights' prior to 'Id al-Fitr ending the Fast. Linking it to the 10th of Muharram is surely unsound.

If so—though it could well be that the true Muslim 'ten nights of Dhu-l-Hajj' or 'the last third' of Ramadan are meant—then, implicit in the double sense, the ambiguity, we may read an intention to contrast how those made truly 'free in the land' by Islam—free to adore the living Lord with right ritual and true praise—were reprieved from all their former shame by the coming of the Qur'an.

The point is sustained by the sequence in verses 6–13 followed by the contrasted response to good and ill by the faithful Muslim. The retribution that befell the tribe of 'Ad is one with the fate of Iram (the Nabatean city of Petra thus named for its founder) and of Egypt (with its pyramids and/or 'border-stones'). Thamud had gone the same tragic way. These condign examples of requital and damnation reinforce what was ever the moral context of the celebration of the natural order. The well-loved concluding invitation to the trusting soul perhaps explains why the entire Surah is inscribed around the Taj Mahal.[19]

However controversially Surah 89.1–5 may be read, there is nothing in the same way subtle or ironic in the Quranic hymns that weave their celebration of the created order around the names of God.

> 'He is God. There is no god but He. He knows the hidden
> and the evident. He is the merciful Lord of mercy. He is
> God. There is none but He. He is the King, the holy One,
> the Lord of peace, the Keeper of faith, the watch-Keeper,
> the all-strong, the ever powerful, the Self-aware in His
> greatness. Glory be to God above all that idolaters conceive.
> 'He is God, Creator, Maker, Fashioner. His are the most
> excellent Names. All that is in the heavens and the earth
> magnifies Him, the Almighty, the all-Wise.'

Or:

> 'Do you not see how it is God whom all things praise in the
> heavens and in the earth and the birds also on wings of

---

[19] Shah Jehan, as he watched the mausoleum in building from his prison across the River Jumna, had ample reason for the godly fortitude under adversity which the Surah (v. 27–30) commends, and the gift of *itmi'nan*, or peace of heart. For he was incarcerated by his own son, the rigorist Aurangzib, the ultimate ruiner of Mughal glory. The Taj Mahal, as an exquisite monument of the love of man for woman, will always be rebuking vulgar feminism.

flight? Each truly knows its prayer and its praising and God
knows their every deed. For to God belongs the kingdom
of the heavens and of the earth.'

Or:

'Glory to God in the evening and in the morning of your
days . His be the praise in the heavens and in the earth. His
be the praise in the hereafter. ... He is the all-wise, the
ever-aware. He knows what enters into the earth and what
emerges from it, what descends from heaven and what
ascends to it. He is the merciful, the forgiving.'[20]

These and kindred passages, coming cumulatively through the formative
years of the Qur'an in Mecca take the visible, tangible, audible world, the
world of wind and work, of scene and sight, of change and chance, as all
bayan—'evidentiality', or 'that which manifests and discloses', the essential
'clarifier'. The term describes both the Qur'an itself and what an English
poet called 'the book of nature'. It could be almost the 'rhetoric' by
which the natural order 'tells its wondrous tale.'[21]

It is in the instinct of *bayan* to seek cognisance and anticipate
assent. Hence the intriguing interrogatives of Surah 55.1-30, repeated
some eight times and using the dual form of the pronoun and verb: (lit.)
'Which of the blessings of your Lord will you two deny?' The dual form,
with single intent, is used in the *Labbaika* with which the pilgrim greets
the Lord of the Ka'bah on coming to Mecca. The dual usage is said to
have been a device also of Arab poets, in a sort of 'spreading' of the range
of appeal, 'you and you' suggesting how inclusive the intention being
conveyed. Or is it possible to move the duality into the force of the verb—
'dispute and dismiss' as negatives with discernibly different angles on
what 'denial' means? As here:

'The earth He established for all living creatures, with its
fruits, its palm trees and their fruiting dates, the grain in the

---

[20] Surahs 59.22-24, 24.41-42 , 30.17-19 and 34.1-2.
[21] Joseph Addison (1672-1719), *The Spectator*, 'Ode, No. 455 On the Qur'an as *bayan*, see Surahs
55.4, 16.89 and 75.19.

blade and herbs of fragrance. Which of the blessings of your Lord will you discount and deny?

'Man He created from a potter's clay while jinn He created from flame of fire. Which of the blessings of your Lord will you discount and deny?

'He is the Lord of the points of the sunrise and of the setting sun. Which of the blessings of your Lord will you discount and deny?

'He made the confluence of the two waters and the bound between which you may not pass. Which of the blessings of your Lord will you discount and deny?

'From these came the pearl and the coral. Which of the blessings of your Lord will you discount and deny?

'His also are the ships which stand out on the face of the waters like banners. Which of the blessings of your Lord will you discount and deny?

'All that is on the earth is passing away. Only the face of your Lord abides, in majesty and glory all His own. Which, then, of the blessings of your Lord will you discount and deny?

'All beings in the heavens and the earth are suppliants to Him. Every day He is at work. Which, then, of the blessings of your Lord will you discount and deny?'

The appealing refrain, with its urgent persuasive quality, is reminiscent of the question we have noted earlier: 'Am I not your Lord?' The liberty with which humans move in the dual setting of their consciousness, the outward that is inward, tells a magnanimity carrying also a summons to attendant wonder. Thomas Traherne (1637-74), the fine poet of 'Salutation' and other songs, had he known his contemporary Edward Pococke (1604-90), the erudite pioneer of Arabic study in Oxford, would have found the Qur'an congenial in this context.[22]

There is little in the Arabian landscape that escapes the eye of the Qur'an, alert also to the history discernible in its shifting face. What we might now think of as its 'natural theology' in no way detracts—as some

---

[22] Surah 55.10-30. Traherne in his *Centuries of Meditations* and his sundry poems exulted in the mystery by which birth had ushered him into a world of perennial wonder and infinite surprise.

in the Christian tradition have feared—from the crucial place of things 'revealed' via sacred word. Rather the two spheres are seen as mutually corroborating the *bayan* (which is one of the Qur'an's titles)—the 'credentials' by which Allah, if not 'known', is truly 'traced' and 'evidenced'.[23]

This central 'God and nature' theme with humans in cognisant register—or callous, brazen negligence—is explicit in the concept of *ayat*, or 'signs', by which all natural things and events 'signify' as to Allah's mercy and power.(The word is also used for verses of the Book, making for an inclusive theology of revelation.) The *ayat* are followed frequently in the text by the participle *la'alla*, 'perhaps', and a variety of verbs— 'reflect', 'understand', 'consider', 'give thanks', and 'sense mercy'. The perennial case for comprehension, for a participation of mind and soul in the experience of existence, argues that life should be a daily appreciation of the sovereignty of Allah. Yet it is clear from the urgency of the appeal that the option of inattentiveness and discounting remains, as if to say to one and all in this 'sign-world' sense: *anta hillun bi-hadha-l-balad*, and 'perhaps you may be aware.'

v

There is an urgent contemporary relevance for us today in this dimension of the Qur'an. Its immediate bearing on the current temptation to technological arrogance, to depreciation of the body as less than a sanctuary, to callous exploitation of the natural order and to a bland consumerism, is evident enough. We have to know ourselves as *not* in a cosmos meant for violation. The good earth needs human freedoms that are reverent, tentative, discreet and perceptive. 'Meet 'tis the ground is holy.' Islam can claim from its scripture to 'bless all green things upon earth' in kinship with the Latin *Benedicite*.

This reverence, however, is accompanied by what seem to many readers remnants of an old animism, survivals from a mind-set which Islam's unitarian message superseded and repudiated. What, then, of the

---

[23] Islam has to make the proviso out of its insistence that 'knowledge' of God is not open to us mortals, but only knowledge of His ways and of His law. The divine nature, despite the command to use the Names, is not only ultimately ineffable (as all would agree) but essentially incommunicable (as Christians would not).

frequent jinns and *qarins* of the Qur'an as if it were still, in measure, a world of daimons and spirits? Embarrassingly for some Muslim exegetes, these mysterious beings are evident enough in the Qur'an's world and might prompt the question whether the Prophet's message of divine 'Unity' was not significantly compromised by their survival as from a *Jahiliyyah* of pluralism that all-inclusive divine sovereignty had doctrinally banished.

A whole Surah (72) is named for them. Surah 46.29-31 has them listening to the Qur'an as Muhammad preaches. Whereupon they went as warners to their own kind, carrying word of 'a Book' vouchsafed from on high to Moses and urging them to pay heed to Muhammad. In Surah 6.39 'the jinns and humans' are alike the addressees of revelation, though the former are 'created of fire' and the latter 'of clay-mud' (15.27 and 55.14-15)—the one, as it were, from a fiery furnace, the other from a potter's kiln. Like humans they are capable of both belief and unbelief, and of sectarian schisms (72.11-15). They were able also to recognise the wisdom of Solomon and are destined to be judged eternally as corporeal beings.

If, as *qurna'* (s. *qarin*) jinn are 'attached' to individual humans, whether as 'protectors' or 'beguilers', we would seem to be still in an animist world at some remove from that human autonomy under a single heaven assumed in the notion of *khilafah*, as authentic human 'dominion' over a good earth, disenchanted of all superstitious agencies that intervene to harass or deplete it. If so, we are still in the régime of fear, vividly indicated in the two final Surahs, of the Qur'an, the two 'refuge-seekers', and far from the meaning of 'refuge in Allah' as liberating from these fears. For in Surahs 113 and 114 we sense the atmosphere of apprehension around imprecation, and spell-binding, and the spiritual contrivances of envy, 'whispering in the bosoms of men'—the atmosphere, in short, of the *Jahiliyyah* from which Islam was intending deliverance. Yet 'refuge', from such fears, in divine 'unity' might still suggest some kind of co-existence between the two with 'refugees' secured from daimons they still credited.

Rightly read, however, Muhammad's message as from one 'free in the land'—including the freedom from fear (106.5),[24] in 'this land made safe' (95.3)—is not ultimately betrayed by the Qur'an's giving

---

[24] Though the sense in 106.5 may well refer, not to fear from jinn-attentions but from marauding tribes on the Meccans' caravans—their 'assembling' and transit—often at risk—being the context of the Surah. Yet the two sources of apprehension could well combine, if human depredations were plotted or incurred by jinn-connivance.

ample place to jinn and demonology. That verdict can stand on two counts. It needs to be realised that animism is not dispelled from apprehensive, unsophisticated, popular minds except as a gathering process of emancipation. What matters is that the liberating reality be in place and firmly proceeding—as indeed it was in Muhammad's essential mission. That there were survivals from the past is evident enough in the legacies of rituals in the pilgrimage and indeed the practice of circuiting the Ka'bah and prostration, as well as other feature of the pre-Islamic world. Some elements could be found congenial and compatible inside an uncompromised *Tawhid* or others innocuous enough to need no eradication. On such issues between what purists would passionately repudiate and others would hospitably integrate, Islam would be occupied through all its centuries.[25]

The point of a necessary gradualism in cleansing the animist vernacular world within an unmistakeable unitarian mission was well phrased by H A R Gibb. Islam was 'essentially revolt against Arabian animism.' As such

> 'What Muhammad did … was to superimpose upon the deposit of Arabian animism a supreme controlling power in the personality and activity of an all-powerful God. But under this supreme disposer the Arabian legacy persisted.'[26]

Hence the continuity, even within the text of the Qur'an, of a sense of daimonic powers, of malevolent agencies and 'familiar spirits' requiring countering invocations and reliances to thwart and defeat them. What mattered in the movement of time and culture was that the absolute confession, *La ilaha illa-Allah*, was firmly in place, under which the old phenomena could die away as beliefs and fears or be absorbed as symbols

---

[25] Examples are legion. Muslims things like *mawlids* celebrating Muhammad's birthday, Sufi invocation of saints, charm-taking from Quranic slate-washing etc, could be non-Islamic for those Muslims, e.g. Wahhabis or Kharijites, who deplored and denounced them. By these last long-established Muslim cultures could be, and have been, dubbed as still in *Jahiliyyah*. There could be no more ironic disavowal.

[26] H A R Gibb, *Studies in the Civilization of Islam*, Boston, 1962, pp. 179 and 181. He notes how the harsh conditions of life, as well as a pagan mind-set, contributed to fear of malevolence resident in sacred haunts, natural phenomena or human malice, leading to taboos and phobias requiring vigilance and more than natural protection. Attendant *qurna'* might also reinforce the idea that envies and enmities had incidence inside oneself, to prompt or betray one into 'madness' or 'excess', whereby one became *majnun*, i.e., 'jinn-possessed'.

into popular, Sufi and other, versions of Islam. In that way if the victory of monotheism was not, or ever, absolute in the common mind it was superbly entrenched in the all-commanding doctrine.

The other reason why, on the last analysis, the role of the jinn does not jeopardise the doctrine of Unity is the human 'caliphate' in the earth. It belongs with how the evil jinn in the Qur'an are party to Satanic conspiracy against the human 'empire', earlier studied in this chapter. They connive with Satan as emissaries of the wiles and guiles we human have to repudiate anyway. So it would be odd to think them outside, or independent of, the human privilege. We simply have to accommodate them (i.e. in our thinking not our heeding) inside that whole Quranic vision of the human crisis. They are just an ongoing instalment of that 'listening-in to', and disputing, divine counsels, as in the original 'myth' of Surah 2.30.

There is thus no question of the jinn not being subject to divine power or exempt from the all-inclusive worship due to Allah alone (51.56). We can comprise their significance inside eschatology, the divine resolution of all things in final judgment which is the ultimate vindication of divine sovereignty against all diamonic pretension.[27] There their molesting devices cease their troubling.

Muhammad's role in the situational features of the Qur'an and these meanings of his 'being a freeman in the land' have assumed, but thus far deferred, the central mystery of his inspiration, the language, the rhetoric, the eloquence that belonged with both. For every situation turned on a verbal deliverance with which it was aligned, and every aspect of his being 'native' to the soil of the land belonged with the words being 'native' on his lips. He spoke the land's Arabic in its most expressive range and power. That language recruited the land's imagery for its parables, its invocations and its trust-swearing 'oaths'. As the bearer of a Scripture at long last 'indigenous' to both land and language, a revelation emulating other 'scriptured' people and now at length gathering Arabs into that supreme dignity on which peoplehood would rest—all turned on 'the weighted word' (73.5)) as 'cast upon' Muhammad in 'the enmantled role' in which it addressed him. There, where the Scripture and the man conjoined, lies the central quest of all Quranic study, the whence and whither of a human agency in a divine summons.

---

[27] It is inside eschatology that Fazlur-Rahman—for the most part—deals with jinn in the Qur'an. See his *Major Themes of the Qur'an*, Minneapolis, 1980, pp. 121-43.

Chapter 3
'THOU WHO ART ENMANTLED'

i

Of all the terms by which Muhammad is personally addressed in the Qur'an none are more arguably prosaic and merely circumstantial than this at the opening of an early Surah 73: *Ya ayyuhal muzzammil*, 'thou who art enwrapped.' Yet none are more potential of significance inclusive of all the other salutations in study here. It was possible for the great exegete, Al-Baidawi, to assume that Muhammad was 'trembling' from cold until 'A'ishah wrapped a caring blanket round him. Such a bare *mise-en-scène* could never satisfy interpreters of *khuluq 'azim*, and *uswah hasanah* and *Al-Muta'a* and other epithets to which we have yet to come.

For 'mantle'—if we use the word in Surah 73.1—is the famed emblem of prophethood. The Surah, for all its 'night-watch' theme when 'wrapping' may well have been normal and wise, is about being 'charged with a divine message' which the half of those watches will bestow by the onset of the 'recital', that enjoins its own rubric of fidelity: 'Recite the Qur'an as it should be recited.' The rest of the Surah—as we must see—gives clear hints of the nature of the revelatory rendezvous it tells.

The following Surah (74) opens with a similar call: *Ya ayyuhal muddaththir.* 'O thou who art enfolded,' where again, the meaning may be quite literal yet may also suggest vocation and garb as a symbol of, or means to, the disciplines through which the destiny is reached. For, as in Surah 73, the context is plainly that of commission, a summons into witness. If the 'wrapping' were purely incidental to the time and place, even the temperature, it would seem strange for it to be the very form of address on so awesome a mission.

Traditions, however, suggest a link between 'covering'—whether prophetic 'mantle' or not—according to which Muhammad asked to be *muddaththir* at the onset of the experience of *wahy*, by reason of 'trembling'

46

under its 'weight', or of feeling cold and anxious.[1] It can hardly have been, at this early point, that he was alerted to Elijah or Elisha with their symbolic 'mantle' conveying the succession between them. They figure only rarely in the Qur'an, the one in company with New Testament figures, the other with Old Testament patriarchs.[2] In any event, the 'mantle' as the sign of a series could only be relevant in a backward sense, seeing that the Qur'an presents Muhammad as 'sealing' or finalising the whole long sequence that had originated with Adam. From that angle, a 'mantle' salutation in Surahs 73 and 74 could even be the more impressive but only in retrospect, as and when any sense of the Qur'an's ultimacy supervened in Muhammad's consciousness—a point on which it is impossible to reach any conclusion.

'O thou who art enmantled,' then, can carry for us the significance of a 'mandate' whether or not *in situ* it was merely a reference to the pre-dawn cold. The descriptives that could become names bestowed on Muslim children[3] were substitutes for the personal name so rarely used in the Qur'an. There is fascination in that very fact. Muhammad was being addressed, if not in a capacity, certainly in a posture of receptiveness and it is in that setting he is saluted by what is meant to recruit it and take it further. It is this incipient 'enfoldedness' we have to explore, its antecedents thus far—insofar as they can be told—and the long entail of the prophetic *Sirah* in Mecca and Medina.[4] Already, in the very form of these near equivalent greetings around garb and vesture, the essential 'office' rather than the individual man is where the significance resides. The words are highly personal with the intensive vocative: 'O thou!' but the import is deeply vocational. The pronoun has to do with an identity

---

[1] Only, of course, in the literal sense, because of limpness or discomposure of body thought to accompany what he underwent in Quranic 'inspiration'. See E W Lane's note in his Arabic/English Dictionary, Book 1, Part 3 under *dathara*: 'It is said that Mohammad when a revelation came on used to say: "*daththirni*: Cover me with something whereby I can be warm."'

[2] Elijah, Ilyas, is listed with Zachariah, John and Jesus among the just in Surah 6.86 and Elisha, Al-Yasa', with Ishmael, Jonah and Lot in Surah 6.87. Elijah, among others, has sometimes been identified with Dhu al-kifl mentioned in 21.85, though others have taken the term, not as a personal identity, but as a word denoting any 'pledged' or 'devoted role-bearing' such as might designate anyone so called by Allah into service.

[3] As noted, for example, by Annemarie Schimmel in her *And Muhammad is His Messenger. The Veneration of the Prophet in Islamic Piety*, Chapel Hill, 1985, p. 110.

[4] For that reason it would seem to be mistaken to use the 'mantle' word in any history ensuing after the *Sirah*. One example is Roy Mottahedeh's *The Mantle of the Prophet*, New York, 1985, a study of the role of the mullahs in 'Religion and Politics in Iran'.

but only for the sake of a destiny, a messenger at the call of a message. That is how the Qur'an throughout sees and presents the *Sirah* of Muhammad. What, then, were the antecedents in the salutation?

ii

The 'question' takes us to the factors in Muhammad shaping this mandate to him, the factors in the context conveying it towards him. For these were clearly mutual, in his being fitted for them and they moulding what he would become. There is much that remains conjectural and obscure about the mysterious interaction of personality and theme in the single denominator of 'apostle', the assuming of the 'burden'—the favoured word in the Qur'an for the vocal and the textual making it 'the Book' it was.[5]

The careful reader of Surahs 73 and 74, early as they surely are, senses that something in the soul of Muhammad is already under way. The night watches seem to be in hand, for guidance to be given about their length and on how they are more readily fitted to Qur'an recital than are the stresses of the day and there is the call to 'bear patiently' what is being urged against him. He is on every count experiencing what perhaps we may call 'prophetic formation'.

Our task is to reach for the influences already at work antecedent to the juncture at which the Surahs find him and to judge the springs within his psyche and the impulses he derived—as far as they can be discerned—from the society in which he moved and had his native nurture. It is a task that calls for a careful sensitivity. Much disquiet, if not anger, has been aroused by those whose conjectures called in question the 'givens' of Islamic faith, pre-judging what could only be the prior duty of any scholarship that stood inside those 'givens'. The sound procedure is to move, as far as may be, from the clues discernible in the Qur'an itself and from the reception Muhammad himself received from the immediate scene. For Islamic scholarship has always believed that the *Sirah*, and the Qur'an within it, were throughout situational, the

---

[5] As, notably, in Surah 94: 'The burden weighing down thy back'. Using Surah 73.5 as a clue this theme was developed (incorporating also the Biblical stress on 'burden') in my *The Weight in the Word: Prophethood, Biblical and Quranic*, Brighton, 1999.

themes being a steady encounter between his mission and his cities' reaction.

It is well to remember that, according to all traditions, Muhammad was already around the age of forty when the issues began to be joined by the onset of his inspiration. The long sequel occupied about the last third of his biography. Forty, in the life-span of that society, was late adulthood, so that there were long shaping factors relevant to the immediate 'event' of the Qur'an's incidence.[6] But what these were and how they moulded what ensued after 609 (or thereabouts) is best studied inside the years of encounter with Mecca/Medina.

Reception is the surest test of content in all such radical religious confrontations. Meanings are defined in what resists or maligns them and what they have for spoken language to carry is taken on in engagement with the vital controversy it evokes. So it was in the Christian Gospels. So it was in the Qur'an.[7] The Prophet's actual *Sirah* during its final score or so years, being the years of its actual incidence, is the best index to his being 'enmantled' by the 'charge' of the Qur'an. After the elements of that engagement have been studied we can better come to the hinterland that preceded it before 609.

iii

The constant atmosphere of affirmation wrestling with its harsh contradiction is the sustained feature of the Meccan Qur'an.

> 'Those who argue about the revelations of God, having no warrant bestowed on them for so doing, have nothing but pretentious pride in their hearts.' (Surah 40.56)

---

[6] Using the word 'event' as the best term to express the Islamic sense of a 'privileged' climax, or metahistory, where faith had its divine data. See further Chapter 7. By 'incidence'— here and elsewhere—is meant the time and place of that 'given' identified as 'revelation'. It would violate Islamic doctrine of the Qur'an's 'uncreatedness' to speak ambiguously of its beginning.

[7] If one could venture a literary analogy, George Eliot wrote of those who reproached Robert Browning of 'obscurity': 'What we took for obscurity in him was superficiality in ourselves.' Muhammad's preaching was proven precisely in the terms of the Meccan antipathy it underwent. George Eliot in *The Westminster Review*, January, 1856, p. 290.

'The leading men among them withdraw advising their
people: "Move off from him and hold staunchly to your
gods. That is what is needed. Nothing of this sort in religion
have we ever heard. It is sheer invention."' (Surah 38.6-7)

'People who ignorantly dispute about God, having neither
guidance nor book to enlighten. When they are bidden to
follow what God has sent down they say: "Indeed, not! We
follow the tradition of our fathers." What! Though it were
the very Satan calling them down to the doom of *Al-Sa'ir!*'
(Surah 31.20-21)

'When they see you (Muhammad) they take you for a joke.
"Is this the fellow God has sent for an apostle? He would
have led us astray from our gods had we not held staunchly
to them." They are just like cattle. No! Further off than that
from the true path.' (Surah 25.41-42, and 44)

'Say: "You who reject faith, I do not worship what you
worship. Never will I be a worshipper of what you have
worshipped, nor will you be worshippers of what I worship.
To you your religion and to me mine."' (Surah 109)

The issues could in no way admit of compromise, though by the same
token there could be temptation to it.[8] It was almost as if 'Thou who art
enmantled' had also to read: 'O thou who art embattled!' Such were the
fires in which the ore of the human Qur'an was smelted, the steel of the
Prophet's vocation cast. 'Do not yield to them' (76.25): 'Do not sorrow
over them nor be oppressed because of their intrigues' (27.70)—such had
to be the set of his spirit, such the situation in which the Qur'an-reader
has to measure the throes in his inner psyche.

Notable among the sceptical queries of the Quraish was the
crucial issue about the Qur'an's being Arabic. That fact—and the superb
quality of its diction—were prime items in its credentials. 'Had We sent it
down upon some non-Arab stranger and he had recited it, they would
not have believed it.' (Surah 26.198-99) The same Surah asserts its 'clear

---

[8] See below, this chapter.

Arabic speech', (v.195) as do several other paasages (41.44 and 46.13). This aspect of the encounter is best handled in the chapter following around the characterisation of Muhammad as *ummi*—a descriptive of great import and liable to sad misreading.

The language question, however, given that the Qur'an's Arabic was indeed its surpassing and corroborating asset, leads into the further matter of its sources. From the suspicions his hearers harboured against him, it is clear that his mission was shaped in a setting where story-tellers, soothsayers and rhyming poets were numerous and popular. That Muhammad was pretentiously among them was frequently alleged in scorn of him. The first Muslims, believing in his integrity, had to concede how, in part, he resembled them, while being firmly distinguished from them as one divinely enabled, as believers held.

Inevitably, the issue of pre-Islamic Arab poetry has been a sensitive one but, for intelligent faith, there is no drawback in the Qur'an's resemblance to patterns familiar—if remotely so—to its human world.[9] Indeed the Book itself brought the challenge to 'bring a Surah like it'. The gibe that he was a mere versifier, coming from enmity to his message, was only what malice did with one of the evidences—as his faith held— of the divine warrant the message enjoyed.

The invocation of eternal nature which is so keen a feature of the early Meccan Qur'an bears striking resemblance to contemporary themes, as noted in Chapter 2.

'By light and darkness, by the earth and the sky,
The trees are perishing. In truth the water will return
As it was in time gone by.'
'By the star that shines brightly,
By the star that shows clearly,
By the clouds that give rain,
By all the birds in the air,

---

[9] A classic case of the tensions involved in respect of pre-Islamic poetry and the Qur'an was that of Taha Husain's *Fi-l-Adab al-Jahili*, as far back as 1927, in which he revised and amended *Fi-l-Shi'ir al-Jahili* of the previous year (both Cairo) after his tenure as a salaried professor in the State University had been called in question by pundits who insisted on 'the inimitability' of the Qur'an in dogmatic terms that admitted of no adjacent studies that might query their 'orthodoxy'. Academic freedom, albeit expert and reverent, has made heavy weather ever since in Islamic academies.

By what is rightly guided,
By the waymarks of the wayfarer.'[10]

Surah 91 opens with the invocation:

'By the sun and the midday glory and the moon that follows after,
By the day telling its splendour and the night that envelops it ...'

And Surah 79:

'He raised the canopy of heaven and set it in poise. He made the night a cover for it and He brought forth its high noon. And then He laid the expanse of the earth, bringing forth waters and pastures therein.' (v. 28-31)

The precariousness of waters and the wayfarer's reliance on landmarks, those crucial 'signs' whereby to navigate the tracks, are kindred themes of the one world the Qur'an shared with its hearers. How else could it have addressed them with its contra-pagan note of one over-all divine supremacy?

It must follow that antecedent to this message kindling in Muhammad's soul was an instinctive sympathy for this poetic dimension in the culture of his people. The context which he came to challenge in its plural worships held the verbal model by which he would subvert and disown its spiritual vulgarity. But it was vital that the literary vehicle, in the admiration it aroused, should not be mistaken as no more than the pagan culture's familiar pride.

Hence the paradox by which the Qur'an's supreme verbal asset was also the ground of its initial Meccan discredit, thanks to what its eloquence told.

---

[10] As Charles Doughty eloquently told in his classic *Arabia Deserta* 'waymarks' are a vital factor in the Qur'an's territory. It was characteristic for Sayyid Qutb to entitle his spirited defence of Ikhwan style rigorism: *Ma'alim fi-l-Tariq*, 'Signposts on the Way,' Cairo, 1981, (published almost two decades after his death.) He was only echoing the Deuteronomist: 'Cursed be he who removes his neighbour's landmark' (27.17) and the proverbialist: 'Remove not the ancient landmark' (27.28).

'Give them to know that you are no soothsayer, no crazy
fellow. Or are they saying: "He is a poet? We expect some
chance of fate will see to him." Tell them: "Wait as you may. I
have my anticipations no less than yours!"' (Surah 52.29-31)

'As for the poets, it is the beguiled who follow them. Do
you not see them around in every valley, wandering in their
trances? Words not matched by deeds.' (Surah 26.224-25)

'We have not taught him poetry: it would not be fitting for
him. For this is solely a *Dhikr* and a luminous Qur'an.' (Surah
36.69)

The poetic *I'jaz* of the Book could only serve for sign to those heeding
the message it conveyed: others writing it off as 'a fraud' were condemned
by their own impercipience.

  The wandering soothsayers and legend-tellers were another feature
of Meccan life with whom Muhammad's detractors could readily link his
words. 'Legends of the ancient people they say. He has had them written
as they were rehearsed to him morning and evening' (Surah 25.4). Did
they have in mind the stories of Dhu al-Qarnain and Dhu al-Kifl, of
Alexander and the corpse of Solomon?[11] These were certainly part of an
oral culture to which the radical theism of the Qur'an was meant to
belong. It had, therefore, to make its way—and Muhammad's tested spirit
with it—inside, and yet against the grain of, its immediate setting.

  Thus the charge against him of being a folklorist dogged his
words. 'Fables of the ancient!' (68.15). Or, it was held against him that he
was a forger of his deliverances. 'They say of the truth when it has come
to them: "This is plain sorcery!"' (46.7) 'They are astounded that a warner

---

[11] Lit. 'the owner of the two horns', (18.83f) and 'the owner of the pledge' who appears
anonymously in 21.65 and 38.48 where he accompanies Isma'il, Idris, and Elijah. Sulaiman
(Solomon) figures in 34.12-14, not only in his control of the winds and his copious
mining of copper, but also for the miracle whereby his corpse, leaning on his staff, only
collapsed to the ground when vermin (?) gnawed it away. There was also the famous story
of the Seven Sleepers (18.9-27). It refers to *Al-Raqim* (v.9) as, possibly, the name of the
village of the celebrated 'cave'. Some of these stories bear on the titles of the chapters of
the Qur'an. They served to reinforce the preaching moral that was always in mind. There
can be no doubt that this story-telling feature links the Book squarely with the Arab ethos
of the time and place.

has come from among themselves. The unbelievers say: "This is indeed a lying sorcerer. Has he indeed made the gods into one God?—a marvellous thing to do!'" (38.4-5). Precedents abounded for this kind of calumny. 'No messenger came to those of earlier times of whom they did not say: "He is either a sorcerer or he is mad"' (51.52).

A Prophet's being 'jinn-possessed' was a gibe that often came Muhammad's way in those Meccan years. 'You are not jinn-possessed,' he was assured in 68.2. Clearly the solace was necessary but he was able to turn the tables.

> 'As for the satans—shall I tell you on whom they come down? They descend on every sinful liar. What they hear they impart and most of them are false informers.' (Surah 26.221-23)

It was no small 'burden' running the gauntlet of a so mischievously perverse and hostile world. There was need for patience such as was often enjoined on him. 'Await with patience what your lord determines. Do not yield to any among them' (76.24). The counsel was necessary both for the intervals that had to pass in his reception of words, but also for the stress stemming from the use his vilifiers made of them. This 'periodicity' of the Qur'an was a large part of its 'wear' in the soul, at least in the Meccan years. Hence 87.8: 'We will take you gently where rest will be yours,' with its gentle play on the words around *Sirah*.[12] 'Be patient, the promise of God is true' (40.55). What was requisite in the apprehension was crucial in the confrontation.

The text and the gainsayers apart, there were also insinuations about mercenary motives in the Prophet's role. In a passage of high rhetoric where Allah engages in heavy satire with the Quraish, He asks Muhammad: 'Are you asking some fee from them, burdening them with insolvency?' (52.40). He had to steer clear of any traps they could lay. 'Shun defilement. Give not with a view to self-increase' had been the mandate from the first (74.5 and 6).

'Say: "For this I seek no reward from you, save that

---

12 *Wayuyassiruka li-l-yusra, yasira* 'to make easy' is the original verb, *yusra* the 'resultant ease or rest'. *Sara*, 'to journey, travel or proceed' yields *sirah*, 'a going', and so 'a record of going', 'career'.

whoever wills shall take his way to the Lord.' (25.57)

Believing response from his hearers was to be the only and sufficient recompense.

Throughout the long encounter with Meccan obduracy and the trial of strength around its sundry devices of scorn, obloquy and insinuation, it was natural Muhammad should come to register the mystery of human ill-will, the capacity to repudiate both good tidings and warning, the tenacity with which guilt and perversity could entrench themselves. In the event, it was these that prompted the option for the Hijrah which, in certain senses, only short-circuited the issue. There was an early anticipation of the problem:

'These men are in love with this fleeting world and put behind them the harsh reality of doom's day.' (76. 27)

Hence, the sustained, at times seemingly fruitless quest for *qawm yatafakkarun*, 'a people giving their minds' to heed. Hence also the steady reiteration that what was being said on his part was no less, no more, no other, than what all Allah's envoys had brought.

'All this is to be found in the earlier pages of Scripture, the Scriptures of Abraham and Moses.' (Surah 87.18 and 19)

'I am not a new phenomenon among apostles, nor have I any forward knowledge of my destiny nor of yours. I follow only what is inspired within me by revelation.' (Surah 46.9)

'Long before your time messengers have been met with derision. But those who taunted them were overtaken by the very thing they had laughed out of court. (Surah 6.10)

In the toll of his engagement with the folk of his native city, Muhammad's sense of authenticity took inner hold within him the more, from the very force of their enmity and the inventiveness of their devices in reproach.

'They said: "What sort of messenger is this who takes food and walks about in the suqs? Why was no angel sent down

55

to keep him company in his warnings? Why no treasure as a windfall for him? Why no gardens for him as his provender?"' (Surah 25.7-8)

The imaginative reader of the Qur'an can tell the human wistfulness that finds itself buoyed by the solace in the lines that follow:

'See what notions they bandy about to describe you, lost in error as they are, and unable to get on the right way. Blessed be He who will indeed bestow on you, as He wills, much better gardens than their idea—with running streams and palaces that He will confer. (Surah 25.9-10)[13]

iv

What, then, was the inner incentive in the soul that sustained Muhammad through this long encounter? The personal address, in the last passage, by the Sender to the sent was—we might say—the 'mantling' the *Sirah* 'wrapped' around him, the psychic experience as a garment of destiny. All the clues are there to the initiation from which it stemmed and which its sequences confirmed. The *Shahadah*—though too tersely—comprised them, namely the urgent assertion of the divine unity and the imperative vocation conjoined to it—Allah and His apostle. These could only take shape in the *Sirah* by the play of the local and personal factors bringing them to climax.

The role of prophet-messengers in the economy of Allah was a salient feature of Muhammad's awareness from the outset and, with it, the conviction that 'messengers for peoples' and 'peoples having their own as messengers' was the constant pattern. This meant 'Books' and 'writings' brought and in turn possessed through the indigenous pattern of divine 'sendings'. Conspicuously exemplifying this order of things was Jewry, exclusively 'people of the Book', so possessively enjoying a status that 'Arabs' no less manifestly lacked. The forebears of Muhammad's generation may have been the wilful auditors of Salih, Hud and Shu'aib,

---

[13] Is it fair to conjecture whence, in the Hijaz, came dreams of 'running streams and palaces'?

but in their remoteness these had left nothing comparable to the Torah of Moses. There was no comparable 'prophet to the Arabs', no 'Arabic *Kitab*' to fulfil the vital role of Scriptures.

We need to make the case in Chapter 4 concerning Muhammad's 'sentness' as the answer, in his own responding psyche, to this hard predicament. To sustain it there was the tradition of those *hunafa'*, 'theists' of 'Arab' lineage via Abraham but outside the line that ran through Isaac and Jacob and engendered Moses. At least the Qur'an's steady pride in its being 'Arabic', and superbly so, chimes well with its destiny to supply the prophethood the Arabs thus far lacked and to do so via a heritage of undeviating worship of One Lord linked with Mecca itself in Abraham, builder of its famous Ka'bah. The monotheists, the *hunafa'* of Abraham's vintage, his *millah* or 'faith-folk' as 'non-Jews', seem to have been a major factor in Muhammad's call. The impetus their repute brought to him also brought together the main strands—things local, indigenous, vernacular, fulfilling both lack and yearning in all those realms.[14]

These influences, however, if we judge them rightly such, could not have conduced to their Quranic fulfilment without long and questing deliberation on Muhammad's part. That dimension takes us to the significance of Mount Hira', the famous rendezvous with meditation, to which—according to repeated tradition—he repaired in the months prior to the event/events to which Surahs 96, 53 and 81 refer.[15] How these supervened on what pre-empted them[16] and how they answered what hungered towards, as does a thirsty land the quenching shower, must always remain the core of the Qur'an's mystery. A wise perception knows that auto-suggestion basely betrays what eventuated but also that entire relinquishment of soul and search could only have frustrated it. Room has to be made in the making of a prophet for the prophet he is made. No 'Book' could be given into a *Sirah* where a *Sirah* had no place in the beginning of its coming to be in human speech and mind.

---

[14] The role of Abraham in Islam hardly serves as a 'unifier' among Semitic faiths (as is often assumed to be the case). For the Quranic Abraham only fulfils his role in clear dissociation from his Hebraic aura. He is the great iconoclast, not the 'seed-progenator', patron of Jerusalem—to be sure—but supremely builder of Mecca's shrine.

[15] See below, the 'vision' and the 'voice', the visual and aural experience of *wahy* in its first dramatic entrance into his personal consciousness, making for the heightened self-awareness which is the central concern of these chapters.

[16] 'Pre-empt' in the strict sense that there was a deep pre-engagement for what they would become when they transpired.

The stress Muhammad underwent in the actual deliverance of
the Qur'an to his hearers was noted for emphasis in Chapter 1. It certainly
was present in its 'deliverance' to him in the incidence of the initial
occasions of inspiration. It seems well to read back from the one into the
other the vivid words of Surah 18.6: 'You are grieving to the death
(bakhi'un nafsaka) over the way they are.[17] Muhammad was in deep anxiety
about the evidences offered by the society around him, of corruption,
decay and malaise—the features that the term *al-jahiliyyah* denoted. They
were born of pagan pluralism and the patronage of feuding tribes, and
the incipient fatalism of a grimly mortal world. It was a world capable of
female infanticide answering the precariousness of the common scene,
despite the prestige of the city and its commerce. The ledgers of its
merchants seem to have loomed large in the mental horizon of the
marauding tribes, bought off by some version of protection racket as
their way of sharing the profits.

It is also well to ponder the *mise-en-scène* out of which
Muhammad's recourse to Mount Hira' and meditation came within the
several tensions inside the 'Abd Manaf tribal clan to which he belonged.
It is clear that as his mission began and its local encounter intensified, he
had the powerful protection of his uncle Abu Talib, who, however, never
became a Muslim. The several branches of the clan claimed and exercised
their respective privileges relating to the environs of the sacred precincts
and their custody. The inter-association between them and their *haram*
enclosure, with its holy well of Zamzam and the 'corner' of the *Iltizam*,[18]
was certainly a decisive element in the interrogation of his spirit. What
did such a custodianship imply, given the implications of the different
perspectives of those *hunafa'* ? Muhammad's eventual sense of vocation
was no abstract vision exempt from the constraints of family and kinship-
heritage. Its emergence came in the bosom of domestic, local bonds and
ties, readily fertile in conflict and emotion.

Arguing—as we must—from the *Sirah* as it ensued via the *Sirah*
in its mental genesis, it would appear plain that Mecca's trading instincts
and its pattern of usury figured largely in Muhammad's misgivings about

---

[17] A fair translation of the phrase *'ala atharihim*, lit. 'at their traces'. The renderings differ—
following after them', 'over their footsteps', 'sorrowing over them'. *Bakhi'un* has the sense
of both anger and grief.

[18] *Iltizam*—the pilgrim ritual of pressing the breast against 'black stone' at a corner of the
Ka'bah, as opportunity affords, or can be made, during the *tawaf* or ritual circumambulation.

his society. It may be thought that the hostility to usury only became central as antipathy hardened on other grounds, namely the religious quarrel over plural worships or, as a weapon, was necessary in the post-Hijrah conflict by which the Quraish could be enfeebled. Other consideration, however, counter that cynical view. The Qur'an's stress on alms for the poor, on the obligation of *Zakat* and the steady reprobation of extortion and deceit in commerce, suggest a deep economic urge in the Prophet's impulse to withdrawal where his disquiets would find their positive commission.[19]

Whatever may, in this way, be discerned or conjectured, the ultimate impulse to all that tradition tells us about Muhammad's experience on Mount Hira' springs from the inner secrets of his personality, 'Thou who art enmantled.'[20] Rigorists have refrained—for the sake of their view of *wahy*—from language about 'genius'. Historians have found the word compulsory, sensing the elusive, psychic and spiritual elements at work in the personal origins of great religions. What, in the figurative sense, was the 'mantle' that 'enrobed' Muhammad in that sequence of visitations or epiphanies which his mission translated into the *Sirah* thus laid upon him?

There is one immediate point to register. It stood firmly in the 'tuition' and hortatory 'guidance' of humankind as assumed in and by the Hebraic tradition of prophethood, though free of the ethnic particularity of that tradition. It perceived itself, via its Arabicity, 'a mercy to the worlds'. But, in conforming to prophetic 'messaging' and 'warning' and 'exhorting', it had no 'Messianic' dimension,[21] in the sense that its reliance for 'success' stood in the clarity, the urgency and the veracity, of what was

---

[19] They also seem to have been a large factor in Meccan hostility to Muhammad when preaching reproached malpractice and exploitation. See W Montgomery Watt: *Muhammad: Prophet and Statesman*, Oxford, 1961. Surah 68.10-15 would be a case in point.

[20] Here, unlike other passages to be noted soon, the language is direct, employs the personal pronoun and places the command to 'rise and warn' at the very core of his identity. It is the most immediately 'role-bestowing' of all the titles or descriptives by which Muhammad is given to 'know himself'—not in the Socratic terms of some philosophic 'Who am I?' but as a prophet's self-awareness.

[21] In contrast to the gathering 'lesson' on a Messianic destiny which—according to the Letter to the Hebrews (5.9) —Jesus underwent during his Gospel *Sirah*, or life-path. I tried to develop the entry on Messiahship there in: *The Education of Christian Faith: Literary and Critical Encounters with the New Testament*, Brighton, 2000. No 'Messianism', in any such sense, was necessary or present in Muhammad's *Sirah*, seeing that the whole emphasis was on 'law' and 'warning'—unless, of course, we see a sort of 'something Messianic' in these alone.

'uttered'. It did not stand in the tradition of 'saving expectation', whereby the predicament of uneducable perversity, proven immune to hortatory persuasion, would need to be 'redeemed' by more than sound advice, by the love that sacrificially 'bore its wayward sins'.

That fundamental characteristic of a (solely) preached message led at length to the counter strategy of the Hijrah with its different kind of persuasion. Thus the *Sirah* was fundamentally conditioned by the theme of its initiation as a summons to 'warn' and to 'recite', to rehearse the rule and claim of God. In the Hebraic tradition of an exceptionality of theirs with Yahweh, Jewry relied on the covenant of Sinai as under-writing all that proved urgently 'expectable' from Yahweh in the light of exile. Hence the sundry shapes of Messianic hope which the Christian faith identified by their perceived fulfilment in Jesus and the Cross—a fulfilment which inaugured what it necessitated, namely a relevance in redemption open to all kindreds of the world. Muhammad's sense of vocation, born outside the Hebraic covenantalism, nevertheless renewed the régime of law and prophethood and thereby forewent the Messianic.

How, then, should we understand that *mysterium tremendum* in the summons to 'recite'? It is striking that though Muhammad is the immediate party to all that transpired, it is told nevertheless in the third person. So Surah 81.15-28.

> 'NO: I swear by the planets in their revolving and declining courses, by the brooding night and the breathing dawn. This is truly the utterance of a gracious bringer of truth, one imbued with strength and authenticated before the Lord of the Throne, demanding obedience and worthy of trust. Your kinsman, then, is not out of his mind. He saw truly, saw the vision on the bright horizon. He is not one to keep jealously to himself the transcendent mystery. This is not the word of some accursed Satan. So, where are you heading? This is a word addressing and alerting all sentient beings, everyone who is willing for the straight path.'

'I swear'—there is the immediate speaking self but 'your kinsman ... he saw ... he is not one ...'—the telling is as of one reporting about another. Is this a measure of how an individual identity is taken over by a sacred office so that the speaking one is initiated into what is other than himself?

The pattern is the same in Surah 97 where Allah tells of 'angels and the Spirit descending' on the 'night of power' with no mention of Muhammad upon whom that 'descending Qur'an' comes on 'a night of peace until the breaking of the day'. The human recipience—for such it was and had to be—lacks all mention. Is this to indicate how all embracing, how total, the transcendent will?

Again in Surah 53.1-18, which is the most explicit of the events on Mount Hira', and which vindicates Muhammad after some interlude of actual preaching, the third person form of narrative remains.

> 'By the star and its setting, your kinsman has not been led astray, nor is he under delusion. He does not speak by some whim of his own. This nothing else than a revelation imparted to him. One of awesome power has taught it him, a being of supreme strength, who stood on the height of the horizon and then approached, coming down to within two bows' length, even nearer, and then revealed to his servant what he brought.'
>
> 'The vision he saw his heart did not deny. So will you take issue with him over what his vision is? In truth, he saw him in another vision by the Sidrah tree—the garden of refuge is close by—when the Sidrah tree was wrapped in a covering. His gaze was transfixed, never turning from the sight. Truly he saw the greatest signs of his Lord.'

What is unmistakable in this passage fraught with mystery is the intense interplay between Muhammad face to face with his hearers and Muhammad fused with the conviction born of vision. It was in grappling with its fulfilment in the one that he possessed the reality of the other. 'Nothing else than a revelation imparted'—told itself in the answering urge to utterance. So it had been in Surah 96: 'Recite in the Name of thy Lord.' The paradox that impersonalises him in the narrative—'he saw,' 'he saw, his gaze was fixed,' 'never turning from the sight', 'he saw'—personalises him intensely in the appeal: 'Will you (Meccans) take issue?' and in the direct address: 'Recite in thy Lord's Name' (96.1).

What was clearly an overwhelming personal experience of encounter with revelatory visitation is, nevertheless, told in studious avoidance of the pronoun 'I'. 'Your companion', 'your comrade', 'your fellow'—as the translations go of *sahibukum*—makes him a third party to what transpired, even though it powerfully commissioned him, and only him, to be its mouthpiece.[22] Could there be a clearer appeal, on his part, not only to his being truly an indigene and genuine, but also that status as displacing his private name and, with it, neutralising the kinship nexus, of which, nevertheless his hearers need to be re-assured? 'Nothing else than a revelation imparted to me' is what he will not say:' ... imparted to him' who now proclaims the 'imparted' thing, fronting their incredulity. The vision has absorbed the Muhammad of mere kinship familiarity into the apostle of Allah.

But what are we to understand by 'One of awesome power'? The visionary 'teacher', 'a being of supreme strength', stands 'on the rim of the horizon' and 'comes down' those 'two bows' distance, revealing what he revealed'? The vision was undeniable but 'his heart' *(fu'aduhu)* did not 'deny'. What do we understand by this other organ of reception which brought its own submission to the sight?[23] What held the gaze found ardent consent from the inward depths of being, where fear, alarm or anxiety would otherwise have doubted what, so greeted, could not have been authentic.

Whatever the point intended by 'the mantle' in Surahs 73 and 74, it serves well to symbolise what the vision of Surah 53 conveyed to Muhammad, namely the 'mandate' of 'voicing' the 'revelation' revealed— a task already underway, as the narrative shows, before its authoring crisis has been told.

The 'other vision' of Surah 53 is usually understood as referring to the *Mi'raj* or 'Ascension' of the Prophet, beyond the Night Journey of 17.1 to Jerusalem. So much is suggested by the celestial imagery of the shady lotus tree and the garden of refuge, clad in the enveloping calm of Paradise. Its position in the Surah only confirms the central truth—to be seen as crucial to all else—of the constant interplay between the authenticity of vocation and its immediacies in the responding *Sirah*.

---

[22] The term occurs also in 34.46. We note in Chapter 4 how important it was that Muhammad was of their own kin and not some alien import, and so suited to 'an Arabic Qur'an'. *Sahibukum* has also been taken to mean an emphasis on his being 'human and so mortal', or that the plea that he is well known among them offsets any charge of madness.

[23] *Qalb* is the other usual word for 'heart' as that 'upon which the Qur'an was sent down', i.e., not the lips alone. It is said that *fu'ad* denotes more the pulsating, rather than reflective, action of the heart. Hence 'ardent' here.

An objective view, in the context of religious history, is surely to see the epiphanies or visions the Qur'an records of Muhammad as mediating between the conscious soul-quest of which traditions tell on Mount Hira' and the active word-mission that the *Sirah* fulfilled. They intercepted, we might say,[24] the yearnings of a seeker and conveyed them to the energies of a campaigner. The inner nausea around a moral and social *jahiliyyah* was galvanised into a correcting mission. A brooding aspiration after a 'native' gift of people-defining Scriptures was rewarded in a destiny to be its human means. What had inwardly drawn Muhammad into the muse of withdrawal found answer in the outward enterprise to which its climax conveyed him. Or, in more abstract terms, it was a metahistory where a religion found community in faithful celebration of its meaning, via the tangible evidences of the *Sirah* comprising its founding story.

It is such metahistory Sayyid Qutb is identifying when he writes in *Fi Zilal al-Qur'an*:

> 'The true nature of this event is that Allah ... out of his benevolence, has turned to that creation of His called "man" ... The period that followed the event was twenty-three years of direct contact between the human race and the Highest Society.'

and in *The Meccan Crucible*:

> 'This direct link between heaven and humankind ... these words (of God) find their descending way to man. What a blessing it is that God was aware of him, has turned to him, has linked him unto Himself and has chosen of his human genus a Messenger to whom He reveals his words and his habitat, the earth, to be their descending place.'[25]

Such is the language of an interpreting faith. Those who stand outside it—as Muslims are outside other metahistories that have a comparable

---

[24] In the strict sense of the word, i.e., 'met along their way,' as implementing what they awaited.
[25] Eng. trans. *In the Shade of the Qur'an*, by M A Salahi and A A Shamis, London, 1979, Vol. 30, p. 220-21. Zakaria Bashier, *The Meccan Crucible*, London, 1978, pp. 96-100.

role for the faiths possessing them—can best handle their scepticism, if such it be, by conceding the *de facto* reality of given faiths in given metahistories and, leaving the critiques to the academic realm, that may, or may not, sift them, and try to appreciate and apply whatever abides or avails for the guidance and benediction of secular society.

For founding 'events' always consist in the issue they historically have, as with the Torah of Sinai, the 'Enlightenment' of the Buddha, the Gospel of 'the Word made flesh', or the Qur'an of Muhammad. Sufi devotion may make what it will of that 'mantle', its antecedents and its sequence, while theosophy will conjecture about the 'genius' of *Al-Insan al-Kamil*[26] but the direct historian will be in the presence of a religious phenomenon best evaluated by what preceded it and eventuated from it, in the persona and the *Sirah* of Muhammad himself. That leaves us still more squarely with the psychological theme involved in all the titles it conferred upon him. It is one to which we must return in Chapter 7.

There is perhaps one clue here in the Qur'an's phrase about *Sharh al-sadr* which gathers to itself both psychic and mystical significance having to do with the implanting of the word reported in Surahs 53, 81 and 96. *Sharh*, when applied to a text or document, has almost the sense of 'exegesis', i.e. the 'drawing out' of what is latent, while *sadr* means simply 'bosom' or (crudely) one's 'chest.'[27] Thus Surah 94.1, enquires: 'Have We not opened for thee thy bosom?' The phrase comes in Surah 20.25, as a prayer of Moses: 'O my Lord, open my bosom for me and ease for me what I have in hand.'[28]

The bearing of *Sharh al-sadr* on Muhammad's Hira' experiences may be in mind in the general term of *sharh al-sadr li-l-islam*, 'the opening of the heart to Islam'. But it is noteworthy that all believing Muslims are those for whom this blessing has happened (39.22), for it is how Allah deals with those He wills to guide (6.125).[29] However, 'opening of the

---

[26] The Perfect Man', a favourite term encapsulating belief in Muhammad as 'spiritual genius' and 'supreme exemplar of the human meaning'; see, e.g., Annemarie Schimmel: *op. cit.*, note 3, pp. 134f, 219 and 231 with citations.

[27] The English idiom 'something on my chest' would be too vulgar; 'the bosoms of men' are the prime arena of Satan's wiles in the Qur'an, cf. Surah 114. But see, further, Chapter 7, note 16.

[28] Or 'my task' or 'what I am commanded.' For it is the 'burden' that most 'straightens' the spirit, so that the two halves of the prayer tally.

[29] The verse goes on to state that Allah 'narrows' or 'constricts' the bosoms of those whom He does not will to guide. 16.106 refers to those who have 'opened their bosoms to kufr (unbelief)' have His wrath upon them. In such passages responsive action is volitional and yet, somehow also fated.

bosom' is contrasted with the state of being *da'q al-sadr*, i.e. constricted and confined. Surah 15.97 observes of Muhammad: 'We know well that your bosom is tense ('narrowed') over what they are saying,' a comment and comfort that confirms the fact of things fervently reciprocal between Muhammad recipient and Muhammad announcer of the word.[30] Thus the intaking of meaning into the receptive heart is steadily conscious of its public conveyance as liable to daunt the spirit and constrict the speaking self—a fact fully corroborated by the Qur'an's frequent allusions to Muhammad's need of vigilance in the presence of demonic mischief or malign distraction. This situation, inside *wahy* and the *Sirah* bearing it, deserves a careful study. For it was one in which his persona, carrying the office, was critically self-aware.

v

The issue becomes evident in address to Muhammad in Surah 11.12-13.

> 'It may be that you are leaving out part of what is revealed to you out of distress of heart *(da'iq bihi sadruka)* at what they are saying, namely: "Why has no treasure been given him from above? Or why has no angel come with him?" whereas you are simply a warner and God has everything within His charge. Or are they saying: "It is a forgery on his part"? Say: Then you bring ten comparable Surahs, your own concoctions ...'

If this passage and that in 15.97 are suggesting that some temptation to compromise the message was present for Muhammad in the stress caused him by the taunts of his adversaries, then there could be no clearer evidence of how embroiled inside his personhood—his *sadr*—the entire mission was. The reality of a 'receptive' or a 'distressed' 'bosom' would, either way, completely attest his personal engagement with the word of revelation.

Being 'enmantled', then, as also being 'embattled' meant, in turn, being 'entangled' or 'enmeshed' in the whole situation of Quranic

---

[30] For here, as elsewhere frequently, the actual content of' the Qur'an supervenes on things circumstantial and vocational inside the *Sirah*.

mediation, i.e. the conveying of the 'speech of God' via the self-in-action of Muhammad into the human realm of hearkening and obedience. The pressure to adjust the inexorable mandate of the Book's entrustment in his care to the placating of his scorners and critics of his message could only mean that his fidelity was a personal crisis in his very psyche. It meant, further, that his victory over the stressful trial sided him with Allah in a deeply existential way, for which we might perhaps enlist the Hebraic idea of 'sympathy' with God.[31]

The point may be expounded by reference to the 'divine council' at which certain Hebrew prophets were said to have been present.[32] Surah 2.30 has angels in that role in line, perhaps, with Isaiah's report of God's question: 'Whom shall I send and who will go for Us?' Any such 'for Us' on God's part means that prophets are enlisted for His truth's purposes. Whether or not they are any party to them in their conciliar heavenly origins, they are certainly partners in them down in the moil and mire of the human scene. They are called to be concretely on behalf of the divine will where all its heavenly provenance bears on time and place. When time and place threw up the kind of perversity in hearers that Muhammad knew as *da'iq al-sadr* among them, he was in active identity with Allah's counsel and cause.

Sharh al-sadr, then, can only fully mean this identity in its positive quality of trial overcome and mission fulfilled. Seeing that *sharh al-sadr* is so clearly associated with the theme of the Night Journey and the *Mi'raj*, we may perhaps take these to mean, in some sense, Muhammad's 'audience' in divine counsels. If so, the experience of soul-constriction and inner turmoil at the hands of an obdurate world would be the due corollary of the status that 'enmantled' him.

Though Islamic mysticism has been only too ready to mythicise the Prophet's stature in its own terms, Muslim piety has tended to resist any thought of his having been exposed to possible compromise.

---

[31] Abraham Heschel, in his definitive work *The Prophets*, New York, 1962, develops the concept of 'divine pathos' into which he sees prophets like Jeremiah entering as the very condition of their ministry. The theme is not readily congenial to the Islamic mind yet, clearly, as when Muhammad stood out against adversity to his commission from Allah he was, by the same token, 'on behalf of Allah'. In that sense there was an identity between the divine ends and the human means.

[32] In Jeremiah 23.18 it is the mark of the true prophet in contrast to the false ones who 'send themselves' (Cf. Jeremiah 14.14). When refusing to be drawn into proffered compromise with the pagans is not Muhammad standing by—if not 'standing at'—the council of God?

Nevertheless there are clear testimonies in tradition to the actuality. There was the personal factor of strong Quraishi pressure on his staunchly protective uncle, Abu Talib, to whom delegations came from time to time, urging him to cease succouring Muhammad or perhaps—as some traditions suggest—proposing some compromise whereby Muhammad might propagate his 'Allah' without expressly denouncing (or in Quraishi terms vilifying) the gods on whom their lucrative custodianship of pilgrimage crucially depended.[33]

Despite the deep clan tensions, Muhammad held his ground. The claim of the Unity of Allah could not co-exist with any such *modus vivendi*. Whatever the precise date of Surah 109, its stance prevailed: 'To you your religion, to me mine.' However, there seems to have been— according to some tradition—more question over the notorious 'Satanic verses'. The passage now runs:

> 'Have you (pl.) thought about Allat, Al-'Uzza and the third Manat, the other goddess? Do you have male children and He the females? That would be a very unfair allotment!' They are nothing but names: you have coined them yourselves and your fathers, with no warrant at all from God. They are merely following supposition and their own wishful thinking, though guidance from their Lord has truly come to them.' (Surah 53.19-23)

Did Muhammad, at some point, under stress of hostility—and that deeply within his own clan circle—incline to some mutual conciliation for the sake of his protecting uncle? Could he, as it were, have conceded those three Meccan goddesses to the Quraish, while adding that they were merely 'names' anyway, thus letting them keep their illusions while he still disavowed them? In that way they and he, theirs and his, might co-exist in peace.

Or was his characterisation of them as 'mere names' a deliberate repudiation, signalling no compromise—as the very local, and sharp, case-making that follows indicates? The 'no warrant from God' ruled out all tolerance of them, while 'mere names' not fit to quarrel over *could* have

---

[33] See, for example, Sir William Muir, *The Life of Mohammad*, ed. T H Weir, rev. ed. 1923, pp. 68, 87-88.

once meant some ready, if uneasy, conciliation. There the traditions ambiguously leave the infamous 'Satanic verses'.

Either way, Muhammad emerges in line with 'the counsel of God'. If ever made, the concession was loyally withdrawn and the absolute claim of the solitary Allah upheld. Piety will want to dispute the traditions that record some tentative compromise as only false and malicious. But that Muhammad's mission was prone to, and beset by, pressures to compromise seems inseparable from any intelligent reading of the nature of prophethood itself, any adequate reckoning with the realities of the Meccan scene.

From all such careful study of the vicissitudes of the *Sirah*, both here and as relayed from Chapters 1 and 2, or remitted to 4, 5 and 6, it is evident that being 'prophet of Allah' was no abstract or self-vacant role but deeply grounded in the psyche, a transaction in the total self both intelligent and intuitive. Analogies about a flute in the lips of a flautist or a pen in the hand of a scribe will not serve. That covering 'mantle' on Mount Hira' had more to do than offset the cold night air or comfort a shivering body. We may not say or think that the more we ascribe to the Spirit the more impersonal becomes the instrumentation of the text.

On the contrary, the surer Muslim faith would be in the Qur'an's being 'from God', the more insistent must be the confession of the personal travail in its being through Muhammad. Is not so much explicit in the very shape of the *Shahadah* whose two halves do not explain their juncture but profoundly assume it?

Thus, it is neither Muslim nor adequate to say with Ali Dashti that the Qur'an is Muhammad's 'initiative in proof of his innate genius', nor with Jalal al-Din Rumi that 'he was not there at all, for the speaker in reality was God.' The former writes 'to dispel a phantom' and see prophethood as 'the mental and spiritual genius peculiar to an extraordinary individual', for whom 'the angel personified the aspiration long latent in the depths of his being ... Years of meditation concretised the idea ... The voice (if genuine) was the voice of Muhammad's own soul.'[34]

By contrast, in his *Discourses* Jalal al-Din Rumi sees the Prophet 'transported out of himself'.

---

[34] Ali Dashti, *Twenty Three Years*, Eng. trans. F C R Bagley, London, 1986, pp. 25-53.

'Now that such words are being born from him he realises
that he is not now what he was at first. This is God controlling
him ... It became realised that it was not he who was
speaking: God was speaking.'

Rumi's language could be taken in two ways, one incorporating the
responsible/responsive prophet for whom we have argued, had he not
gone on to invoke a most bizarre analogy. It had to do with stone birds
through whose mouths cunning plumbers have routed lead piping to
create a garden fountain.

All possessed of reason know that the water does not issue
out of the mouth of a stone bird, it issues out of another
place ... God delivers His words by means of any letters and
voice and tongue He desires.'[35]

A right mind about the soul of the *Sirah* in the Qur'an matters because of
the fact of the two in the long reception of the Islamic community.
Religious faiths of long tenure in human history are necessarily
institutionalised, not only in structures of society but in perspectives of
mind. In any inter-religious meeting these must be allowed. For long
receptions of their order have to be conceded—and understood—in terms
of the conviction they have brought to pass and the centuries have
sustained.

' ... the words sufficed
To compel the recognition they preceded.'[36]

What the Qur'an is religiously held to be by the household of Islam has
the status that religious holding finds it to be. Such is the way of all
metahistory in the dimensions of faith. But the holding has to be intelligent
and open, a commitment carrying well the onus of its integrity. From all
that was entailed in Muhammad, 'enmantled' and so 'embattled' and thus
in turn 'enlisted' and 'enmeshed', we move to other features of the *Sirah*
that reinforce the case. The descriptive of Muhammad as *al-rasul al-ummi*,
notable among them, occupies the next chapter.

---

[35] *Discourses of Rumi*, trans. A J Arberry, London, 1961, pp. 51-52.
[36] T S Eliot, *Four Quartets*, 1959 ed. London, p. 53.

Chapter 4
AL-RASUL AL-NABI' AL-UMMI

i

Among all the terms the Qur'an uses in addressing Muhammad in his capacity as *Rasul-Ullah* none is more in need of alert interpretation than *Al-Ummi*. It occurs only twice in Surah 7.157 and 158 as qualifying the two other descriptives of him as 'envoy' and 'prophet'. A variety of English equivalents have been tried but none exactly fit its whole significance.

'Native', 'Gentile', 'illiterate', 'unlettered', 'of the common folk', are all on the way to its meaning but leave too much at stake to satisfy the Arabic. *Ummiyyah*, the related noun, is contemporary Arabic for 'illiteracy' in the normal sense, i.e. a total inability to read or write. We have seen good reason in the previous chapter on 'the enmantled one' to exclude that sense of *ummi* as applied to Muhammad in the incidence of the Qur'an, despite the long orthodox Muslim view that finds the 'miracle of the Qur'an' in its bestowal on a literal incapacity of that order. 'Unlettered' in the sense of not being a habitual scholar, much given to cloistered learning, could serve to translate *ummi* and would sustain the truth that the Qur'an was not the product of any human cult of erudition. There were no academies for 'men of letters' of that sort in the Prophet's mental hinterland.

'Native' is nearer to what we seek, if we could rid it of the gratuitous elements it has often had since imperialism adopted it. We needed to note in Chapter 2 how deeply Muhammad was possessed of, and possessed by, his native land. Prophets and their 'own country' proverbially went together and that is certainly how the Qur'an sees it. Surah 14.4 says: 'We have not sent any messenger except in the speech of his own people.' The *ummi* term requires us to bring together this 'native' factor *and* the commission to prophetic utterance in an envoy's task, as combining to tell its full meaning. The word fuses together what is local, verbal, inspired and 'popular'—in no crude sense—i.e. meant to and for 'a people'.

It is via this term *ummi* applied to Muhammad that the whole

Judaic dimension in the background of the Qur'an comes into focus. Jewry was known by the descriptive: 'the people of the Book'. Those two nouns, in a dramatic way, made Jewish identity. They were indeed 'a people', tribal, ethnic, cohesive, an exclusive community made so by the common possession of a Scripture—common, that is, to them alone and not possessable outside their ranks, their births, their family of tribes. They were the only 'people with that Book': 'that Book belonged to no other people.' In this mutuality of 'Book' and 'people' they were in no way *ummiyyun*—the plural of *ummi*.

Arabs, by contrast, sadly and forlornly, were *ummiyyun*—people lacking a sacred Scripture of their own, a holy Book in their own tongue, a folk to whom no prophet had come. There are only three occasions when the Qur'an uses the plural word and each time there is an evident contrast with Jews. 'Those to whom the Book came and the unscriptured ... (3.20) and 'This springs from their (i.e. 'the people of the Book') saying: "We are under no obligation to the *ummiyyin*."' (3.75)

'Unscriptured', then, is the nearest English can come to the meaning of this elusive word, singular and plural, 'Gentile', not in the New Testament sense or with the New Testament sanction for that word's obsolescence, but simply as unlike Jews by virtue of being 'holy bookless'.

ii

Muhammad is thus addressed as *al-ummi*—the 'envoy' from within that condition (as no 'messenger' could fail to be) to his 'native people' in the task of *al-Rasul al-Nabi'* (the shared descriptives) making good the lack of 'an Arabic Qur'an'. The Jewish factor had been involved in a double way—positive and negative. The demonstration of peoplehood via scripturedness could generate a yearning to be likewise possessed of sacred revelation and thereby ethnically sanctioned, solemnised and guided from on high, as Jewry had been. Seeing, however, that the Judaic remained insistently privatised with Jews, inalienable, unshareable—thanks to its fulcrum on them, their story, their exodus, their territory, even their diaspora also—any Arab emulation could not fail to register resentment of that isolationism, when Jewry in Arabia proved to have little approval for the Qur'an as counterparting their own scriptured dignity. Being uniquely 'scriptured' was the insignia of their identity, a privilege not to be foregone. The Jewish stimulus—if we may so speak—in the historical antecedents of the Qur'an could hardly fail to turn into controversy and enmity when the Islamic Scripture was fully realized as the Arab/Arabic 'text from heaven'. So painfully it proved in the Medinan period.[1]

Such then is the wealth of meaning gathered into this single word *ummi*, both as a part-clue to the Quranic story and as an index to the vocation of Muhammad. There were ample reasons why 'peoplehood by Book' and 'Book had in peoplehood' should seem on both counts an enviable status where, as in Mecca and beyond, there already was a proud oral tradition of poetry, and a language with a remarkably disciplined grammar and a versatile vocabulary. The *ummi* word captures that psychic situation on every count. Should we understand the persona of Muhammad mysteriously responding to this environmental impulse tending to a scriptured destiny? To find it so need in no way compromise the Islamic perception of divine initiative. The Qur'an itself employs the *ummi* term and embraces all its subtle implications.

Surah 62.2 says: 'He (Allah) it is Who has sent among the *ummiyyin* a messenger of their own number to rehearse to them His revelations.' It might at first be thought that this *ummi* condition ignores how frequently the Qur'an presents its message as 'confirming what is already in the hands' of its recipients. They were not unaware of previous revelations and these were being invoked and reiterated in Muhammad's words. The Qur'an presents its contents throughout as consistent with, and confirmatory of, all earlier Scriptures (Surahs 2.41, 3.3, 4.47, 5.56, 35.31 *et al.*). The contradiction is only apparent. Careful reflection makes it clear that the point about *ummi* is reinforced. It was not that previous Scriptures were wanting but that they were not possessed in the 'native' Arabic. There had been a long sequence of prophets, like Salih, Hud and Shu'aib of whom the Qur'an tells, sent to 'Ad or Thamud and other hearers, but these had not scripturalised Muhammad's people.[2] These were in no way—as yet—'people with their authentic Book'.

When, in an extravagant way, the novelist Benjamin Disraeli took his hero, Tancred, to the Hebrew East he had him say:

---

[1] It was mainly then that there was a hardening of sentiment against the Jews, consequent, for the most part, on the tensions in armed struggle and the vicissitudes to be studied in Chapter 5. See below. However, the theological factors were present from the beginning. Jewry had yielded a paradigm which was not for copyrighting elsewhere.

[2] These so-called 'minor, prophets (also extra-Biblical, unless Shua'ib be Jethro) were significant in Muhammad's preaching as historical figures. Their mission was probably wholly oral. They represented the *ummi* truth of tribal nexus.

'There is a qualification of blood as well as of locality necessary for this communion ... the votary must not only kneel in the holy land but he must be of the holy race.'

By 'communion' he meant the solidarity of a scriptured people. He added: 'The Creator speaks with man only in this land.'[3] For this in Arab terms the *ummi* state was waiting. Divine revelation had to have due regard for the ethnic and local particularities so dearly cherished by humankind. If, as Muslims later said: 'Allah was only heard speaking to Muhammad' it was in that way, that way only, his people ended their *ummiyyah*—in fact by his mission, in event by his 'manifest victory' with the text.

Maybe also we should see here a further sense to that 'freedom of the land' explored in Chapter 2. For the precincts of Mecca and the route-maps of the Hijaz were the necessary locale of the Book's being 'an Arabic Qur'an'.

It is the emphasis on that phrase which underlines the *ummi* theme. It comes five times in Surahs 20.113, 39.28, 41.3, 42.7, 43.3, while as *hukman* (law-code) (13.37) or as *lisanan* (tongue) (46.12)—synonyms for the Qur'an—the same stress is laid. The state of being Arabic is crucial to its being Scripture as 'God's Word'.

The emphasis on its Arabicity is no ground for refusing leave to translate—as has often been alleged—as if the meaning could never be divorced from its Arabic form. On the contrary, the fact of its being Arabic belongs in every case to its being intelligible among Arabic speakers. Clearly there could be no point in the *ummi* logic otherwise. A 'people without a Book' could not be contented by a text they could not 'be the people of', while having it also as 'a mercy to the worlds' (Surahs 21.107 and 34.38).[4]

The issue of the Book's Arabic was also to the fore in the vexed task Muhammad had in vindicating his credentials even when duly 'scriptured' by his deliverances in that tongue. Surah 41.44 urgently takes 'foreignness' out of the equation in controversy with the Quraish in Mecca. It was well that the rigours of encounter between such agnostics and the

---

[3] Benjamin Disraeli, *Tancred*, London, 1847, Chap. IV, Sect. iii.
[4] 'We have sent you (s.)' entirely as a 'mercy to the worlds' (21.107) is in the context of the only verbatim Biblical citation in the Qur'an, that from Psalm 37.29: 'Verily the earth is the heritage of My righteous servants.' David in the Qur'an is one of the four major recipients of sacred Books.

contents of the Qur'an were so eminently met by the excellence of the Quranic Arabic. The point of the challenge made to them on solely linguistic ground ('Bring a Surah like it!') occupied us in the previous chapter. Surah 34.44 was emphatic that Muhammad was uniquely 'prophet to the Arabs', to whom he was distinctively their messenger:

> 'We have not brought them any scriptures for them to take into their reckoning, nor—prior to you—have We sent anyone to them with admonition.'

The intimacy between him and them, his as theirs, could not be plainer.

iii

'The Book' warranting 'the people' and prophets being always the human means to 'sacred books'—these were the themes through which the factor of Jews and Judaism was at work in the forming of Muhammad's mission. The single word *al-ummi* captures it inclusively—the human means to the 'scripturising' of his own people, in his own speech, on his own soil, among his own kin. The three words of Surah 7.157 inter-depend—*Al-Rasul* and *Al-Nabi'* as the greater and the lesser synonym and *Al-Ummi* as the *sine qua non* of each in the Arab/Arabic/Arabian incidence of what Jewry had exemplified in chronological priority.

Thus the third descriptive has to be read, whether by neutral scholarship or by Muslim allegiance, as belonging within the self-consciousness of Muhammad himself. His vocation has to be seen as fusing an impulse from the world of Judaism with a destiny towards the education of the Arab soul. The interior aspects have been studied under 'Thou who art enmantled' in the preceding chapter. The point here is that in being *Al-Ummi*, Muhammad can be seen as at once in debt to things Judaic and in deep rejection of them. Both aspects are to be comprehended in the one descriptive. Judaism conferred a stimulus and made it the more evocative by not allowing it to leave their copyright, so that—in the event—it came to be emulated by what ensued into rejection.

It was frequently in this way that the Jewish factor worked, enlisting a certain kind of debt-awareness and then a strong disclaimer.

'Had we caused it to be a Qur'an in an alien *('ajamiyyah)* language, they would surely have said: "Why were its revelations not made intelligible? What!Foreign, non-Arab, and you are an Arab?" Say: To those who believe, it is guidance and healing.'

Clearly a Persian Qur'an—as a wrong language in the wrong place—would not have met the *ummi's* need.[5] The adequacy of the Arabic was also partly to the Arabic's suitedness, repairing the *ummi* state in the most handsome order. There would be nothing niggardly or mean about the bestowal of the vital nativeness. The quality of the Qur'an's *I'jaz*, or 'eloquence' figured large in its credentials. It was the refutation of the charge that—whatever his Arabic diction—Muhammad was receiving it from a foreign source.

'We know well what they are saying, namely: "There is some man or other who is teaching him." The language of the one they are alluding to is a foreign tongue whereas this Qur'an is in clear Arabic.' (16.103)

That text is preceded by the assurance: 'The Spirit of holiness has revealed it from your Lord in truth.'

This vital inter-relation of prophets to peoples and of the tongues of either to each was familiar enough in all antecedents. Even so, Muhammad's *ummi*/'native' quality as *Al-Rasul* had to run the gauntlet of this hard scepticism born of pagan scorn or personal enmity. His being 'one of them' could not shield him from incredulity, least of all when he came to 'the resurrection of the dead'.

'By the Glorious Qur'an. Nay, but they show surprise at a warner come to them from among them and in their disbelief they say: "This is a stange thing."' (50.1-3)

Shall 'the dust of the dead' ever live again?

---

5   The word *'ajami* somewhat resembles 'barbarous' in English from the Greek, i.e., a speech that sounds uncouth in other ears. Language is the ready means of 'zeno-depreciation' if not of zeno-phobia.

Muhammad, in his *ummi* capacity, and they as *ummiyyun*, came perfectly together in that what he brought into their midst was entirely fitted to where they were in their untutored locale. The intimacy of him to them, or theirs to him—present in the circumstances of the Qur'an's incidence—was sealed in the common Arabic speech. When, finally the Quraish capitulated, it could be said that Islam had taken the Arabic tongue to itself as, at one and the same time, the fulfilment of Arab peoplehood and its binding with their soul. An Arab paganism had yielded in the triumph of an Arabic Scripture. What by its absence had been a perplexing source of dismay had become a kindling, compensating satisfaction.

It follows that the three terms of Surah 7.157, 158, addressing Muhammad, define—in doing so—the Judaic factor implicit in the forming of his mission. The three synonyms inter-define themselves. Hence the later credal shape of Muslim 'confession' of 'prophets and books'. How should the three descriptives be understood, whether by neutral scholarship or by Muslim allegiance, as accomplished in the self-consciousness of Muhammad? His vocation has to be seen, via the meaning of *ummi*, as fusing an impulse from the world of Judaism with a destiny in the education of the Arab mind as to the Oneness of God. The three descriptives, in their unity, provide the surest clue to the shaping of Muhammad's single commission. For thus as *Al-Ummi* and *Rasul*, Muhammad is at once in the Judaic idiom yet strenuously at odds with it. The debt is to be the germinal concept of 'enpeopled revelation', and 'Scriptured People'. The conflict stems from the clear incompatibility of the stimulus that availed with the sequel that was attained. The tension that transpired and stayed with the sequences of the Qur'an left its abiding mark on the whole ethos of Islam as still in some sense a 'Semitic' faith.

For here the adjective *al-ummi*, qualifying *al-nabi'*, both indicated what fused into Muhammad's vocation *and* also meant its ultimate irreconcilability with the Hebrew tradition. The divergence came from two reasons. The one was that—for Jewish eyes—prophethood from God as an ethnic reality was limited to Jewry as 'chosen people'. It could only speak in Hebrew.[6] The second was that this other ethnic prophethood in its Quranic incidence was not 'covenant-based'. It was not, as in Biblical terms, 'the law and the prophets', after Sinai and Exodus: it would rather

---

[6] As, indeed, did all the Hebrew prophets with the rare exception of some Syriac in the Book of Daniel which, in any case, is not strictly 'prophetic'.

be 'the Prophet and the *Shari'ah*', with things codal ensuing, via Qur'an
and Tradition and community, from Muhammad's having been *Rasul-
Allah* by his personal destiny and not out of a community's history such as
made the covenant of Sinai.[7]

As we have seen elsewhere, the covenantal dimension in Islam
returned not to Moses but to Adam, in the cosmic pledging of humankind
to divine Lordship in the terms of Surah 7.172 with its question: 'Am I
not your lord?' and the concurring assent: 'Yes, indeed, we so acknowledge.'
That inclusive perception of how Allah was with humans, how humans
were under God, was corroborated by the dominion/*khilafah* entrustedness
of the creation to the creature by gift of the Creator. Islam, therefore,
would always be in tension with Jewish self-understanding on both counts.

The inherent Arabicity of the Islamic Scripture as indispensable
to the faith was held to be consistent with a universality of ethnic
membership. Muslims might speak any tongue even though their liturgy
must needs be in the single language of the Qur'an. An Arab ethnicity
(i.e. one as *ummi*) had been crucial to the Qur'an's mediation but it had
been mediated to and for a whole world as Muslims believed and as they
demonstrated by the speed and spread of their imperial expansion.[8] These
strains of contrast are all implicit in that *ummi* word.[9] Despite the initial
expectations, founded on what had been positive in Muhammad's relation
to the Jewish matrix, incompatible they proved. That story is all within an
exposition of Surah 7.157-158.

iv

That a 'native' Arab, sensing in that *ummi* status the sorry lack of 'native'

---

[7] The Semitic quality of Islam and the Qur'an via Abraham will come later but does not
affect the foregoing differential. As the *ummi* preacher Muhammad is a different figure
from the Moses of Sinai. The reversed form of 'Prophet and Law' (instead of 'the law and
the prophets') is highly significant in Islam.

[8] That there were tensions between Arabs and non-Arabs in those decades is not in doubt.
There had been earlier tensions between pre-Hijrah and post-Hijrah recruits while he
lived. But the racial distinctions did not override the basic 'level ground' of Muslim and
Muslim.

[9] It is for this reason that *goy* (pl. *goyim*)—the Hebrew term by which to denote all non-
Jews—will not fit the sense of *ummi* inasmuch as it remains a permanent and ethnic non-
scriptured condition, seeing that only Jews are validly scriptured, whereas the Qur'an
claims to have finally scripturalised all peoples. The *goyim* rendering for *ummiyyun*, was
suggested by C C Torrey, *The Jewish Foundation of Islam*, Yale, 1933, p. 38.

Scriptures, should have yearned for its making good, was an impulse[10] about which Jewry could in no way complain yet could scarcely approve. The seeds of inter-alienation were already there waiting to become active. There was the Muslim tribute of emulation to the Judaic principle of people-identity via Book-possession via prophetic mission of duly ethnic birth. Yet, as Jewry knew and held it, that principle was not for emulation. It belonged within an ethnicity that Yahweh had made unilateral. He was, to be sure, 'a universal Lord', but He was not 'an international God.'[11] He might be sought by 'strangers' flowing to Jerusalem. These, however, could not properly expect—under His aegis—to be independently 'scripturalised', seeing that a particularity of land and race was essential to the whole-experience that, from the seers through Hosea to Malachi, had yielded the holy writings to their people.

This vital logic worked itself out in the whole sequel of Muhammad's mission and its bearing on the Jewish diaspora presence in the Arabian peninsula. There were aspects of that presence, many of them still obscure, which contributed independently to the stresses and conflicts that ensued. Furthermore, the fact of diaspora itself and the inner psychic urge to preserve identity tended to sharpen the latent need for disavowal of the non-Jewish *ummi* pretender to scriptural standing. Aside, therefore, from whatever circumstantial factors obtained, the inherent antipathy stemmed from the significance of an *ummi* messenger among Arabian *ummiyyin*. For the hallowed nexus between prophethood and Jewry, and with it the prerogative of Yahweh, were at stake.

It followed that Muhammad's Qur'an readily acknowledged a certain plurality of 'books' via ethnic 'prophets' and linked the first squarely with the second. Moses—in very frequent mention—has the Torah (2.53, 11.110, 21,48, 25.35, 37.117, 40.53, 41.45 and 45.16),[12] David has the *Zabur* and 'Isa (Jesus) the *Injil*. The theme, deeply problematic as it is, of the Qur'an 'confirming' earlier books, at least recognises the legitimate diversity of 'messengers', the people-directed nature of all prophetic

---

[10] 'Impulse' here passes no judgement on the motives, present or absent, in Muhammad's becoming *Rasul-Allah*. The whence and whither of his 'inspiration' have been pondered in Chapter 3 inside the phenomenon of his being 'enmantled'.

[11] In the words of H M Orlinsky (*Studies in the 2nd Part of Isaiah, Vetus Testamentum*, Vol. 14, Leiden, 1977, p. 41) 'Not one of all peoples … were God's coventanted people. Yahweh is not an international God … He is the God of Israel exclusively.'

[12] In 2.53 and 21.48 Moses' Torah is termed *al-furqan*, 'the criterion', sharing that descriptive with the Qur'an itself.

vocation, thus 'confirming' the rights of *ummiyyin* to an inclusive privilege.[13] A scene of sharp altercation between Muslims and Jews in Surah 4.47 seems to intend this in stressing 'what We have revealed confirming that which you (Jews) possess.' Is there not a hint of 'let us participate in scripturedness seeing that the core-message is one and the same'?—unless a status shared is a status invaded. The claim to 'confirm' clearly belongs with holding prophethood to be 'de-exclusified'.

Despite the questions around the content of the Surahs, especially those assigned to Medina, how composite or unitary, it seems clear that there was a marked change of perception in the Qur'an about Jewry— from one of anticipation and expectancy to one of controversial exchanges and incipient hostility. The latter were, of course, dogged by issues of complicity or neutrality in the passions of armed conflict. But, these aside, the inner substance, had to do with on the one hand—the perceived pretentiousness of an *ummi*—and on the other the inviolate standing of 'the people of the Book'. The fact that, in measure, Muhammad was in debt to Jewish contacts, even perhaps Jewish tutors, for elements of the Qur'an's allusions to Jewish *Haggada*, only made the final tensions more acute.[14] In the very act of 'indigenising'—if we may so speak—what the Qur'an claimed to be 'confirming' from earlier revelation, Muhammad was inevitably engaged on two fronts. His own standing *vis-à-vis* his pagan Arab hearers, stoutly tribal as their loyalties were, laboured under the onus of reinstating a monotheistic faith taking issue with all their vested interests, psychic, economic and communal. The sources they alleged to be 'foreign' were inseparable from the themes and the warrant of what he claimed to be 'Arabising'. The pains and burdens of that paradox were traced in Chapter 1.

Thus the obstinate 'native' resistance of the Quraish was, by their lights, only the other side of Muhammad's being bound to fulfil an *ummi's* vocation in a Judaising way. For such Judaising lay within the constraints

---

[13] Though 'confirming' has usually been taken as referring to the 'contents' of revealed texts, it may also be read in this other sense of reproducing the basic principle of texts to peoples and of texts via bringers of those peoples' kin.

[14] The passages that align readily with Jewish *Haggada* and lore are examined, together with word-borrowings from Hebrew and Aramaic, in Torrey, *op. cit.* (note 9), Chap. 2. On so-called 'foreign vocabulary' in the Qur'an see Arthur Jeffery, *The Foreign Vocabulary of the Qur'an*, Baroda, 1938. The phrase is, of course, reprehensible to those who understand the Qur'an's being 'pure Arabic' in a literal sense, as excluding all loan words.

of the *ummi* situation as defined—precisely defined—in not yet being scripturalised, the destiny of which Jewry was the historic monitor. Or, differently expressed, his *ummi* vocation spelled, at one and the same time, a will to be autonomous in respect of debts in retrospect and a destiny to be in need of them. It was this experience, this anomaly, that Muhammad underwent and the Qur'an documents, in the steady transformation of the Jewish factor from affinity to repudiation.

Its sequences, of course, moved within the entire history either side the Hijrah. Surah 29.47 indicates that earlier scriptuaries (Jews) 'believed' in the Qur'an's message, though the preceding verse tells of 'argument' with them, discerningly claiming the common content of all revealed books. Jews, like all other hearers, were inside that 'perhaps you may understand' that has always been present in prophetic preaching. The Qur'an does not ignore how 'unheeding' Jews were even under their own Moses (cf. 2.73). It is this clue to how accused they must become which develops later, as evidenced by such passages as Surah 3.64-74, where disputation passes into acrimony.

It seems clear that there were mingled elements of sharp disappointment and puzzled dismay in Muhammad's quest for Jewish recognition as something due, as of right, from a prototype he had validly fulfilled by the pattern they had shown, namely 'kinship prophethood'. When the realization hardened that the pattern was 'natively' betrayed by the Arab reading he drew from it, the implicit rejection could only be explicitly returned. Post-Hijrah Islam became steadily independent of its Jewish sources, developed its own worship patterns, ended its Jerusalem *qiblah*, inaugurated Ramadan and formulated strong indictment of Jewish lapses from truth—all, as the Qur'an understood, by divine behest. Then the very writ of Islam came to reside in a final revelatory ultimacy that would still comprise its debts in its text but live beyond them—even against them—in its structure and its soul.

Whatever may be said concerning 'abrogation' by the lawyers in respect of legal prescripts, the abrogated text stays in the Qur'an.[15] Nothing is elided, so that even what may no longer run as writ remains to remind of a one-time presence despite its final obsolescence. Insofar as

---

[15] The principle of *naskh*, of *nasikh* ('what abrogates') and *mansukh* ('what is abrogated') whereby a later revelation was understood to cancel' or 'displace' an earlier one. There was long debate about the principle in practice and as to why the *mansukh* remained in its textual place.

scholars and exegetes will to discern it, the Jewish dimension abides in the Qur'an, whether as, deposit or as discard. Surah 18 is a notable example of narratives concerning Alexander (Dhu al-Qarnain) with his feats of engineering and martial fame, the Seven Sleepers of Ephesus and Gog and Magog, as well as stories in the Moses cycle.[16] It clearly belonged with Muhammad's *ummi* quality to participate, not only and crucially in the stimulus of Judaic prophethood, but also in the lore and legend that came with its legacy as heirs might cherish these.

They were, however, only incidental to the fascination of the Quranic milieu. The core, surely, of the *ummi* character of Muhammad's prophethood, its being both with and without its antecedents, lies in the figure of the Quranic Abraham, or 'Ibrahim'. The Prophet's role as *ummi*, we might say, recruited the Biblical figure to find him 'native' to a territory that could adopt him out of Jewry and locate him inside the story of a people 'biblicised' by 'an Arabic Qur'an'.

Abraham emerges as 'neither a Jew nor a Christian but as a *hanif*', an Arab 'monotheist', whose *millah* or 'community' is a different sort of 'chosen people', earlier in being pre-Mosaic and truer in being denizens of Mecca in its pure origin (Surahs 2.135, 3.67, 3.95, 4.125, 6.161 and 16.123). As noted in the previous chapter, the tradition of a residual Arab monotheism may well have moved Muhammad's sense of prophetic destiny. The association of the *hunafa'* with Abraham, in an other than Jewish role, joins a 'native' strain with a shared forebear—a measure of what Muhammad's being *ummi* achieves. For the Jewish lineage was ineradicable: what had transpired was its enlistment into Arabism.

So Ishmael replaces Isaac. The harsh dismissal of Hagar finds no mention in the Qur'an. Abraham and Ishmael together become the builders of the Ka'bah, the authentic founders of the shrine, the habitués of the well of Zamzam (Surahs 2.124-131, 13.35-41). 'The 'seed' dimension, so central in the Judaic, is still present here but via Ishmael and rooted in 'submission'. It is intriguing how the very terms *islam* and *muslim* are woven into the fabric of Abraham's 'obedience' to Allah, alike in the hallowing of Mecca and in the readiness to offer his son at divine bidding. Thus in 2.128, Abraham prays hard by the shrine-in-building: 'Make us *muslimin* to You and of our seed a people *(ummah) muslimah* to

---

[16] The Nativity narratives of 'Isa may be the same provenance via the Christian contacts of the Prophet. See Chapter 8.

You.' In 37.103, where the scene is the Moriah one of the 'offering' of the son, both he and Abraham *aslama* 'surrendered'.[17] These passages add that 'right worship' is being established.

Thus the role that the Quranic Abraham plays fills a double significance. It 're-establishes' an *islam* at Mecca via a progenitor antecedent to things Mosaic with their 'covenant' at Sinai and it justifies an ultimate incrimination of Jewry, insofar as they refused to recognise an Abraham at Mecca. They become 'those of the people of the Book who disbelieved' (Surah 98.2). It might be possible to read in the distinction alleged in the Qur'an between Jew and Jew over Muhammad an index to the course of the relationship. Did his sensitivity for their accord and their early, complacent attitude suggest that they assessed things as tolerable, if not negligible, whereas when his claims became more confident and urgent their disavowal of him became more urgently fixed? So much that is obscure turns on the range and character of Muhammad's Jewish contacts in the Meccan region, but all, in their incidence were the outworking of what it meant to be—among them—*Al-Rasul al-ummi* and for them to be deeply relevant bye-standers at an Arab phenomenon of prophethood. Thus, the early mildness on either side turned into harsh reality. Even when there came the highly symbolic change of *qiblah* and clearly Muhammad saw how pivotal a thing it was, the Qur'an was still anxious to have it acknowledged as 'truth from *their* Lord' by those 'recipients of the Scripture' (2.144) while being, for his part, a *qiblah* 'of his pleasing'.

In the deeply confrontational Medinan sequel with the armed engagements and the confrontations they entailed, the Qur'an was ready to enlist against Jews the strictures of their own prophets, accusing their heedlessness and obduracy. Muhammad's own experience of their rejection could thus become a fresh appeal to Jewish precedent about Jewish hardness of heart in which to fit his own assurance.

From this angle it is the more remarkable that no reference, still less appeal, was made in the Qur'an to the most long-suffering of the Hebrew prophets. It seems an odd conjecture that Muhammad's alleged Jewish rabbi neighbours in Mecca held back from ever referring to them for reasons about which we are left to speculate.[18] Silences and absences too often elude elucidation. Such is their habit. However it be explained,

---

[17] The son is not named, while nine verses later (v. 112) Abraham has tidings of the birth of Isaac. The Aqedah narrative does not figure in Surah Ibraham, (Surah 14).

[18] The suggestion is made by Torrey, *op. cit.* p. 67, on the ground they would be too 'abstruse' for him.

the non-presence of an Isaiah, a Micah or a Jeremiah in the Qur'an is deeply significant. How relevant their anxieties would have been, when Surah 20.2 referred to Muhammad's 'distress' over 'this Qur'an', or (18.6) his being 'consumed in soul-grief', in going after unbelievers. It may be that those Biblical precedents, those figures 'acquainted with grief', were hardly congenial to the emerging drift of the Qur'an's development when physical encounter grew more demanding. Or, perhaps Jewry in Arabian diaspora had also left them in some limbo, in grouping around the Torah and the fathers of the race. How much, however, awareness of a Jeremiah might have contributed to a Qur'an's measure of an *ummi* destiny prior to the Hijrah, his sublime monotheism and his urgent dissuaders about 'chosen-people' presumptions that misjudged their place under the sovereignty of God.

The same would apply more strongly to the Jeremiah-like dimensions of the Jesus of the Gospels, those aspects of the Christ that underwrote the Christology of the early Church. These, however, will more appropriately come in Chapter 8, which attempts a study of the inner consciousness of Jesus. Meanwhile, the *ummi* status of Muhammad in the Qur'an, as making good for his Meccan/Medinan scene the 'divine-Book-in-hand' privilege Jewry had exemplified, believed itself to be fulfilling and confirming all that divine 'enwording' had granted to 'all the prophets from Adam to Jesus'.[19] To these the *ummi* condition had needed to be added: in the adding it believed itself fulfilling the last, and universal, prophethood. We are still in quest of what this 'seeding', of which the given Qur'an was the fruit in time and place, could have meant in the inner awareness of Muhammad and his *ummi* status. 'Scriptuarising' in these Quranic terms, however, opens out another—and very modern—issue which enquires whether, even in the utmost state of being 'lettered', we humans have any 'knowing' satisfaction.

v

Contemporary philosophic musings around language may seem worlds away from the Qur'an and Muhammad's recipience of heavenly words. But their challenge to the assumptions of 'logocentrism' press hard upon

---

[19] There is perhaps a certain irony in the Qur'an in the *Ummi Rasul* making good an 'omission' of Arab place and race from prophethood, while having significant omissions from the tally of all preceding messengers—those who belong in that gap between Elisha and Jesus (reckoning Jonah, Yunis, as a narrative figure in parable).

any enquiry as to what was happening in the *Tanzil* of the Qur'an and, therefore, what can be meant by its perpetual *Qira'a* or 'recital' as 'the speech of God'. For the import of 'deconstruction' reduces all language to a human device, an illusion which never conveys meaning because it only 'trades' it. Seeing that the Qur'an—and Muhammad's experience in it—are so confidently 'logocentric', addressing this philosophic interrogation of *all* language-use has to have place in reckoning with what is often called 'the phenomenon of the Qur'an'.[20]

This is so because the classic Muslim way of understanding *ummi* as telling an actual 'illiteracy' strongly underwrites a literalist readership on the part of most Muslims. It does so despite the superbly eloquent quality of the Qur'an and its highly charged rhetorical power. It also tends towards a neglect of the crucial distinction made in Surah 3.7 between 'things categorical' and 'things figurative' in its verses. For a strong literalism is liable to find all things 'categorical'. That apart, the concept about how divine mediation of meaning works in prophethood as perceived in the orthodox sense of *ummi* makes the Qur'an—on those premises— more vulnerable than almost any other Scripture to the problematics of language as these are disconcertingly broached by 20th century 'deconstructionists'.

There is heavy irony, as well as a certain logic, in the fact that, when *ummi* is made to mean an unparticipatory 'mouthpiece' of what is verbally given for 'recital', the resulting text will shape a reading mentality similarly verbalist in possessing it. That this has long happened is evident enough in the vital place of calligraphy and recitation in the life and usage of Islam. The Book is essentially to be learned by heart in the duty of *hifz* so that its verbal sequences carry its aural 'feel' as well as its meaning in the Muslim soul. Likewise the perfect transcription of its sentences is the vital art in and for devotion.

In these aspects, the Qur'an is not a writing *about* something more ultimate than itself.[21] It is in itself, as Book and text, the very 'Word

---

[20] As, for example, Michel Foucault (1926-84), *Les Mots et les Choses*, Paris 1976. We have no direct, unmediated cognisance of reality.

[21] With the proviso that it is 'about—in a simple sense—what is inscribed on 'a preserved tablet' in heaven. See Chapter 7. It is not even about that: it carries that in Arabic on earth. The point makes it different from the New Testament which is derivative from the prior—and prime—divine 'Word' which is the Christ. The Qur'an is not about any such event or person in Muhammad: he is the mouthpiece of a text that is already document, whereas New Testament penmen cause a 'document' to come about concerning a Person, Christ.

of God'. The contrast with the New Testament is complete. For there—to be explored in Chapter 8 to clarify this Quranic situation—what is written, in the form of the Gospels and the 'oddity' (in Islamic eyes) of 'Letters', has to do with Jesus' personality and with the 'event' within it of the Christ of God. There the ultimate revelation is believed to 'happen' and what comes to be 'written' is derived from it and ranks inferior to it, as the record where the ultimate 'Word made flesh' is 'had' by the faithful in an access understood to be 'sufficient', not 'infallible'. It is an access which invites and assumes a discerning readership under, as faith believes, the enabling reality of the Holy Spirit—enabling which had place in the writing and avails for the reading.

This New Testament situation in no way exempts its possession from the language issue as recent language theory poses it. It does, however, greatly ease it, as compared with the concept of textuality by which the Qur'an is normally received as Scripture, and 'it is written' carries the kind of sanction with which an *ummi* recipience in the traditional sense endows it.

This 'it is written' derives from an 'it is uttered'—if we have in view the earthly Qur'an. The order is reversed if we are alluding to the heavenly Qur'an on the 'inscribed tablet', so that what is 'uttered' is the pre-existent Word. It comes again to be a writing via the 'recital' of it conveyed to—and so by—the *ummi* Prophet. Despite the blending of that 'recital' with situations as traced in Chapter 1, and despite the literary 'genius' and power of the Arabic explored in Chapter 3, it is as something scribally pre-determined and divinely 'languaged' (if the term may be allowed) that dominates how both the status of the Qur'an and the stance of its readership should be understood.

It is precisely such 'languagising' even in inter-human realms, that recent 'grammatology' distrusts and queries. Such critique is even more pointed when 'divine language' is in view. Texts, the argument, runs, intend to preserve speech, to 'capture' meaning, to send 'truth' onwards as though housing reality in some assured way, so that language 'tells'. But, being 'logocentric' this way, surely we delude ourselves. 'Writing' is a sort of 'absence', a supposed preservative around which discourse must continue. Such discourse implies that no transcription of meaning is ever 'final', ever 'gets reality right'. This must be ever more the case in what purports to be 'eternal script'. Can it escape the flux of time into which it seeks to mediate what abides? Its very textuality will be caught in the culture-sense of its time-incidence. Must it not be said of revelatory 'language' that because of

> '… the progressively wider range of spiritual experience with which it is forced to deal, the further it proceeds the more precarious it gets'?[22]

If so, what, in Islam with a verbal Qur'an has been 'history' in its there-and-then, could only belong with ongoing here-and-nows through 'discourses' finding what 'ideal' reading alone can make contemporary. Maybe, in this way, the Qur'an's language has to be taken as 'performative', not 'informative', only 'telling' in the sense of 'stimulating' action, not of 'defining' truth. In that way, it might ride with the concept of *ijtihad*, as the reader-factor in all logocentric meaning, if *ijtihad* were not excluded from what belongs to the Qur'an.

Clearly what is done with texts by believers holding them such, matters crucially, but what they do with them must begin with how they see the textuality inhering there. It is here that the normal Islamic view of the *ummi* character of the Prophet, corroborated in calligraphy and recital by memory, and habituating Muslim minds in their readership, is so strongly at odds with sceptical contemporary reckoning as to what language can do—sacred language most of all. The Qur'an is the supreme case in point from this angle. The New Testament as we have noted, is logocentric in a very different way as also are, though again distinctively, the sacred Scriptures of Asia.

It is not likely that Islam will take, or even need to take, the deconstructionists too seriously. They may tell us that language is no neutral, no independent, vehicle of truth. But they offer no alternative to their scepticism. If 'indeterminacy' is all and only a subjective 'significance' can be managed, with language only 'espacing'—transacting—meaning, the existentialists will remind us that we still have to 'live and have our being', decide and belong. Even those who undermine meanings still go on advancing them. The iconoclast can well become his own idolater. For the agnostic, of every type there will always be 'questions to beg'. It will

---

[22] Clifford Geertz, *Islam Observed: Religious Development in Morocco and Indonesia*, Chicago, 1968, p. 14. See also Jacques Derrida, *Of Grammmatology*, trans. G Chakravorty, Baltimore, 1974.

still be possible, if not imperative, to live by light and love of answers that are not in doubt.

Even so, in all honesty, *ummi* prophethood—in the usual sense—and its entrustment with a logocentric truth in the familiar Quranic terms, leave today's Muslims with vital responsibility of mind. Perhaps the classic sense of that *ummi* word can be revised to tally more duly with the actualities of the Quranic situation. The script of the Qur'an need not be found less inspired, or less divinely given, from being less miraculously granted. That it 'is obviously not intelligible by itself'[23] will always be the case, and readership will be the more proper in being more ready for the fullest role of mind and heart.

Readership in such terms will want to penetrate—as here in these chapters—into the meaning of Muhammad as partner, 'freeman', genius, mentor, visitant and, by all these capacities, certainly recipient, of the text. To be sure the Book allows his personality 'space' within it only on its own terms of the verbatim 'reciter' of what he hears from heaven. Only seldom do we find him portrayed there preaching to hearers grouped like people around Jesus in the Gospels. There are very few picturings of the immediate scene or of its human incidentals. Muhammad is at once heeding what is divinely said to him and repeating it in fidelity to 'them'. As an addressee for addressees, he is often almost like a third party as in 'obey the Prophet' or 'one has taught him.' The first person pronoun rides with the third. The Qur'an is dominated by the sense of 'the pen' whereby God 'taught man what he knew not' (96.6). Muhammad is 'A messenger reciting from pages of pure Scriptures that contain books of supreme value' (98.2-3). Who and how he is, otherwise, is of no present import. The concept of the scriptured is the whole content of the Scripture.

Could we then think of the Qur'an as 'heaven's aphorisms—deliverances complete in themselves and only not sufficient to themselves in that their earthly incidence needed time and place and human voice? The destiny of the last could be wholly taken up in that voice-capacity. Yet, even so, the entire import of the aphoristic world had to turn upon response to him, upon controversy of which he was the brunt, upon encounter which could not be other than personal and deep. So we reach the final paradox of the *ummi* situation—that of the 'voice only crying' but out of its 'wilderness' as the crowded arena of bitter engagement

---

[23] Fazlur Rahman, *Islamic Methodology in History*, Karachi, 1965, p. 9.

where the person in the voice becomes central to the drama in which at length the meaning is complete.

vi

The foregoing study of the aspects of the phrase *Al-Rasul al-nabi' al-ummi*, the intriguing reaches of that *ummi* word, have duly taken us into the comprehensive mystery of revealed truth, of any Scripture 'teaching man by the pen what he knew not.' The attention to recent language analysis and the subjectivity of words may have seemed extraneous to any normative Islam and irrelevant to Quranic study. Wiser reflection learns otherwise. For, in its own uniquely problematic way,[24] the Qur'an involves Muslims, via the *ummi* issue, in the central theme of 'revealed' religion. Theories of language in no way create what was always there. They merely underline its presence in their disconcerting way and so summon any positive reliance on the feasibility of sacred scriptured truth to livelier examination of that confidence. Muhammad's being allegedly, feasibly *ummi*, in what sense and in what terms, is the Islamic version of that common task. For man to cry 'Thus says the Lord,' or to heed the call: 'Recite in the Name of thy Lord,' may well seem presumptuous or arouse the query: 'How could he know?'—which is only a way of asking: 'Is he not *ummi*?'

It is clear that the phenomenon of scriptural revelation belongs within the feasibility of prophethood and both within the economy of God. That theology on human part is impossible without language is only a way of saying that the reality of God must include the significance of revelation.[25] In discounting both, Michel Foucault was fond of two analogies about language in general. The one was 'imprisonment', the other archaeology. They amount to the same confinement of meaning in its own hinterland of psychic or economic factors, forbidding any genuine verdict on reality. It is intriguing to note that the Qur'an itself uses both analogies and, in using them, suggests that on their own showing they can

---

[24] Uniquely problematic, for the reason noted throughout, the exceptional stress on a non-participatory form of Muhammad's becoming 'verbal' with the text, having what the Qur'an calls *al-balagh*, the 'communiqué'.

[25] If we are to speak intelligibly about what transcends, it can only be because what transcends is of a nature to allow of it. This will still be so even if we hold that we are proceeding only from natural theology, i.e., what we take as rationally accessible.

be surmounted, so that the alleged veto on authentic knowledge is overridden. Archaeology never supposes that the museums it supplies are all there is about what it knows. To know we have the hinterland of a past is not to think we still inhabit it.

Surah 47.24 asks, of the unbelievers: 'Do they not reflect on the Qur'an or is it that locks are on their hearts?' *Tadabbur*, there, is a vital concept of lively thought that, inviting sane 'minding' of the text, promises liberation from ignorance and/or illusion. Unless we are only 'liberated' into other prisons, prophets with scriptures are no gaolers, and in any event, a language that lets us suspect we might be confined spells no final prison.

The Qur'an too is interested in archaeology. Surah 40.21 and 82 muse on the *athar*, 'the traces', of ruined powers once mighty in the land, while 36.12 reads precedents as 'footprints' still discernible in history. According to 46.4 such an *atharah* (s.) like a vestige, confirms a text. What is 'writ' scripturally can be 'writ' otherwise on the face of the earth which—as in Chapter 2—some 'read' as a telling landscape, while others delve beneath it as archaeologists of truth.

Thus to turn analogies of despair on their head is not to be at an end of the problems deconstructionists propose. It is to move out of their insistent negativity and begin again to trust the arguable integrity of scriptured faiths, insofar as they take cognisance of the task such integrity must require. In the case of the Qur'an, this issue we have reviewed thus far as to Muhammad being *ummi* and the wide range the term embraces, has to reach towards a prophetology, a doctrine, that is, of his personhood as instrumental to the Qur'an. Have Chapters 3 and now 4 left us with the paradox of a supremely 'illiterate literacy'?

This requires a study of the significance of *Tasliyah*, the 'calling down of blessing upon Muhammad in greeting him with peace' that Surah 33.56 ascribes to God and enjoins on Muslims. If the *ummi* theme has, in measure, taken us to Jewish antecedents, it may be that *Tasliyah* points to Biblical, perhaps even Christian, factors in the background. It occupies a chapter following. Meanwhile Qur'an-study has to reckon with Muhammad post-Hijrah.

Chapter 5

'TILL WAR LAYS DOWN ITS BURDENS'

i

The one Surah (47) that bears the Prophet's name directs:

> 'When you come up against the unbelievers in conflict carry
> the war to the death until you have defeated them. Then
> take prisoners for subsequent release or for ransom until the
> toils of war are ended.'

'Toils', *(awzar)* could well be translated 'burdens'—the 'toll' that weighs
on armed combat. It is the central feature of the Medinan Qur'an, the
sequel following the Hijrah from Mecca. The obdurate city that had not
yielded its pagan sanctuary to a preacher's persuasion would soon be
engaging with the meaning of his departure. As a gesture repudiating the
idolatry, but by no means the destiny, of the prior city, such was the whole
logic of migration to Yathrib. The implications of refuge in a potentially
alternative *haram*, or sacred 'city-state', were plainly confrontational.

     Our main concern throughout these chapters being the
significance of the Qur'an for the persona of Muhammad and of that
persona in the incidence of the Qur'an, the place of the Hijrah in that
double theme is obviously crucial. By emigration from Mecca Muhammad
incurred a radically new dimension of prophetic experience, one—
indeed—that interrogated the whole nature of *Rasuliyyah*, the state of
being *Rasul*. Hitherto, by the Qur'an's own reiterated directive, he had
been only and exclusively a bearer of *balagh*, a 'messenger', commissioned
to no other task than that of preaching. The transition to belligerence, to
the politics of war and captives, of booty and ransom, meant totally new
and problematic measures of *sabil-Allah*, 'the path of God'. These, in turn,
spelled new and different psychic reckonings with his inner self, with the
ethics of his mission, and the place of his own emotions in the economy
of the Qur'an. It was one thing to be harangued in the suqs by hostile or

disdainful audiences, another to be perceiving them as *hizb al-shaitan* in the passions of battle-array.[1] The man and his meaning crossed their Islamic Rubicon in the terrain between the two cities.

It was a watershed also for the very Arabic of the Qur'an. *Wahy*, in that ever exclusive tongue for revelatory 'burdens', would now be involved away from the religious theme of *Tawhid*, to directives about political allegiance, the handling of the vicissitudes of war and the growing legislation around its fruits in community and conduct. Aspects even of Arabic vocabulary would change, so that *rasul* itself had new referents and the *fitnah* that had earlier been the persecution of 'witnesses' became the subversion of their cause by conspirators within. Or it could even be the inhibitions about active service felt by fathers fearing to leave orphaned children.

The narrative of events on the ground as the Meccan/Medinan encounter was joined is familiar enough and need not be rehearsed here in full. Yathrib had first to become 'the city of the Prophet', the 'redout Medina' it needed to attain to be.[2] For, initially, Muhammad's reception there had been as of one accepting no more than the protective sanctuary, volunteered by no more than a minority of its people, the *ansar* who had invited him on the strength of their interest in Islam via the 'teacher' they had earlier requested. Their initiative had been a veritable 'rescue' from the nadir of his adversities in Mecca and the dark failure of his venture to find a like haven in Ta'if.

Still lukewarm or hostile Yathribites had to be wooed or implicated into his cause, and there were the numerous tribes around, either dubious in their 'neutrality' or suspect in their postures waiting on events. There were strategic advantages in Muhammad's tenure in Yathrib, lying usefully on the flank of the Meccan trade routes northward and among tribes accustomed to deriving their own profits from the treaty-art of 'non-molestation'. The situation was loaded with potential mischief either way. The Quraish had every reason to be wary, having let Muhammad out of their city-precincts, with all the implications of the tenacious mission he had evidenced against their paganism—a mission

---

[1] 'The party of Satan' is only loosely ascribed here to the battle foes of Islam in the post-Hijrah campaign. More strictly it belongs in the Qur'an to dissidents and malcontents within the ranks whose disloyalties contrasted painfully with the virtues of *Hizb-Allah*. See below.

[2] 'Redout' here seems the apt word, meaning a place of refuge, with a hint of precariousness but more than a hint of robust potential for security and courage.

now announcing, by its very Hijrah from their family and fealty, a new chapter in its reckoning with their obduracy.

It was a chapter which, on every count of antecedent circumstance and local setting, could not fail to be sharp and physical. Muhammad had read his warrant for the Hijrah in their sustained resistance to his verbal task of spiritual dissuasion from their plural worship. Yathrib, by becoming Medina, would serve notice on them of a different pattern of dissuasion. It was one they would be in no mind to recognise until physical defeat and diplomatic worsting had brought them to it.

The first decisive engagement at Badr proved Muslims, on their *Yaum al-Furqan*, well able to match the Quraish, having joined issue and vindicated a cause no longer derisory or despicable but impressively 'on the way'.[3] The next encounter at Uhud might be dubious but, even so being, it could be interpreted as salutary in underlining the necessity of that vital Muslim virtue of *sabr*. Meanwhile the tribal environs of Medina, several Jewish groupings among them, were being steadily induced or cajoled into bringing their assets into Islam.

At length, Muhammad's Islam attained a strength and prestige adequate enough for him to take up his spiritual relevance to Mecca— beyond all martial means to it—by prospecting a pilgrimage back to it. It had always been crucial, from the moment of his exit, to disavow any permanent exile, any intention to constitute some equivalent to it in Medina. Mecca had no equivalent. It was uniquely the house of the sacred Ka'bah, the shrine of the patriarch Abraham, whose ancient adamic purity had to be retrieved from long pagan aberration. So much had been in the original call on Mount Hira'. The Hijrah had always been a purposive not a perpetual decision.

When, on the rising tide of his intention, Muhammad came armed for pilgrimage he was refused admission. The Quraish, however, agreed that he and his followers might have access to Mecca the year later, coming unarmed and having the vacated city 'free' to them for a pilgrim-time. This was the crucial 'pledge of Al-Hudaibiyyah', by which also the two parties agreed each to return to the other any persons newly acceding to their ranks, i.e. Meccans accruing to Islam in Medina, or renegade Muslims reverting to their Meccan kin.

---

[3] Surah 8 comments on this *Yaum al-Furqan*, the time that 'discriminates' the precarious *islam* of pre-Badr circumstance from the new *élan* and prestige that 'Day of decision' at Badr had set in train. (8.41)

These provisions caused keen dismay among eager Muslims, as did also Muhammad's acquiescence in the demand that he sign the accord in his personal name, and not as *Rasul-Allah*. To that detail we will return. For the rest, the Muslims need not have been dismayed. Ultimate victory would make the 'returnees' clause pointless and meanwhile Muhammad had confidence about the way the human traffic would go.

Al-Hudaibiyyah was to prove a sort of diplomatic Badr. It established Islam as treating on equal terms with the prestigious Quraish whose own position it drastically weakened on the same count. When 'the return pilgrimage' duly took place both factors were rekindled. It was the prelude to the final capitulation of the Meccans when at length confronted by a power of force they no longer had the will, the guile, or the wiles to counter. Rather they yielded to the logic of the strength which the Prophet's Allah had bestowed upon His messenger—a strength their own goddesses and patrons had proved incompetent to match. Why should they perpetuate a barren loyalty to deities so manifestly inadequate to fulfil the supreme business of deities, namely to vindicate their devotees? The events ensuing after the Hijrah had been a trial of strength between the sanctions of paganism and the sovereignty of Allah. The latter *qua* Islam had the double vindication—Allah's and Islam's—of 'manifest victory'. 'The toils of War' were ended, having reaped their rewards.

ii

The present duty is to try to comprehend this story as it transpired within the personal self of Muhammad. That proviso of the Quraish at Al-Hudaibiyyah about his not signing as *Rasul-Allah* seems to have been a calculated humiliation, in that the Quraish were still repudiating his 'messenger' pretensions and re-asserting their own, still implacable, devotion to their pagan lords. It should be clear that they were dealing with him as a personal adversary with no other credentials than those of an upstart renegade. Muhammad, for his part, had been minded still to treat with them that way. Their calculus was merely local and—in sequel—petty, but uncannily they had high-lighted what would be significant for all future centuries, namely the critical unison of two descriptives—a personal identity, this man Muhammad, and Allah's 'envoy', in a politico-religious situation.

As we have studied in Chapters 1 to 4, that unison had been

present in the entire pre-Hijrah Qur'an. Its place in the Medinan scene is still more crucial, given the contrasted milieu of armed encounter and the power-dimension, both so strikingly and obligatorily absent from the Meccan ministry. What was, what could have been, the incidence within Muhammad's soul of 'the burdens of war' until they 'were laid down'? With what inner brooding were they broached, allowed, assumed, intensified and pursued to the end? By what counsels were they sustained, by what misgivings attended, by what warrant concluded? The questions go to the very heart of religion, to the core of Islam. They have echoed through all its Hijri centuries and are urgently contemporary as its fifteenth evolves.

There is, perhaps, an inkling of moral issues consciously present in these dramatic years in the observation in Surah 8.67:

> 'It is no part of a prophet's business to hold prisoners until he has the land under vigorous control. You (pl.) had in view what this present world might afford, but God looks to the world to come.'

The singular and the plural here, the conscience of the Prophet and the acquisitive impulse of followers, were in constant inter-action in the entire story. For campaigns that shape 'burdens' for leadership afford occasions for popular ill-discipline. Battles and skirmishes that are not won without the impetuous are often tarnished by the ensuing ardour for their gains.

More deeply, however, the question of liability and propriety on the part of commanding control is clearly alive in Surah 8.67. Literally translated the Arabic says: 'it is (was) not to a prophet (*nabi'in*: any prophet) that there should be to him captives after he has wrought war's slaughter in the land.' Or does it mean '... so that he may bring havoc on the land,' depending on how one reads the particle *hatta*?[4] There would seem to be no question of 'prisoners' while battle is in full cry. Clearly 'prisoners' are

---

[4] Muhammad Asad in his commentary, *The Message of the Qur'an*, Gibraltar, 1980, seeks to confine the sense of 'prisoners' to those taken in a *Jihad*—when presumably their retention as 'captives' is warranted. Thus he makes the verse into a prohibition of enslavement in any other circumstances so that 'the acquisition' of a slave by 'peaceful means, or retention thereafter is entirely prohibited and amounts to a prohibition of slavery as a social institution.' There is, however, no mention of *Jihad* in 8.67, unless that be the meaning of 'subduing the land'. Asad notes that 47.4 enjoins the freeing of captives when conflict ends.

a distraction if taken before martial engagements are ended. Does the verse then sanction combat to the death until the issue is decided?[5] More likely, the passage could be read as a warning against combatants bent on taking prisoners with a view to personal gain from their subsequent ransom or their value as barter or as slaves.

The intricacies of exegesis apart, the arresting phrase is: 'It is not right, due, proper, or seemly, in any prophet's scenario to take captives until ...', however a right reading should conclude the sentence about the land's subjugation. The prescript is an explicit limitation on the lucrative passions a war situation arouses, a mitigation of what could become its excesses. By the same token, the precise check to these, however identified, becomes a legitimation of the conflict itself. It would be idle to think to argue any case for pacifism from the Medinan Qur'an—though one might well be drawn from the innocent preachment under the provocative duress of the Meccan years.

Thus 'what is fit and right for a prophet' in the ambiguity of 8.67 plainly contains, if it does not resolve, the supreme issue of those martial events in the dunes and land-routes between Mecca and Medina, namely the religious role of war and the martial role of religion. That was the reason for an otherwise tedious focus on the verse. It clearly hints at the all-embracing question as to what 'is to, belongs with, appertains for', the prophetic role.

iii

In addressing this vexing theme of the post-Hijrah Muhammad and of the Medinan Qur'an, it is important to keep two factors in clear view. The one is that we are dealing, not with the aberrations of a religion, but with its definitive and ever constitutive history. The other is the contemporary setting of Arabian society. If, in the side-issues around booty, spoils,[6] captives, ransom, absence without leave, subversive behaviour and the like, war imposes its own necessary regimen whatever the 'holy' auspices, the social order of its immediate context and the culture of its

---

[5] I.e. 'no quarter given.' It is clear, however, that prisoners were taken and exchanged by both sides. The rest of the verse seems to make clear that 'prisoners for later gain' were in the mind of some fighters and it was this 'a prophet' ought to disallow.

[6] 'Spoils'—*al-anfal*—being the title of this Surah 8.

time and place must carry major responsibility for its character. A founding religion can hardly 'found' itself outside the culture-bearings in which it is found. Even so, given that it aspires to a universal relevance, a finality across all times and territories, it must be capable of transcending the constraints of that founding context, the inhibitions of its first locale, as and when it perceives them to have been alien or inhibiting to its true and real 'intention'.[7] As and when the passing centuries bring that duty into focus and conscience thrusts it into urgency, the burning question will be what that 'intention' was and in what terms it dynamically endures and renews.

Can there be doubt, whether among insiders or intelligent outsiders to Islam, that the 'intention' of Islam had its first abiding definition in pre-Hijrah Mecca? Had the 'intention' at its heart been to create a caliphal hegemony on behalf of a political Medina and its heirs, or to affirm a faithful theology of divine Unity in the terms of Meccan witness? Not the one without the other, many will answer but what, then, of the divine Unity tied into the crippling vicissitudes of a waxing, waning, human institution such as war is?

The point is implicit in the Hijri calendar itself, by which Islam dates its history from 622. It is customary to interpret the decision for that date as inaugurating the sequel that followed. But sequels flow from what initiated them. In Muslim understanding, what happened in *wahy* is eternal and, therefore, dateless at any single point.[8] Nevertheless, dating what determined all else could well locate itself where the cumulative Meccan Qur'an stood complete, if the vital faith in *wahy* as divine guidance was to have any celebratory timing for its eternal relevance.

All reading of a Hijri calendar apart, this care for the 'intention' of Islam, and this centring of it in the Meccan theme, return us to our central study—the incidence of all the Medinan events in the personal psyche of Muhammad. That those events were vigorous, robust, forthright, assertive, even ugly and violent, is not in doubt. The mood of some of the Medinan passages is strident, harshly peremptory and necessarily

---

[7] Borrowing the basic term *niyyah*, the 'intention' required before and in all the ritual acts of Muslims. See more fully in Chapters 7 and 9 its potential for the ongoing self-perception of Islam and also later in this chapter.

[8] 'Dateless', that is, in its ascription to eternal source. Naming it so does not ignore or exclude the obvious fact that the Qur'an, in its *Tanzil*, impinges on particular points and occasions in a time sequence—'timings' which were important for exegesis of the meanings.

aggressive. Reluctance to fight, born of cowardice or domestic affection, has to be overborne by sterner readings of duty and valour. The legitimation that war must generate to sustain its perils is everywhere assumed and enforced against all reservations of soul or fear. Divine anathemas are invoked on all who doubt or impede its onward way. Martyrdom in battle and the pledge of paradisal bliss nerve the warriors' wills. The concept of *Jihad* avails to spur the will to sacrifice, the passion to overcome.[9] 'God absolves from their iniquities those who have faith' (47.2). There is a sense of legitimate retaliation, seeing that 'some have been unjustly expelled from their dwelling-places simply for their words in saying: "Our Lord is God" ' (22.40).

Hostility is not to be wilfully provoked, but where it is read as real even 'massacre' becomes a lesser evil than 'subversion', though, preferably, the slaughter is better done away from sacred vicinity(2.190-91). The case for *all* areas holding a sanctity that should be immune from blood-shedding does not allow itself a voice in the Medinan world. 'In the path of God be ready for what it will take, and do not—by the work of your own hands, contrive your own destruction'(2.195). The Quraishi tradition of 'sacred truce' (months so vital to the ease of pilgrimage) can duly be broken in the Muslim 'cause' (2.218), seeing that impeding Islam is a greater crime.

When around the time of Badr the former *Qiblah* of prayer to Jerusalem was turned around to Mecca, Muhammad's personal stature was heightened—beyond the surprised demur of his faithful—because revelation warranted him. His increasing eminence corroborated, and was corroborated by, events in the field. The fate of obdurate tribes now extinct, invoked in Mecca to underline the *balagh*, served in Medina to hearten the fighting ranks by casting their foes in the same role, they being executants of a like judgement. Those questions of booty, ransom and 'spoils of war' became, as success increased, the theme of that strange unison in all this action of 'God and the Apostle'. To be sure 'the spoils of war are God's,' but Surah 8.1 adds: '… and His Apostle's'. Hence it follows: 'Obey God and His Apostle.' The more vital the discipline, the more urgent the command,

---

[9] The doctrine of *Jihad* in the import of these passages (as contrasted with the—later evolution of the term to enclose 'inner struggle' of the personal heart for purity of mind—the conflict with evil desires) means the legitimation of due violence in the 'cause' of true faith. Its antecedents go back to the concept of 'holy war' in ancient Israel. See: Gerhard von Rad: *Holy War in Ancient Israel*, trans. from the German by M J Dawn, ed. 1991, Grand Rapids.

the more intimate the inter-play. It was the very progress of the story, its initial jeopardy, its gathering achievement, that cemented the connection between what only Allah validated and what, in historic terms, only Muhammad effectuated on the ground. When issues were still in doubt, indeed utterly daunting to the weak in faith, his reassuring pleas for 'steadfast patience' – in being the more crucial—became the more assuredly leaderly. His mandate, known by a preacher's tenacity in Mecca, moved into an aura that was awesome on the battle-fronts.

The testing ground of Muslims became the crowning ground of their Prophet-leader. His was the articulate morale that stayed their faltering minds, ripening their sense of being led into a mystique of those divinely sponsored.

> 'If you have suffered wounds, wounds have befallen other folk too! That is how it goes in days of battle that We make to fluctuate among men, so that God knows who are believers and that He may take martyr-witnesses from among you ... Prior to actually meeting it, you were eager to court death: now you have seen it before your eyes.' (3.140,141, 143)

The courage they had learned under Muhammad's banner they might need to maintain if he were to succumb to wounds and die. For he, too, was mortal (3.144). Such sober realism in a salutary reminder, nevertheless served to underline his indispensability to Allah's will.

It has to be remembered that through all these military events the Quranic revelation was in train with them, interpreting their significance, exhorting the participants, and confirming the sequences as divine ordaining. Thus the severely martial engagement of Muslims felt, or inwardly told itself, to be the co-movement of Allah's omnipotence. For a studious mind, standing outside and doubtless mentally aloof from that awesome equation, the whole can only seem a strangely perilous situation, fraught with impossible dimensions of human tension and temptation.[10] When the concentrated saga, bearing these well-nigh

---

[10] Using 'temptation' here in its basic sense of 'test' and 'trial', the *fitnah* that tries the mettle and—by the verdict of the action—defines the doer. By the Quranic concept of such *fitnah*, the Scripture of Islam is well aware of what 'tries' all selfhood, that of believers most of all. It tends, however, to locate the sources of *fitnah* in circumstances that minister to fear or in the outward machinations of others.

unbearable pretensions under God, reached its term in success, it was well the Qur'an should cry to its agents:

> 'When God's help comes about, and conquest, and you have seen people come crowding into the religion of God, then sing the praise of your Lord and seek His forgiveness . To be merciful was ever His wont.' (Surah 110)

That *istighfar* ('forgiveness-seeking') might somehow have to do with qualms of conscience, yet only over what might have unwittingly blemished what in its whole programmatic enjoyed not only divine succour but divine commission.

Perhaps the reference of the *istighfar* had been to the vagaries of camp-followers, of devious adherents, the like of whom, in their time-serving, their gain-seeking, all war campaigns gather round their conflicts. There is ample evidence in the Medinan Qur'an of such *nifaq*, an ugly feature of events when the 'cause' between two definable parties waged its course with neutrals, real, would-be, or pretending, on the margins. When 'he that is not with us is against us' is the military theme, then either fear, or cunning, or malice are the more evoked. To be aware of such *munafiqun*[11] only draws the other confrontation into frenzies of suspicion so that the compassions that are human drown under the exigencies that are political. 'Causes' too readily find conscience expendable and, making the tests of loyalty obsessively unilateral, only excite a self-serving emulation of expedience.

iv

How, then, should the religious mind estimate and read the narrative of the Medinan Qur'an, holding to the emphasis made earlier that all ensued in conviction about the approving, indeed, enjoining mind of God? Ends justify means, we say, but only if the means have not suborned the ends. The entire Medinan enterprise had to do with the ways and right of

---

[11] These 'hypocrites,' (better: 'those who dissemble out of ill-will and make conspiracy') have frequent mention in the Medinan period. They were an inevitable accompaniment of power situations, the hazard of a winning cause.

God. It belonged religiously with Allah's rule of justice and compassion. Its due assessment can only rightly be in that entire context.

On the part of many outside Islam—given the enmities in the history of centuries—there has long been a superficially adverse judgement about Medina-in-Islam which has lost sight of its deep religious impulse. Accordingly, it has talked of character degeneration undergone, as if the Meccan mission had been diverted into something like personal brigandage, sustained by self-mandating manipulation of divine authority.

So to predicate is only sadly to distort and wilfully elude a far deeper issue and, so doing, never to reckon with how Islam traditionally formulates its own thesis, which is to hold authentic its Medinan story and perpetuate its logic as the due, indeed, the comprehensive, expression of religious power. What the Qur'an knows as 'the night of power', the *lailat al-Qadr* of Surah 97, was, indeed, the mediation of the Qur'an on that unknown night in holy Ramadan, but it was a 'power' of word entirely meant for, and served by, the power Medina achieved in the political 'establishment' of Islam and the physical surrender of the pagan one which the Quraish had striven to perpetuate against it. The city of the preacher and the city of the victor symbolised one Islam.

If, thus, we firmly hold together Muhammad's Meccan meanings concerning God and humankind, and his Medinan campaign, it follows that Islam, so constituted, raises in insistent form the ultimate religious problem, namely that of truth and power. 'It is no part of prophethood to take prisoners' (8.67) is a principle any Isaiah, any Jeremiah, would applaud. They would more likely be 'prisoner-taken'. Should it ever be proper to prophethood to be—or seek to be—in any position to do so? Was the basic ruling of Surah 2.256: 'There is (ought to be) no compulsion in religion' flouted in the Medinan story? The verb behind the noun there, *ikraha*, figures in Surah 10.99, when Muhammad, still—it seems—in Mecca is asked: 'Would you compel men to be believers?'

In the strain of the Meccan scene the yearning so to do could hardly have been absent, though steadily held at bay. Ought the Hijrah then to be understood as now a contrary ruling and a contrasted option? The teaching, to be sure, would continue to the hearts of the Yathribites, but did his initial refugee status among them—and his withdrawal from the Meccan sanctuary—mean that the power factor had to follow? Whatever the immediate post-arrival 'intention', the sequel gave an early answer and the sequel, by its own momentum, proved what Islam took a 'perfected religion' to encompass with full legitimacy.

That situation is exactly expressed in the frequent Medinan dictum: 'Obey God and obey the Apostle.' The coupling the *Shahadah* makes between 'Sender' and the 'sent' is there renewed as the whole ethic of Islam as that ethic emerges from the Medinan setting.[12] It signifies a complete identity between the will that is divine, the role that is Muhammad's and the whole duty that is the believer's. It is a moral situation that rules out any inner hesitancy or misgiving, whether on the part of the Prophet, or in the bosom of the Muslim. It leaves no room for 'conscience', or rather, what would be 'conscience' in an open situation of personal appraisal, has been taken over by an all-embracing mandate. This is so entire and inclusive that the very notion of 'conscience' is not merely elided but never comes into conscious purview as a relevant factor. What might be called 'a theocracy-in-the-soul' steers the whole policy by what becomes an automatic pilot. External study confronts a deep psychic experience of sheer mandatedness in the Muhammad of those post-Hijrah years. There may have been many such examples in leadership but few so assuredly 'theocratic' yet also a 'human-heroic'.

It suggests we study further the place of 'conscience' in theism. It is noteworthy that the term is absent both from the Old Testament Hebrew Scriptures and from the Qur'an.[13] The reason in either case is not far to seek. For when divine 'law' is believed to be 'sent down', and thus 'in charge' of 'its faithful' by an inclusive warrant, the notion of some personal assessing of its directives, with any presumption to query, amend, revise or refuse them, would be close to a blasphemy. 'Holy writ' is not to be thus subjected to moral *lèse-majesté*. Who is the believer to question his Lord?

Some revisory rubric on the part of 'conscience', or, rather, a duty wholly to shape one's own ethical liability was a dignity that Stoic thinking, in the Graeco-Roman context, learned to claim as inherent in

---

[12] The command to 'You that believe' occurs in Surahs 3.32 and 171, 4.59, 8.1 and 41, 24.54, 47.32. 58.13 and 64.12, all but 64 being Medinan. The deep issue for any psychic study of prophethood in Quranic terms is to ponder what it could have meant to Muhammad— in his consciousness—to use and reiterate these words, demanding 'obedience' to himself, as at the same time to God, and to do so in respect of 'the Apostle' not a third party.

[13] The word *damir* is absent from the Qur'an. For the Hebrew situation re 'conscience' see A Finkel and L Frizzell (eds.), *Standing before God: Essays on Prayer in Scriptures and Tradition*, New York, 1981, where Michael Wyschogrod writes on 'Judaism and Conscience', pp. 313-28. Also discussion in my *The Weight in the Word: Prophethood Biblical and Quranic*, Brighton, 1999, Chap. 6, pp. 88-101.

being humanly alive. The Christian New Testament, with its Hebraic dimension rooted in that context, baptised that same dignity in its Christ-devotion.[14] It would seem that, in this regard, Medinan Islam stayed obliviously conscience-less.

There are, however, deeply Quranic reasons for looking again at that conclusion, if only in order to discern the grounds for a contrary verdict—grounds that could be of profound meaning for an Islam now in its fifteenth century.

In any event, the persona of the Prophet is always involved. Even in the most absolute reading of divine dicta the human agency is still present and never wholly superseded by an overbearing fiat or *Deus dixit*. More importantly, if Allah—as in those verses—is not to be obeyed without the Prophet being obeyed also, perhaps there is still room for his conscious decisions coming into the purview of the divine ordering. As *wahy* has it, he is being prompted in association with God. May this not comprise at least some element of what the Stoic mind would have called 'being alert to one's selfhood as moral'?

That hope can well be undergirded by exposition of the basic Quranic emphasis on human *khilafah* and *amanah*. The former is familiar enough as the Biblical 'dominion', the caring entrustment with the good earth by which theology is charged with ecology and human entrepreneurial relation to nature calls for a consecrating reverence and moral liability. The *amanah* is of the same order. As Surah 33.72 runs:

> 'We offered the trust to the heavens and the earth and the
> hills and they refused to undertake the burden of it, being
> apprehensive of the responsibility. Man assumed it.'

If we read it rightly, this human acceptance to be 'liable' for the mystery and meaning of existence may well admit, perhaps even enthrone, 'conscience' in Islamic realms also.

The commentators offer different interpretations of this *amanah*. Was there a time when the now 'natural order', 'the heaven, earth and hills', was rational and capable of self-discerning 'volition'? So some have

---

[14] Conscience is frequent in the Letters of Paul. As a youth in Tarsus, home of the great Stoic teacher, Athenodorus, he may well have listened to lecturers of the Stoa, contributing to his Jewish sense of human liability for personhood, for right and wrong as issues, so urgently, realistically, told by such as Amos and Jeremiah.

held. For, otherwise, no *amanah* could have been offered them. Is their refusal of the burden just a mythic way of saying that they are subjects of a 'natural' order and gladly non-volitional? Is this reading meant to underline the contrasted human privilege of volition and, with it, the duty to 'undertake' the physical liability the faculty of reason incurs—in other words to 'have a conscience'—the concomitant of consciousness itself? It is evident that the pursuance of *khilafah* must all the time entail the 'custodian' in ethical issues which no 'trusteeship' can evade. What will be left of 'entrustment' if these are entirely pre-legislated from on high? If any *khilafah/amanah* is authentic must it not be less than totally subjected to omnipotence in the range of its conduct?

Further, may not those twin concepts, in measure, apply to prophethood—the supreme privilege of all? For, as with the day-to-day individual *khilafah* of each and all of us, prophetic *wahy*—not least when it issues into political aegis and decision—is fraught with still larger dimensions of liability into which, as from *amanah* itself, some 'conscience' might enter. In that case, God's will might be more fully co-active with Muhammad's perceptions of the role he discharged whether in Mecca or Medina.

But are we reading 33.72 and *amanah* aright? Some exegesis takes the term to mean 'the entire doctrine of Islam', or duty to perform the Five Pillars and ablution, others again confine it to the chastity of women. Syed 'Abd al-Latif, however, links it squarely with the *khilafah*, 'the giving of the vice-gerency to the *khalifah* , man.'[15] *Amanah* is, then, 'the Trust',[16] understood as 'fidelity in faith-keeping', a concept that can hardly obtain in the absence of responsible discrimination employing that rational sense by which, as 33.72 indicates, humankind is expressly endowed. Perhaps also the *dhikr*, or 'reminding', central to the Qur'an, may have to do with this alert liability, no less than with the explicit text as something recited.

In sum, then, the *khilafah/amanah* theme, so crucial to Quranic humanism, must be seen to entertain some measure of 'conscience', and so give genuine place to the moral self of a man, of a Muslim. That, by the

---

[15] *Bases of Islamic Culture*, Hyderabad, 1959. See also his trans. of *Tarjuman al-Qur'an*, Bombay, 1962, by Maulana Abu-1-Azad, with *humanitas* as the 'field' for the fulfilment, via our vice-regency, of the expression of faith in divine *Tawhid*, p. xviii.

[16] The capitalised 'T' is used by Yusuf Ali in his *The Meaning of the Illustrious Qur'an* (many editions since Lahore, 1934).

same token, it must also enter into the human-ness of the Prophet—an aspect so frequently stressed—seems duly to follow, however mandated—as we have seen—Muhammad felt himself to be in excluding criteria of conscience which, in a different age and scene, would certainly need, even demand, to be applied. The question *now* is whether conscience can find a larger writ in the Muslims' trust of their Islamicity.

v

Whether or not it is valid to conclude from the foregoing that—liable for reasoning volition as we are in our human *amanah*—there is place in Islam for its exercise in 'faithful believing' will be endlessly debated. That debate must also attend to arguable measures of personal volition in Muhammad's Medinan policy, if we are discerning some co-activity in the meaning of *Tanzil*.[17] That, in turn, will depend on how we read all the personal issues discussed in earlier chapters. In any event, there is one over-riding point for contemporary Muslims and studies of Islam, namely the location of all in that 7th century and the territory of its two cities.

Whatever may, or may not, have been the volitional factor in Muhammad's own *amanah*, as recruited into Meccan ministry and Medinan affairs of city-state policy, the central theme of the Qur'an's finality means that believing, Muslim *amanah*, carries responsibility for Islam's here-and-now reality. It must be right, though neither for exoneration nor incrimination, to locate the Prophet's own role as *Rasul-Allah*, with his summoning to obedience as also 'obedience to Allah', as belonging to the scene and setting of that time and place. That brings into focus the old traditional histories with their ready recognition of his stature and his prowess, as it does also the apologias of modern times that rightly stress the perils and pressures of Quraishi venom, the weight of vested interests in pride and prestige, the conspiracies of treachery that made the post-Badr years so violent and haunted a drama.

It would be futile to read the Medinan Muhammad by the criteria or the perspectives of today's world. For the *de facto* situation of a past

---

[17] The measures discussed earlier in Chapters 1 and 3. Cf. the observation of Syed 'Abd al-Latif *(Bases, op. cit.)* : 'The Prophet had simply to follow ... the law or regulations revealed to him from time to time or as suggested themselves to him in consultation with his companions.' P. 169.

culture and ethnic incidence is not to be reckoned by the *de jure* perception of a different time. But, if we have accepted 'the *amanah* of the heavens, the earth and the hills', neither are we exempt from its judgement. This is the paradox now, of all Qu'ran-study, namely that a religion which once legitimated itself in a Medinan scenario can now no longer do so. For, by a ripening of capacity with *amanah*, religion in those armed terms is disqualified by what it once approved. That 'there be no compulsion in religion' has become a more absolute principle, a more rigorous scrutineer of what earlier evaded it.

Muslim apologia may well, and roundly, repudiate this verdict and continue to approve and salute the forceful defence the Prophet made of the truth of divine Unity, the 'manifest victory' he achieved against 'the forces of evil'. But doing so, they will only the more engage themselves with the nature of *amanah*, with the liability religions have for what they let religion be and do. To renounce that responsibility is to cease to be 'religious'—being which takes us to the ultimate reach of that authentic volition by which we are 'custodians with God'.

This realisation may have far yet to go in contemporary Islam, so minded are many to recapitulate the original Medina which they still possess in their Qur'an. Its presence there, however, like all else, is not outside *amanah*, even as contemporary Judaism has the text of Joshua and ancient tribal *Jihad* in its ken, either to emulate in some resembling Zionism, or to relinquish in the compassions of the great Isaiah. Scriptures were always for a wise *tadabbur*—that ever present duty of a textual *amanah*.[18]

The other case is that 'trust' with sacred text has still to acknowledge the actuality of the Medinan Muhammad in the there-and-then with a salute to the efficacy of his polity as the locale presented the context in which *wahy* might decree his pattern and so engage his persona and do so in uninhibited assurance as to *sabil-Allah*. It has to be noted also that—given the over-all scenario—there were several aspects of moral restraint, not least the magnanimity with which surrendering Quraish and their minions were handled. Things that were 'no part of a prophet's business' were acknowledged in 8.67, while 47.4 enjoined that captives should be freed at war's end, and over-all 'burdens' *(awzar)*, not glamour, was the word for what belligerence involved. Good will can discern an element of pity in the word, however far some Muslim history has been

---

[18] *Tadabbur*, 'intelligent reflection' on the Qur'an is enjoined on all in Surahs 4.82 and 47.24.

ready to glorify the tribulations, the massacres, the passions and martyrdoms of armed strife.

We seem, in short, to be left with an option, either to enthuse about the prowess of the Medinan story, holding admirably legitimate for all future time what it then comprised, or accord it a 7th-century realism with reservations taught by a more inclusive perception of the onus on religions to be only patiently religious. Either way we will only be reading, in our contrasting terms, the nature of human *amanah*.

Would that second reading, it might be asked, mean that there was no place for power in religion, that *Din* had no truck at all with *Dawlah*? The question is warranted. Ought Christian faith to have so long accommodated Constantine and consented, with such relish, to be a 'Christendom' and for so long? Can any faith proclaim itself wholly apolitical and live in a real world? Was there not a Biblical vision of a nation, that was 'holy', by virtue of a 'priesthood' that was 'royal', i.e., vested with political relevance? Could/should Islam have been itself, only in Meccan terms of prophethood, exhorting and suffering?

Answer has to reckon—as noted earlier—with the issue in the defining origins, rather than in subsequent experience obscuring what these had been. The central place of *regio* in *religio*, of *Dawlah* as the organ of *Din*, came, for Islam, in its Prophet and its Scripture as integral and inaugural—unless it is allowed somehow to hold pre-Hijrah Mecca definitive of Islam itself, with the Medinan dimension like a kind of Constantine 'revision' of a prior 'text'. The unity of the Qur'an would seem to exclude that view unless we can urge it by arguing that the time-and-place factor, in making Medina *then* necessary, made it also non-perpetual.[19]

To borrow the 'Christendom' parallel, it is clear that Muhammad was his own Constantine and had that role *within* what constituted *the* Islam, as Islam was meant to be. Thus —the thirteen years in Mecca aside—it would forever lack any Muslim parallel to those three centuries

---

[19] This could be where the whole course of thought is leading, namely an Islam which agrees to see itself again back in Mecca. The long ruling concept of *asbab al-nuzul,* the immediate 'occasions'—points in time and place—necessary to understand what was 'sent down to them', may be enlarged to reckoning with the there-and-then of 7th century Mecca/ Medina as 'explaining' why Islam was the way it was. Given that 'times change' and that Islam is 'final' for them all, there may be ground for arguing that present 21st century time re-appraises, by its own light what *Tanzil* tells us now. This need not mean excluding things from the Qur'an but only reading them as apt for a past that has gone.

of Christian powerlessness and suffering. They for all time remained as monitor of whatever a different Christendom might become with its powered empires and statehoods.

But if 'lack' them Islam did, what of that? Was not its incorporation of successful power its supreme asset and the very essence of its genius?[20] It has been instinctive for Muslims so to think and there is much realism in their assurance. What is a faith without the means to regulate and control society, seeing that the role of power is paramount?

Verdicts here take us into the very estimate of what religion is and needs to be. Given that religious faith has to address the issues of power, it may not well do this if too closely identified with its organs and its exercise. For then it may surrender its ability to accuse, to indict and restrain the corruptibility of power. It will forfeit its own capacity for verity and integrity, its ability to monitor the things of justice and compassion, given its own invested interest in what power affords of institutionalised avarice and ambition. The *Dins* of *Dawlahs* have, throughout history, demonstrated these snares only too well.

Moreover, it properly falls to religious faith to be the patient mentor of human tragedy, to have room for the vulnerable by an evident vulnerability of its own, out of which it may interpret and share the bearing of wrongs which no state-power can retrieve and will often ignore. It cannot be the servant of patience and hope if it is itself walking pretentiously in the corridors of power.

Its real business in those corridors is in the integrity it fosters in citizens who hold it, in their capacity for creative community, their co-operative readiness for minority groups and the moral pressures they can bring to the themes and the temper of state-power. The idea of 'theocracy'—or something pretending to it because a faith dominates—was never either viable or intelligible. Given the *khilafah/amanah* divinely assigned to the human order, what we loosely call 'the secular' has always (for Islam and all other theisms) been inside the purview and the volition of us humans—and deliberately so, according to both the Qur'an and the Bible, by God's lively resolve. This must mean that 'the secular' has its legitimacy as the realm awaiting its 'consecration' as the 'sacred' whether by dint of law or of sacrament. Thus, it is not finally a political but a

---

[20] So many Muslim apologists have been urgent to argue, often drawing a contrast with 'Isa (Jesus) as not gifted with a Quranic situation, nor perhaps a Muhammadan tenacity, and so needing—among enfeebled disciples forsaking him—a supernatural 'vindication' by his 'rapture' to heaven.

religious destiny or, rather, political as the corollary of the religious—a role which religion can only authentically play as 'watch-keeper for the transcendent'.

Moreover, it is clear that the political order can, at best, only attain a modicum of justice and honesty in the givens of human nature and society. There will always remain areas of wrong the state order can never even identify for what they are, still less redeem. Those 'remainders' of tragedy and pathos will always need, from religion, the ministry of convictions with which it is possible to love against all odds.[21] The integrity of religious faith is compromised if it covets, or employs, sanctions such as political aegis affords. For then, by the compromises inherent in power, it is disqualified from bringing the caring love which alone reaches those ultimate depths of human wrong, both done and suffered.

This sense of the built-in limitations of power in the task of religion in society argues that its identification with the state can never rightly be sanguine, still less total. For then it will have forfeited the judgement it must always bring on the wilful aberrations or crimes of the body politic.[22] Its watchfulness for all things ethical, as paramount in its duty, and its capacity to have a conscience inside it own realm of doctrine and law, will be the crux of its vocation. The question, therefore, follows whether all that was so confidently characteristic of Islam's origins—in their Medinan not their Meccan shape—can well remain authoritative in contemporary terms. Chapter 9 can take up the burden later.

It also follows, from this sense of religion as politically obligated but not politically annexed, that minority faiths can participate in the ethical task of citizenry sharing that sense of how their faith-commitment belongs in their loyal nationhood. That majority religion acknowledges this valid role for minority ones, and that the latter rise to it with the courage and the vigour innate in their identity, become vital requisites of their co-existence. If the state is, in these juridical terms, partly 'secularised'

---

[21] Echoing, from Friedrich Nietzsche—of all people—the words he once used: 'In order that love may be possible God must be a person ... The answer was to discover a religion in which it was possible to love.' *The Antichrist*, Sect. 24, trans. A M Ludovici, Edinburgh, 1911, p. 153.

[22] It is striking in this context in the different tradition of Hebrew prophethood how independent of the structure of power the great prophets were. Their sense of divine 'anger' and justice, as well as compassion and pathos, made them the very conscience of the nation in radical accusation of its régime—and all in the name of divine Unity. They could never have fulfilled that calling in tandem with rulers.

and faith its vigilant ethical monitor, the case for inter-faith collaboration is complete.

In those terms, however, there can still be place for a traditional dominance, or 'seniority,' which in many realms Islam will still enjoy and be fulfilled in doing so. History leaves long legacies of culture and practice and is not reversed when a plural climate supervenes. Pakistan has clearly demonstrated how difficult, even of definition, is political 'Islamic statehood'. Outside that form of its definition—or even inside it—there is the greater quest for its ethical definition, the definition morally alive to the perils of politics alone and spiritually ready for ethical energies from outside Islam.

vi

Such reflections on the Meccan/Medinan mutuality in Islam's origins, while urgent for our contemporary scene, have been a parenthesis arising from study of 'war and its burdens'. Two final issues remain. The first is to ask whether 'war ever laid down its burdens'. The second it to try to resolve the central theme of Muhammad, made so acute in the Medinan time, of his 'capacity' in the double nature of prophethood.[23]

The pattern of Medinan Islam having been set, it proved somehow centuries-long congenial, even as Constantinian precedent in Christianity—Eastern, Western, Roman, Reformed—enjoyed a self-perpetuating warrant for so long.

It is true that a victorious Muhammad, back in Mecca, was magnanimous in the exercise of power and in receiving the submission of his kinsmen and the townsmen who had so bitterly opposed him. There was no instinct to be vindictive and a future Salah al-Din could emulate that same quality. Force, it was clear, had been purposive and not bent on a random brutality. Yet Medina—though for only some three decades a ruling capital—had somehow foreshadowed a long future as the symbol of what, by its nature, found sustained momentum.

Historians have long debated the precise factors in the far-distanced outward thrust of Islamic armies, whether opportunistic or

---

[23] 'Capacity', as a word functioning in two senses, exactly captures the situation. One may say: 'I am here in my capacity as,' e.g. policeman, inspector etc. while—so being—'I have the ability' to discharge it, being no fool.

spontaneous, haphazard or deliberate. Did initial local adventure turn into global intent by factors of a desert or a faith, of psyche or climate? However they are read, there was war to Tabuk and onwards over the frontiers of what had been Roman Arabia and an impetus that would, via Jerusalem and Damascus, incorporate the southern Mediterranean and stretch beyond the Taurus, the Tigris and the Pyrenees. 'Till the war lays down its burdens' had an ironic ring when the Qur'an itself was closed in Muhammad's death. A wider irony was to follow.

Immediately there had been the *Riddah* when some, at that point, believed that their *islam* had been only to him prudently and not to his faith religiously[24] so that his life ending, their allegiance ended too. The energies of Abu Bakr were required to foil that misconception. There followed the troubled politics of the next three caliphs, each of whom died by brutal murder and thence the tragic emergence of the Shi'ah. Islam then acquired an abiding minority verdict, against the notion of the tranquillity of power, from a bitter perspective of suffering and duress. It would be long before the Shi'ah enjoyed occasions of supremacy but when they did they tended to emulate a Sunni sense of the policy that used it in Medinan terms.

When, for long periods, under minority disfavour, the Shi'ah communities persisted as the underlings, they did so with their doctrine of *Taqiyyah*, of only 'apparent' docility that had in no way surrendered either its disavowal of Sunni rule or its ambition to cast it off. By *Taqiyyah* or 'pretended quietness', they were nourishing the hope of favourable occasion to be the political masters themselves. They were thus inherently politicised even when they were circumstantially discreet. They cherished and visualised their own 'Medina' inside their own version of a pre-Hijrah condition. Only in certain Sufi forms and perceptions of discipleship to Muhammad did Islam diminish and even renounce the impress it had received from the Hijrah and its meaning,

These apart, Islam would never again be in a Meccan situation, until—arguably—via Western diaspora and historical vicissitudes it became so after the turn of its thirteenth century. Whether in Babur and the Mughals to Aurangzib, or Sulayman and the Ottomans, it would fulfil itself by armed expansionism and even when sundry Turks or Mongols or

---

[24] See Surah 49.14-18 with its intriguing distinction between an *islam* as (political) 'submission' and *islam* as actual belief. 'Faith had not entered their hearts.' These were ready to end allegiance when Muhammad could no longer claim their fealty.

others invaded it in pagan marauding, its religious quality subdued them to its faith and they turned to emulating its martial confidence, restoring its defining Medina as the insignia of their territories.

It was in those terms that the post-Hijrah image of Muhammed guided the long centuries in their renewing replication of the post-Hijrah policy. For that sustained reason the entire story brings back the source of thought to the double 'capacity' of Muhammad—the 'office' in word and deed engrossing the man and the man yielded to the vocation for which the 'office' required him.[25] The issue stands in that frequent 'third person' situation—the Prophet, the Apostle—the word simultaneously referring to the word-user himself, a 'first person' situation too, The oft-reiterated: 'Say!' brought both together. The duality was still more crucial when the word was: 'Obey!' commanding what was at once objective in the 'office' and yet subjective in the man.

Muslim assurance may well take this in the stride of its religious submission but scholarship is bound to think around all the psychic implications. It will be wise not to do so crudely or in a spirit of polemic. For it is dealing with the sanctities of multitudes across many lands and times and, as we have seen in Chapter 3, the complexities of 'inspiration' are many. Yet that issues abide cannot be ignored.

There were times in Medina when the interface of things personal and things prophetical—both being equally Quranic—became strangely merged with regulations about access in the entourage, due reverence in audience and immunity from all that might impugn authority. That *ansar* and *muhajirun* alike readily allowed it so, is evident from the contrasted waywardness of the *munafiqun*. It is also plain from their dismay about the technicalities of the pledge of Al-Hudaibiyyah when Muhammad had tactically yielded to his persona abandoning its 'official' quality. That stipulation by the Quraish had been deliberate. For they were treating with a tribal foe and disavowing a status in him so inimical to their pagan perception of themselves and of their city's stake in pilgrimage. He would not be foregoing the identity again, nor had he ever done so *ab initio*.[26]

---

[25] In his masterly work, *The Prophets*, New York, 1955, p. 6, Abraham J Heschel expresses this situation Biblically when he writes of 'a moment of identification of a person and a word ... the prophet is ... one with what he says.'

[26] Once, that is, the full assurance of his prophetic identity had supervened. There were those early hesitations which needed such dispelling as in 'Your Lord has not forsaken you' (Surah 93.2f.) and the heartening words of Surah 94: 'Have We not established your reputation?' dispelling any such dubiety.

For, to have done so—that single tactical occasion apart—would have been to betray his whole experience as both at once inward and outward, private and public, a destiny felt and a destiny fulfilled. The issue has been implicit in the very nature of religion, wherever a singular personhood has fused with a final Scripture. Nowhere has the issue been more critical for faith than here with Muhammad in the Qur'an, the Qur'an in Muhammad. It is in quite different, and far less word-located terms, that Jesus is present in the New Testament or the Buddha in the Dhammapada.

> 'O Prophet: Say to the prisoners who are in your hands: "If God knows any goodness in your hearts, He will give you something better than what has been taken from you. He will forgive you ..." If, however, they will some act of treachery against you (s.) their treason is already against God. So He has given you (s.) power over them.' (Surah 8.70-71)

The whole theme of *Hizb-Allah* identifies the majesty on high with the immediacies of armed engagement, not 'as in heaven so on earth', but 'as on earth so in heaven.' The Prophet's fortunes are the measure of transcendence. There is no realisation that the very notion of a *Hizb-Allah* might be a kind of blasphemy if we mean what we say in *Subhan Allah*: 'Exalted be He.'

> 'It is no right of a believer, man or woman, to retain
> any opinion of their own in any matter on which God and
> His Apostle had ruled by decree. Whoever goes counter to
> God and His Apostle is in grievous error.' (Surah 33.36)

Doubtless it was the exigencies of battle-array and a war situation that demanded this rigorous discipline but what of these being the divinely chosen setting for ultimate *Tanzil*? Are 'occasions of revelation' a larger, sterner issue than usually realised?

> 'Believers! When you come to confer with the Apostle make
> a free gift of alms before your conference. That will be a
> better course of action for you and will make for a purer

intention ... Obey God and the Apostle. God is aware of all
your actions.' (Surah 58.12)

The reference is to *sadaqat* not *Zakat*. Either are an offering to Allah thus
intimately linked to a session of counsel with Muhammad. How does 'the
better course' resonate for the private soul of either the Prophet or the
believer?

In a tense situation when 'the dissemblers opined that the
confederate (enemy) clans had not finally withdrawn' (i.e., were still a
genuine threat to the Muslims) and wished themselves out of harm's way

'... the believers saw the confederate clans on the march
again they said:"This is exactly what God and His messenger
promised us. God and His messenger had it right!"' (Surah
33.22)

The outcome of those eight fateful years is celebrated in Surah 48:

'It is an evident triumph We have achieved for you (s.).
God's purpose being to forgive what was wrong in you
in the past, and what may yet be, thus making good His
grace upon you and guiding you into a straight path. God
aids you strongly towards victory. (48.1-3)[27]

With those singular pronouns the story is told. The unison is
complete in what has been a narrative of 'God and His Apostle'.

How either scholarship or faith should resolve the significance of
that unison remains the ultimate spiritual task of the Islamic mind and of
outsiders rightly-minded for it. It is one that deepens further into the
theme of *Tasliyah*—the 'celebration' Allah makes of Muhammad, a
'celebration' in which angels and believers are summoned to share. To this
we turn in Chapter 6, where 'the burdens of war' are laid aside and the
blessings of God employ the Muslim soul.

---

[27] 'What was wrong' is an enigmatic clause, prompting endless reflection, yet critically
capturing the entire theme of 'the burdens of war'. That 'something wrong' had been
implicit is conceded (as also in Surah 110). It follows that the obligation to reckon with it
is *not*—by this token—unQuranic.

Chapter 6
TASLIYAH OR THE SALUTATION
OF GOD

i

The several terms of address with which Muhammad is saluted in the
Qur'an—'free of this land', 'thou enmantled one', 'the being-scriptured
messenger'—and the added fact that, being said to him, they are reiterated
on his own announcing lips, leave us in no doubt about the partnering
theme which is the fascination of these chapters. Separately and together,
the descriptives serve to alert the reader to implications within the psyche
of the Prophet as being, at once, the third and the first party to their
meaning, the one denoted and the one denoting, as the twin realms of
divine revelation.

Nowhere is their import in this double sense more signally
confirmed than in the *Tasliyah* of Surah 33.56, the 'greeting' which 'God
and His angels' have for Muhammad and which all Muslims are enjoined
also to bring.

> 'God and His angels call blessing upon the Prophet. O you
> who have believed, you also call blessing upon him and greet
> him with a greeting of peace.'

The verse is faithfully obeyed in the formula: *Salla Allahu 'alaihi wa sallam*
said, written or printed by devout Islam after every occurrence in speech
or script of his personal name. The meaning and range of this *Tasliyah* (the
noun drawn from the root verb in the imperative) open out wide vistas of
Islamic thought and practice, both devotional and theological. It is these
which warrant, indeed, invite the ventures that occupy Chapters 7, 8 and
9 following.

A first duty is to explore the context of 33.56 in the Surah of 'the
Confederates'—the *Ahzab* or 'partisans'. The setting is Medinan around,
perhaps, the fifth year after the Hijrah. Despite, or perhaps because of, Islam's
heightened standing after Badr and Uhud, it was still beset by conspiracy and
intrigue in the bitter atmosphere of its own confiscations and tensions both

with pagan Yathribites and neighbouring Jewish tribes. Immediately prior to the *Tasliyah* verse, there are directives and injunctions about respect for the Prophet's wives and access to his domestic entourage. There are rebukes for those who slander or annoy, either him or his wives by malice or innuendo.[1] Verses 57 and 58 of the Surah 'tell the curse of Allah' upon all such maligners and traducers in both this world and the hereafter.

It might be inferred from this mundane and unseemly setting that the great *Tasliyah* verse, in its isolation, its remoteness from any profound theology of divine adoration such as belongs with the early Meccan scene, has to be read as countering by contrast the vulgarity of contentious defamers of Muhammad and his family. 'God and His angels celebrate' his fame: he is extolled in the paean of heaven. Therefore all defamation by Medinan contumacy stands shamed into disgrace as utterly despicable.

But if we read the context that way, Muslim piety—not to say generations of Muslim mystics—have read v.56 in the most ultimate terms. It has never meant, for these, the rescue of Muhammad's persona from sordid calumny and base ill-wishers in the there and then: it has meant the due acknowledgement of his destiny and of the esteem in which he is held in the counsels of the Most High. *Tasliyah* has to be read, and the writ for it obeyed, as to the supreme envoy of 'the Night Journey' and the ascent into the vision and the mind of God as the experience mandating the whole Qur'an.

This deep ambiguity in the verse-context of *Tasliyah* is sharpened by the sequel in 60 to 73, where harsh notice is served on the adversaries of Islam. These, thanks to their 'sedition', will not abide much longer in the Medinan vicinity and are set under a divine wrath, the overwhelming requital of 'the last Day', the 'double penalty', of 'the mighty curse'.[2]

ii

What, precisely, should be understood by the two verbs *salla* and *sallam*, used of 'God and His angels' and of Muslims conforming to divine

---

[1] It is clear that by this time in the *Sirah* both the growing prestige, and the gathering conflict, around the Prophet raised urgent questions about house-security and conspiracies whether of makers of scandal or traders in calumny.

[2] It remains a problem for Quranic exegetes to balance these threatenings with the 'free' call to Islamic allegiance and the 'uncompelledness' of faith (Surah 2.256). The reason, doubtless, has to lie in the sharpening climate of political and military combat.

example? *Sallam* as greet, is less elusive, with its sense of 'seeking', or 'bestowing', 'wellbeing', ousting all traces of ill-will and conferring benediction altogether divine, or duly human. *Salla* is more difficult of precise translation. The immediate sense is: 'he prayed' or 'he performed the prayer-rite'—a meaning which could not apply to God. Nor is *Tasliyah*, as the verbal noun from *Salla*, ever rightly used for the action of human *Salat* or ritual prayer. It is reserved for what Surah 33.56 tells of Allah doing and of humans emulating, in respect of Muhammad. It is the preposition *'ala* which controls the unique sense of what is done to Muhammad. *Salla 'ala* occurs in 9.103 of Muhammad 'praying for' those who accede to Islam. Such 'praying upon' (lit.) others means seeking their pardon with God and such 'intercession' (when not vetoed and excluded) may be attributed also to angels or Imams. Thus the term betokens wistful concern and yearning goodwill towards the parties in mind.

When used of Allah in 33.56 *salla 'ala* comes to mean that He 'magnified' Muhammad, 'conferred honour' on him and 'exalted his renown.' These renderings are in line with the pledge of Surah 94.4: 'Have We not established your reputation?' *(dhikraka)*, where the sense has to do with 'vindication' in the context—pre-Hijrah—of Meccan disesteem and the 'burden' of vilification that was 'weighing down his back'. Thus the entire context confirms the theme of a divine corroboration of Muhammad's mission in a setting of resistance and concerted enmity to both it and him. Indeed, there was no separating the mission and the messenger, so that the attesting of the one meant the commending of the other.

This interplay in divine 'sending' between the 'sent one' and the 'sent word(s)' warrants the usage in Islam by which (as we must note below) *Tasliyah* can be extended to all 'messengers'. The explicit command, however, of 33.56, belongs to Muhammad alone. The 'eulogy'—if we may so speak—in divine 'commendation' of Muhammad confers a heavenly imprint of satisfaction and high favour. This, on Allah's part, His angels invoke in their turn and believers echo in saluting alike his scripture and his *Shari'ah*. The Qur'an, we might say, is 'credentialled' from on high in the status by which Muhammad is celebrated both in the heavens and on earth. *Tasliyah* is the summation of the 'enmantled' and the 'designated' dignity we have traced in earlier chapters. What is striking is that the supreme 'laudation' of Muhammad should come in the context of rebuttal, having to do with violations of social behaviour so darkly reprehensible.

Deep theological implications, to which we must come, belong with the sorry vagaries of the Medinan years. Prophetic 'honour' is proverbially precarious on home ground but the Quranic *Tasliyah* comes to mean much more than local vindication. For the injunction to 'celebrate' in this way, by a liturgical formula, the stature the Prophet enjoys, and to do so in recitation of what Allah does, fulfils two vital necessities of religious faith. It thoroughly secures and ensures the absolute grounds of allegiance and it disciplines the responsive human community. Thus the Prophet is fully 'established' as such, alike by divine warrant and for believing emotion. What medieval Latin theologians called the *contestatio* and the *imitatio* are one and the same.[3]

The two might be said to come together in another passage where Muhammad is personally addressed. Again the context has to do with repudiating false charges against him concerning his status as prophet. Surah 68 invokes 'the pen' and 'that which they set down in writing,' and continues: 'In the grace of your Lord, you are not jinn-possessed.' Calumny dispelled, it adds: 'Truly you have a rightful reward.' 'Truly' again prefaces what follows, namely: *innaka la 'ala khuluqin 'azim*. *Khuluq* is the, arguably, double-meaning word: 'Yours is a character of great moral eminence' and 'You have in hand a great undertaking.'

Various as the renderings are, they conjoin what *Tasliyah* salutes as both delighting God and demanding human acclaim in echoing response.[4] Be it 'the mighty morality', or 'the tremendous nature', the one fuses with the other, the quality of the mission with the identity of the bearer. The authenticity of either abides in the other. Islamic faith believes that Allah has so conjoined the status of the Book and the stature of the Prophet that common eulogy is the due they divinely enjoy and must humanly receive.

'Thou art of a sublimity' is thus the corollary of divine *Tasliyah* and surely belongs among the arresting addresses made to Muhammad and, in his Qur'an capacity, placed on his own lips. The vital word *khuluq*,

---

[3] The two sides of a 'confessional' faith—stated in its due terms and practiced in due obedience.

[4] 'Mighty morality' is Arberry's rendering: 'tremendous nature' Pickthall's. In opting for 'a mighty task', Richard Bell notes that *khuluq* can have the meaning of 'custom' or 'habit', hence the reference is to Muhammad's steady recital of the Qur'an. It is difficult, however, to fit this with the adjective *'azim*, as 'mighty'. (*The Qur'an Translated*, Edinburgh, 1939, Vol. 2, p. 596.)

or 'character', seems here to cover both an inward 'disposition' and the way of life to which it leads—much as the word *din* as 'religion' can have the same inclusions of sense. There are several traditions which read *khuluq* as 'the Qur'an itself'. This would certainly fit the context at the opening of 'The Pen'. On either count, as persona and as 'sent with the Qur'an', it comes close to the meaning of 'paragon'—the Islamic referent by which Islam is both defined and attained.

The 'commendation' of Surah 68.4 brings together the Qur'an and tradition, the first and primary, then the second and supplementary, sources of Muslim law and ethics. *Tasliyah* gives the bond between them heavenly sanction corroborated in human iteration. It is thus the devotional formula, the personal liturgy to solemnise Muslim behaviour, each and every mention of Muhammad's name on lip and tongue enlisted to that meaning.

iii

The import of *Tasliyah*, as Allah's benediction on the Prophet, and the consequent duty of its constant practice by Muslims, are clearly related to the encounter with unbelief. Within the Qur'an the divine approval it confers is frequently responsive to situations of incredulous disdain distressing Muhammad in his preaching. Comparably, on the lips of Muslims the hallowed formula becomes a liturgy of inward reassurance and insistent public confession. It links divine warrant with empirical confrontation.

Thus, for example, in Surah 21.36: 'When those who deny see you they take you altogether for a joke,' while in 25.30, on a rare occasion when Muhammad addresses Allah in the Qur'an, he says: 'Lord, my people have been entirely dismissive of this Qur'an.' 'They have taken it for a *mahjuran*', something altogether 'obsolete', 'a mere pointless relic'.[5] Clearly, then, God's 'celebration' of His messenger is no abstract tribute but a crucial element in the hard strife of truth, a setting where 'they who reject the faith look daggers at you' (68.51).[6]

---

[5] It is intriguing that this noun *mahjur* should derive from the root that yields Hijrah. A 'thing that is out,' a 'discard', that time has let go into 'obsolescence', spells a very different end from the purposive 'Exile' and 'going out' of the actual Hijrah. Such are the vagaries of language.

[6] A vivid rendering of *yuzliqunaka bi-absarihim*—'strike thee down with their glances' (Arberry).

There are two other passages where this vital place of God's *Tasliyah* finds illumination in address to Muhammad. The one is in the early Surah 94.8: 'Make the Lord your heart's desire.' 'Establishing his reputation' (v. 4), as noted earlier, evokes his answering devotion—the conscious realisation of the status in grateful patience. The verb *farghab* is an imperative of 'yearning' or 'quest', the soul-register of the divine commission surmounting all that might otherwise daunt or dismay.

The other takes us to Surah 108 and the theme of *al-kawthar*. 'Truly we have given you abundance.' Beyond the orphanhood and 'destitution' noted in Surah 93, Muhammad is told of a 'plenitude' that transcends as well as includes all outward circumstance. The term has been a rich mine for the Sufi tradition and the philosophers. From the root 'to be copious', it denotes great wealth of quality—unless one opts with many readers for *Al-Kawthar* as the flowing river of paradise (though the immediate context is sharply 'existential' and the Surah early). That there is nothing niggardly or curbed about the divine commission to Muhammad brings the *Tasliyah* formula into the sharp vicissitudes of the suqs of Mecca, and the environs of Medina. Muslim recital of it serves comparably in engagement with the world.

In the post-Hijrah scene it may be well to link *Tasliyah* with *Al-Sakinah*—the protective divine 'presence' by which believers were sustained and guarded in adverse times and places. For this spelled the divine 'approval' of the 'cause' in its active pursuit in the givens of the (mainly) Medinan order. With its echo of the Hebraic *Shekinah* ('peace of Yahweh'), to which Surah 2. 248 alludes in reference to the time of the election of King Saul (Talut), there are four occasions in Muhammad's *Sirah* where he is granted this 'present peace'. Concerning an episode in the Hijrah itself, Surah 9.40 reads:

'When they two were together in the cave, he said to his
companion: "Sorrow not: God is with us." And God caused
His *Sakinah* to come over him and aided him with legions
unseen. Thus did He utterly humble the words of the
unbelievers and exalt the divine word to supremacy.'

Known in a perilous time when the entire future of Islam was in jeopardy, divine 'celebration' was supremely interventionist.

Later in Surah 48.4 and 18: 'He caused the *Sakinah* to come down into the hearts of the believers so that, out of faith's experience, they might grow in faith' (v.18 includes 'and upon His messenger'). Later again 'on the day of Hunain' Surah 9. 26 reads:

> '...when your great numbers, which occasioned you such satisfaction, availed you nothing (and) despite the breadth of the terrain you were caught in tight ambush, God brought His *Sakinah* down upon His apostle and upon the faithful. He sent down armies invisible to you and inflicted loss on the unbelieving forces.'

Thus, if the Psalmist may be borrowed: 'God was a very present help in time of trouble.' The *Sakinah* passages translate into third-party narrative the Medinan meaning of the divinely confirmed vocation, which in primary terms Muhammad knew in the Meccan mandate to preach.

iv

If we are right in associating the protective benediction of the *Sakinah* with the divine bestowal of supreme honour in *Tasliyah*, then the literal sense of *salla 'ala* as 'praying upon' reaches the full significance of the Prophet's 'rank-in-the divine-economy' on every count of comprehension ideally, and of fulfilment actively. There are strong traditions that the incidence of Surah 33.56 in the sequence of the Qur'an belongs with the second year after the Hijrah. It is closely linked with the Night Journey and the *Mi'raj*. Exegesis has been occupied with how the *Salat* of Allah 'on' Muhammad relates to that of the angels and, further, to that enjoined on believers.

It seems wise to link the angelic participation in the divine *Tasliyah* with the angelic reaction—according to Surah 2.30—around the divine intention to assign the *khilafah*, or 'dominion' over the earth to humankind. To this initially they brought a protest of sharp surprise, in demur about the risk entailed in setting up 'deputies' for Allah over the world, in such capricious and potentially brutal creatures 'who would corrupt and shed blood.' Overriding their misgivings Allah enjoined the angels to 'worship Adam', in token of their recognition of the divine purpose for, and with, the human agency. When, reluctantly, they did so, *Al-Shaitan* alone among them refused. He resolved himself into the arch-enemy, the 'accuser' of the human dignity, intending in his scheming enmity, to tempt, beguile and ensnare the human 'trustee', so that 'his case against Allah' might stand proved.

In this light the angels' sharing in *Tasliyah* may be read as sustaining their steady siding—against *Al-Shaitan*—with Allah's will for the human enterprise, prophethood (and Muhammad's most of all) being the instrument to guide, warn, exhort and school humans in due discharge of their 'caliphal' role. In their celebration of the Prophet, the angels are concurring with what we might perhaps describe as the scheme of enlightenment requisite for the human vocation. Whereas the angels' acknowledgement of the human creature was *under* Allah's command, their part in *Tasliyah* is with Him. It is a difference which serves to underline the supremely human role of Muhammad.

Further, there is in angelic *Tasliyah* a sort of defence, or protection, of Muhammad against the wiles of that *Shaitan*. For these extended to the 'messengers' in their ministries to humans as part of an inclusive demonic strategy. The bearers of 'God's language', Muhammad among them, were exposed to traps of speech, 'slips of the tongue' and other temptations on Satan's part, in the discharge of their verbal trust. It was, therefore, appropriate that the angels, being held to their 'approval' of human custodianship, should participate in the divinely protective 'benediction' on Muhammad.

Is it in this context that we should comprehend the many readings of angelic *Tasliyah* in the traditions as having to do with 'forgiveness' and 'mercy', whether in respect of the Prophet or of humans? The term *istighfar*, 'seeking of forgiveness', frequently carried this sense of 'being preserved or safeguarded' from Satanic 'mischief' and the frailties of creaturehood. There are those who would include Muhammad in this need of 'protection', while other esteem of his role in the divine economy sees him as inherently immune from such need. Indeed, saying the *Tasliyah* can then be understood as plea to share in his intercession as of one uniquely exalted in the court of heaven.

Either way, when *Tasliyah* came to be joined to ritual prayer, or *Salat*,[7] 'praying upon' him could be interpreted as meaning that he was

---

[7] It is not clear at what date *Tasliyah* came to be part of the ritual *Salat* or had inclusion at the end of the *Adhan*. Claims were made for a time as early as the first full century of the Islamic calendar, while others no earlier than the third, and others again as late as the tenth. Disparities may be due to uncertainty over a practice only, or any obligatory duty.

the *imam*, or even the *mihrab* (prayer-niche), setting the praying believer on the *qutb*, or 'direction' of Mecca, the abode of revelation and his own birthplace.

But what of human participation in what Allah Himself and His angels do in praise of Muhammad? Was it credible that humans could share in an activity of God? What might any 'praise' of Muhammad, however carefully intended, signify as to the sole glory of God Himself? Might some infraction of divine Unity, some latent, subtle infringement of the veto on *shirk* be implied? That Surah 33.56 enjoined it sufficed to obviate all doubts. Yet the perplexity remained. *Tasliyah*, on human part, meant, in effect, for some in Islam, requesting Allah to 'bless' the Prophet, he taking their place in benediction. In that way there could be a human act of will, as it were celebrating and affirming the divine bestowal, via Muhammad, of all that his persona and his 'sentness' signified. However absolute the doctrine of *Tawhid*, some element of 'association' or 'mediation' with and into the human scene is inseparable from the confession of Unity itself. Some form of 'God and ...', however differently perceived, is inherent in Semitic—and indeed all—faiths. *Tasliyah*, in all its human aspects, belongs within the confession of divine Unity, just as the *Shahadah* also has it in its dual form. Clearly, *Tasliyah* could be seen as simply the devotional corollary in emotion of the *Shahadah's* statement by the mind, whereby both operate in the will.

It might be thought that this conclusion is put at risk by the general extension of the *Tasliyah* formula far beyond Muhammad's own persona to embrace *alihi*, 'his people', the patriarch Abraham and numerous other figures. Surah 33.56 itself enjoins *Tasliyah* only in respect of Muhammad himself so that his singular vocation—as in the *Shahadah*—is consistent with the Unity of Allah. What, however, of these other inclusions in the popular 'calling down of blessing' so that Muhammad's family, Biblical patriarchs and the 'Isa of the *Injil*, are included in the formula?

The answer involved the immediate future of the Muslim community after Muhammad's death and the long pre-Quranic past since Adam, Noah, Abraham and Isaac. Let that past come first here.

While Muhammad's prophethood was thoroughly distinctive and altogether final, as 'the seal of *nubuwwah*', the Qur'an affirmed a noble sequence of earlier 'messengers' in whose train he had followed and whose themes his Qur'an purported to reiterate and reinforce. Accordingly, the 'fellowship' of divinely verbal agencies—so the devotional mind of Islam presumed—deserved in some sense to share the 'celebration'. The theme of the unity of revelation argued that Allah must surely have willed that piety should bring them due honour.

Conspicuous among them was the figure of Abraham, the very precursor of the *hunafa'*, whose ardent prowess made him a destroyer of the idols of his people and a paragon of monotheism. As the Qur'an saw it, he had also been the builder of the first pure Ka'bah, the father of Ishmael and supreme patron of the Arabs.

So the Abrahamic *Tasliyah* ran:

> 'O God, call down blessing on Muhammad and the family of Muhammad as Thou didst call down blessing on Abraham and the family of Abraham and bless Muhammad … as Thou didst bless Abraham and the family of Abraham, throughout the universe.'[8]

It is noteworthy that the historical sequence forward from Abraham to the Prophet of the Qur'an becomes here a devotional sequence backward, thus expressing the culminating quality of Muhammad's role. In one of the narrative passages about Abraham as worshipping Allah alone comes Abraham's plea (lit.): 'Appoint for me a tongue of truth among the last ones' (26.84) which might be rendered: 'And give me a good report in later generations.'[9] The Abrahamic *Tasliyah* could claim to be the answer to that prayer and, that way, the practice has been justified by help also of long tradition.

It would diverge here from our main theme of the soul of Muhammad in the path of the *Sirah* to pursue further the place of Abraham in Muslim devotion. There are, however, two important points about the wider *Tasliyah* and Muhammad. The one concerns the epithets of the godly miscellany, the other the 'celebration' of Jesus.

---

[8] Cited from *Al-Salawat al-Ibrahamiyyah* by C E Padwick, *Muslim Devotions: A Study of the Prayer Manuals in Common Use*, London, 1961, p. 167. This work, now a classic in the field, made a careful, prolonged examination of the manuals of prayer so frequently reprinted and circulated and which afford so rich an access into personal Muslim piety.

[9] The translations vary, depending on how *al-akhirun* is understood. Pickthall has: 'And give me a good report in later generations'; Asad has: 'Grant me the power to convey the truth to those who come after me'; 'Appoint me a tongue of truth among the others' (i.e., the non-righteous); while Bell links it with 19.51, meaning a 'share in the sure repute' of such as Isaac and Jacob. Or one might translate: 'Let me be honest in all I say to others.' The verse certainly affords sound ground for what 33.56 formalises.

Piety attached to each and all individual descriptives. Muhammad being Allah's 'beloved', Adam was His 'deputed' (i.e., as *khalifah* in creation), Noah His 'rescued', Abraham His 'friend', Ishmael His 'offered one', Moses His 'confidant', Joseph His 'expatriate', and Job His 'patient one'. These predecessors and associates of Muhammad brought their significance to his ultimate 'celebration', while their stories furnished themes for faithful meditation, directing the duty of *Tasliyah* towards private soul-search.

Following the Qur'an's own Christology, 'Isa (Jesus) is, of course, Allah's 'spirit' and 'Messiah' (Surahs 4.171, 5.17 and 75 *et al.*). The theme of 'celebrating' 'Isa, however, makes it tempting to reflect on how it might bear on the Christian understanding of Jesus as 'Son'. To yield to it here fully would be too diversionary were it not for the words 'good pleasure' in the New Testament and the light they shed on a possibly common perception of divine agency. Some aspects will better fit Chapter 8 below. In so far as God's 'greeting' of 'satisfaction' is the ultimate sense of *Tasliyah* it might be compared to that 'harmony of wills' implicit in the New Testament understanding of one in whom 'I am well-pleased,' as concerns its presentation of Jesus. The phrase has nothing to do with some abstract 'admiration' or fortuitous 'favour'. It denotes a synchrony of wills, so that what is 'willed' in a divine initiation is also 'willed' in human translation into deed. This, incidentally, is the right point in the familiar phrase 'goodwill among men', which—properly—reads: 'Men whose will is one with Mine.' If Quranic *Tasliyah* 'celebrates' Muhammad's role in those terms of congruence with Allah's 'sending' some kinship of meaning would seem to be present. But it would be well not to press it too hard.[10]

If Surah 26.84 can be cited to justify the devotion that extended 'salutation' to Abraham and, by extension, other comparable *muslims* before Islam, what of the forward inclusion of the *Al* of Muhammad whom Surah 33.56 had not incorporated in his unique 'greeting'? As noted earlier, the immediate context of the passage concerned due deference to his wives and household. This may have prompted their addition to the meaning of the *Tasliyah*. But the reasons, and the precise wording of the formula, went much deeper than 'family' in a literal sense or even than

---

[10] For fear lest Muslim minds would suspect some sinister Christian attempt to 'foist' thoughts of 'incarnation' on to Islamic concepts of Muhammad as he was—and became—in divine employ. In any event, no such aim would be in view. Nevertheless, as Chapter 8 must explore, there are aspects of what *Tasliyah* assumes concerning Muhammad closely akin to how the New Testament writers came to understand and interpret the personal significance of Jesus in his Christ role.

the previous prophets at large as so described.[11] For his 'family' became
the contentious issue between Sunni and Shi'ah after his death. The latter,
citing Surah 33.33 and 'the people of the house' as 'immaculate', read the
'family' as that of the Prophet's cousin and son-in-law, 'Ali, and his two
sons Hasan and Husain. The tension with the Sunnis reflected the times
and circumstances of accession to Islam before and after the Hijrah. More
bitterly, it spilled over into the disputed caliphate in the following decades,
so that the very form of *Tasliyah* and the meaning of 'his family' became
a devotional and liturgical focus of a basic conflict over the very nature of
Muhammad's legacy.

For all, his prophethood was final and irrepeatable and, for the
Sunni mind, heredity had no part in its continuity other than fidelity to
its claims and its political custody in the world—a duty which the prowess
of the Umayyads was eager enough to undertake. For the 'Alids, however,
'the partisans of 'Ali', the sacred heritage demanded the 'seed royal', the
line through Fatimah of Muhammad's sole surviving male heirs. For these,
by Shi'ah reading of 33.33, possessed a mystique of 'light' and 'wisdom',
with which, through successive Imams, the Qur'an alone had a right
exegesis and the companioning of a sound tradition. When the claims of
the Shi'ah were forever hallowed by the massacre of Karbala', their sense
of 'and his family' in *Tasliyah* became the more insistent and fed on many
cycles of adversity.

This deep and often grievous contention apart, piety could readily
make Muhammad's 'family' inclusive of all believers and even of the angels
in heaven. What perhaps we may call the cosmic associationism around
the divinely 'privileged event' of the Qur'an,[12] encouraged the devout to
bring into the range of *Tasliyah* the very archangels themselves, the Gabriel
of the 'lotus tree' 'boundary' of Surah 53.1-18 and Muhammad's vision.
The angels who themselves 'called down blessing' on the Prophet could be
included in its recipience also, thus completing the circle of divine bestowal
and reception of revelation.

> 'O God, call down blessing on Thine angels of access and on
> Thy purified prophets and Thine apostles sent forth as
> messengers, and on the bearers of the Throne, and on Gabriel

---

[11] See Padwick, *op. cit.*, p. 158.
[12] The phrase will be the concern of a concluding Chapter 9, resuming the theme of
Chapter 7.

and Michael and the Angel of death ... and call down blessing
on all the people of Thy obedience, people of heaven and
people of earth.'[13]

This inter-association via *Tasliyah* between the heavenly realm
and Muhammad, between the source of his inspiration and himself as its
recipient, yielded an inter-association the other way between himself and
the private believer. Whatever orthodox theology might say about the
possibility of his 'mediation' with Allah, popular Muslim piety has no
doubts.[14] The duty to recite the formula: 'Celebrate him and greet him
with peace'—thus fulfilling a divine command—became a kind of
petitionary yearning for the benefits of his (Muhammad's)
representativeness before God. Thoughts of 'protection' and 'a seeking of
forgiveness' were already present in the meaning of *Tasliyah*. Its recital
readily became a vehicle of every kind of petitionary aspiration in the
souls of the faithful. Muhammad's 'merit', his vocational 'virtue', would
surely avail for the needy believer. The command to 'celebrate' him in the
terms that emulated what angels did could hardly fail to mean some
residual 'merit' rewarding the devotion that obeyed the call. Human fears
and frailties of every kind in the bewildering and endangering world
were all too apt to answer *Tasliyah* in these terms.

Thus it was that the words of 'celebration of Muhammad' became
almost a talisman, a formula by which to negotiate the finding of lost
animals or provide sacred 'cover' for some emergency or quieten the soul
in a circumstance of suspense. 'No part of Muslim devotion (was) more of
the people,'[15] nor gathered to itself more freely coined traditions in support.
The efficacy of *Tasliyah*, with human wistfulness around it, was told and
retold in the daily exchanges of mosque and suq.

Its recital could ensure the forgiveness even of a multitude of sins
and give hope of safeguard in the horrors of the tomb, with assurance of
companionship in face of 'the last enemy'. Paradise, too, might open itself

---

[13] Cited by Padwick, p. 158 from 'Abd Allah al-Fasi, *Fath al-Rasul*, p. 51.

[14] On whether there can be 'mediation' or 'intercession', the theologians and the folk have
differed. Surah 39.45 says: 'To God all intercession belongs;' 6. 51: 'There is no protecting
friend, no intercessor save He,' 21.28 seems to allow interceders other than Allah but only by
His leave. Whether leave is ever given is an open question. In 53 26 angels may intercede but
only when allowed to do so. In 78.38 in the Judgement, neither angels nor the Spirit save
whom the *Rahman* admits and who speaks aright. Popular yearnings, however, broke free of
these vetoes and eagerly sought—and found—mediators with Allah.

[15] Padwick, *op. cit.*, p. 159.

to the faithful 'celebrant' of Muhammad's fame in the God-given words. Loyal *Tasliyahs* could help weigh down the 'scales' of judgement on the right side at the Last Day. They might serve to cancel the sin of usury. Stories abounded in pious circles of how Muhammad responded to those who—in dire situations—had recited the *Tasliyah* by annulling their guilt or resolving their anxiety.[16]

v

What, in these ways, *Tasliyah* became in the piety of folk Islam only serves to underline the deeper implications that are our main concern, namely the hope to penetrate (as far as seemliness can) into the inner experience through which Muhammad went in being, in his own private persona, the theme of this fame. For, as Islam has it, the very words in 33.56 which enjoined *Tasliyah* fell from his own lips. The duty to 'celebrate' him was voiced by the voice that was his own. It is no part of Islamic thought to think the Qur'an other than his direct speech even in passages where he is himself addressed. With what emotions then—on this ground—could he have heard himself saying, in a setting where reproof was needed of intrusive behaviour around him and his household: 'Allah and His angels invoke on me blessing: you do the same.'[17]

This is, in Surah 33.56, only the most explicit occasion of the problem we have encountered in having Muhammad saluted—not in hearsay or surmise or human deference but in the very language of Allah in revelation—as 'free of this land', as 'of a sublime character", as 'the enmantled one'. The human deference and the devotion only sprang from the initiation that was 'from beyond' and were responsive to its priority. He was, for Islamic faith, the bearer of divine utterance but only in also being himself the crucial theme of what he uttered and that, not—we must believe—by self-will or scriptural autonomy, but by an integrity of vocation. It is precisely this comprehension of what the Qur'an was, and what Muhammad was not in its incidence, which shape the paradox of what he emphatically was, namely the very *qutb* and axis of the Qur'an's being all that Islam holds and perceives it to be.

It is a paradox which we must take up in Chapters 7 and 9, with

---

[16] There are several examples from e.g. *Dala'il al-Khairat*, in Padwick, pp. 157-59.

[17] The paraphrase is crude but only to draw out the implicit point the injunction about *Tasliyah* entails *in situ*.

what light may be had from venturing, in Chapter 8, on a potential, though sharply problem-fraught, study of how and why the persona of Jesus is the making of the New Testament Scripture. Here our best preface to that sequence will be Muhammad as the loved 'associate' of God via *Tasliyah*, not now in the idiom of folk piety but in the heart-language of the poetry of devotion.

Though the fervour of mystical obedience to the injunction of the *Tasliyah* meant the utmost Muslim loyalty, it came to be at odds with the core principle of the *Shahadah* whereby Muhammad was 'the messenger of Allah'. It came almost to mean that he was 'the message', in a subtle enlargement of his being instrument to the Qur'an's text, so that he became also the spiritual referent of divine truth. While the term 'Muhammadan'— though much ignorantly used by outsiders to Islam—had never been tolerated as denoting what only 'Muslim' could mean, it came to be loved and frequent in such phrases as *al-tariqah al-muhammadiyyah*—'the way of Muhammad'. This was the mystical path of spiritual emulation and cult of invocation of the Prophet's merit. His persona became central so that a bond of love between him and the soul of the believer made that soul's *islam* real beyond the surface meaning of the Quranic text as *Tafsir* could attain it.

The goal of this absorption into the significance of Muhammad's messengership was *al-haqiqah al-muhammadiyyah*, his 'reality' as spiritually known by entry into his essence. These concepts, in their obedience to *Tasliyah*, went far beyond the evident, traditional sense of Muhammad as 'the apostle of Allah.' In fact, as a nominal sentence in Arabic, there is no 'is'—the 'is' that English needs to supply. Mystical entry into his 'reality' reads that 'is' in no way as 'was' in bare historical time and place but as perennially abiding in the eternity of Allah. To be sure, classic belief was clear, Muhammad lay buried in Medina beside his first Caliph Abu Bakr. Yet was he not 'alive in his tomb'? The second part of the *Shahadah*, as a nominal sentence, was not a bare statement of historical fact as true for the Meccans who first heard it. It was a statement of metahistory. In His eternity, Allah never acquires what, thereby He earlier lacked. For 'lack' never enters the eternal Self-completeness of *Allahu Samad*.[18]

---

[18] The divine Name *al-Samad*, occurring only in 112.2 and often rendered 'Eternal', means 'one whose resources are wholly His own,' the 'ever all-sufficient one'. This can be seen as elaborated in the words that follow: *lam yalid wa lam yulad*—'He in His being is neither deriving nor derived,' i.e., He is not in that chain of contingency in which we who were ourselves 'parented' in turn are ourselves 'parenting' the next generation.

Furthermore, the initiative on His part by which the Qur'an was mediated to Muhammad in its Arabian time and place was in no way innovative with Allah. Muhammad's human recipience must somehow entail a kind of pre-existence in the divine intention or, at least, an ongoing perpetuation of the role that had ensued in Mecca/Medina. The verbs in the *Tasliyah*, *Salla* and *Sallam*, used both in a factual and an optative sense, in Semitic usage have no reference to temporal relations and can, therefore, carry a meaning that transcends occasions of it.[19] This is in no way to say that Muslim mystics argued from niceties of grammar. Their impulses were deeply from the soul and from a subtle kind of religious intellectualism, which on both counts required this hallowed inter-association of the being of the 'messenger' with the being of his 'sending Lord'.

It did not matter that this led them far astray from the classic understanding of the Qur'an, its stress on Muhammad as unpretentiously human and 'mortal' as all humans are, with a mission that was firmly dissociated from all 'miracle' and 'mystery', save that of its own eloquence— an eloquence which, on the traditional view, owed everything to an inspiration that had not needed him except to be its 'mouth and tongue'.[20] Even so, as this other thinking went, his prophethood, in its unique destiny and superlative quality as 'sealing' all previous instances, needed to be 'inread' in mystical terms. *Tasliyah*—in this way—required a theology defining its meaning in the soul.

While the personal name, Muhammad, occurred only four times in the Qur'an, there was that other name, Ahmad, found in Surah 61.6— the 'praiseworthy' one of whose coming 'Isa had told in anticipation of Muhammad.[21] The two, Muhammad and Ahmad, were derived from the same *hamada* root. Thought on the *Tasliyah* and other factors esoteric led

---

[19] As William Wright's Arabic Grammar has it: 'A Semitic Perfect or Imperfect has, in and of itself, no reference to the temporal relations of the speaker (thinker or writer),' Vol. 1, 3rd ed. 1933, p. 51. So al-madi ('the past') can mean an abiding 'present' with the further sense also that what, abidingly, is, must be let be so.

[20] As noted in Chapter 4 around the implications of an *ummi* messenger and that under *wahy* personal mental and emotional processes were in complete abeyance so that the content might—that way—be more wholly God's.

[21] The passage has occasioned endless debate. 'Isa had foretold Muhammad's coming—a claim that Christians had ignorantly or maliciously refused to acknowledge. If the New Testament was searched for such a prophecy about Muhammad on the part of Jesus, the passages in John about 'another Comforter' were invoked. Long confusions arose around the idea that the Greek for 'Comforter' might be a corruption (wilful or otherwise) of a Greek word equaliyalent to the Arabic word *muhammad*. The issue is more fully explored in my *Jesus and the Muslim*, London, 1985, pp. 261-65.

to a conflation of Ahmad with Ahad by elision of the central 'm'. This aligned his name/title with the Name of Allah that most enshrined the truth of divine unity. *Huwa Allah al-Ahad* (Surah 112.1): 'He is God the One.'

This elision of the 'm' became the theme of much poetic ingenuity with the help of a sacred tradition from Allah, saying: *Ana Ahmad bila mim*: 'I am Ahmad without "m",' as if the central 'm' in Ahmad, derived from the first letter of Muhammad, had found its adored way into the most emphatic of divine Names, God the One'. In a strange way this hidden 'theology' of Muhammad's status as *Rasul-Allah* could almost argue an abeyance of *Tasliyah*, a reason for abstaining from mention of his name out of a veneration of entire silence. 'To speak your name is absolute impudence' sang the poet Muhammad 'Urfi Shirazi, while Mirza Asadullah Ghalib felt that he, a sinner, should not presume to speak at all.[22] That deference was a far cry from the immediate context of 33.56 when Muhammad's 'familiars' in Medina were far too free with their access to his household.

There is no need to stay, here, with the ingenuity with which the poets indulged in fantasy around the letters of Muhammad's Arabic name as carrying significances to be spiritually discerned, except as an index to how far the theme of *Tasliyah* could be devotionally elaborated. How calligraphy cherished it with the pen translated into how piety held it to be inscribed everywhere in pre-eternity. The 'm', 'h', 'm', 'd', of its consonantal structure could be seen—written horizontally—as the human posture of prostration. Its vowels—'u', 'a', 'a'—could also yield hidden clues to mysteries for pious lore. Yet Muhammad, and its near synonyms, 'Ahmad', 'Mahmud', 'Mustafa', remained favourite names to bestow on offspring—a situation which made the *Tasliyah* all the more a dutiful recital when the one and only bearer was in mind.

One fascinating aspect of Muslim devotion to the person of Muhammad is its frequent sanction in traditions of the Prophet himself. What is enjoined in 33.56 is further stressed in his treasured sayings—a fact which returns us to our basic study of his being both the first and the third 'party' to his own significance, at once the theme and the theme-presenter.

---

[22] See Annemarie Schimmel, *And Muhammad is His Messenger: The Veneration of the Prophet in Islamic Piety*, Chapel Hill, 1985, p. 115. This work of piety too is a veritable mine, or quarry, of the devotion that stems from Surah 33.56. Much of it is from Indian and Asian sources.

Given the necessary editing of multiplied traditions in this way, both of and from the Prophet which the great Al-Bukhari and his emulators undertook, the historical provenance of particular traditions is often hard to ascertain. There is no doubt that traditions tell what the mind of the community was coming or needing to feel concerning Muhammad in a process which was really a corporate possessing of his meaning. Even so, and where a tradition was clearly not what he, with his own lips or as his genuine *obiter dicta*, could or would have uttered, the communal sources held, and needed to hold, that 'it came from him.' Thus, however long the chain of *isnad* [23] and however distant from his own immediacies in Mecca/Medina, he was sharing in the injunction to the *Tasliyah* of his own celebration.

Thus, in popular incidence as in the Quranic prescript, the calling down of blessing came within his own cognisance as something happening to him. Therefore, it could hardly fail to mean for ordinary Muslims an ongoing participation in his mysterious stature, as wistful participants in his, otherwise, exclusive relation with Allah. This was the more so when traditions linked with the saying of the *Tasliyah* sundry benefits and comforts solacing the vicissitudes of this vulnerable world.

vi

In so far as the shaping of Muslim traditions around the figure of the Prophet came from a developing communal mind, it was a mind that certainly reacted to influences coming from the broad context of Muslim expansion during the two or three centuries of tradition-making. The process was in measure absorptive both of Hindu concepts and also, it would seem, of Christian theology, however sharply at tension all these were with the canons of Quranic theism. Even so, they represented an intellectual reckoning with perceived implications of the *Tasliyah* and they were unashamedly adventurous. They readily affirmed a 'pre-existent' Muhammad who was 'the Prophet while Adam was still between the water and the clay', i.e., not yet in creaturely being.

---

[23] The *isnad* was the 'chain of attestation' by which classic Muslim 'criticism' of traditions relied on the unbroken overlap of 'transmittors' and on testimony to their reliable character. It did not venture into how feasible or plausible the content could be.

This Muhammad was held to be 'incarnate in all the prophets' and—according to the Shi'ah—in 'Ali and his family.[24] He had sailed in the ark in the loins of his ancestor Noah and had been cast into the fire in the loins of his father Abraham. There was immaculate conception at all points in his physical ancestry so that no two ancestors of his had their intercourse save as pure insemination of innocent wombs.

Where traditions read Muhammad's status in these terms sophisticated philosophy was ready to associate his pre-existent figure with the animating principle of the entire creation, thus approximating to the Greek concept of the *logos*. The divine 'idea' immanent in all creation, linking absolute Being with the world of nature, had its expression in the Prophet of Islam, to be the perfect microcosm of that macrocosm. In some quarters this theme was linked with the 'perfect human' as being 'the copy of Allah', the one in whom the divine Names or attributes found their necessary mirror or innate reality. The 'messengership' of Muhammad in the normal reading of the *Shahadah* now meant that he was the very 'confidant' of Allah.

When this 'theology' of Muhammad's persona—it is no less—took shape in poetry to celebrate his birthday (or *Mawlid*) and other devotional occasions, it would sing:

'Hail to thee, O soul of souls most tender, hail!
Cupbearer of Allah's mysteries, hail!
O pleader for the fallen, hail!
O refuge of all sinners, hail!
O mine of lore, all hail to thee!
O secret of the Scriptures, hail!
O epiphany of mercy, hail!'[25]

The footprint of the Prophet's sandal became a symbol for Islamic art of the mystical implanting on the earth of what the *Tasliyah* saluted in words. As early as Hasan Ibn Thabit (died c. 659 A.H.) we have the hymn:

'He (Muhammad) was the light, the splendour, we followed.
He the sight and the hearing second only to God.

---

[24] R A Nicholson, *The Idea of Personality in Sufism*, Cambridge, 1923, p. 87.
[25] Cited by Emil Esin, *Mecca and Medina*, London, 1962, p. 66. See also E J W Gibb, *History of Ottoman Poetry*, London, 1958, Vol. 1, pp. 245-47.

By God, no woman has conceived and given birth
To one like the apostle-prophet, guide of his people,
Nor has God created among His creatures
One more faithful ... than he the very source of light.'[26]

As if to justify the boldness, the philosophical temerity—for such it was—of these ventures in eulogy, there were ingenious ways of sustaining them from the Qur'an, ways other than the obvious potential of the *Tasliyah* and the Night Journey and *Mi'raj*. They could be linked, for example, with 'the chartered winds in their familiar courses', 'the dispersing, fructifying rain-clouds' of Surah 77 that bring benediction on the earth.[27]

Or, more explicitly, there was the concept of Muhammad as *Al-Muta'a*, 'the obeyed one', stemming from the frequent injunction, noted earlier, 'Obey Allah and obey the apostle.' Beyond its usual political, legal sense, it could be developed into that to which all nature conforms as being the ruling principle of its life and structure, the archetypal spirit bearing 'the image of God'.

This sense of 'the obeyed one' could be linked with Surah 17.85: 'The spirit is by command of my Lord.' The *amr* here ('command') could be read as akin, in measure, to the Greek *logos*, as that by which all things are ordered and through which the design of Allah works in the world and through which all prophets receive their inspiration. If the *amr*, 'from my Lord's warrant', was personified in Muhammad, then his being 'the seal of prophethood' would not be in temporal finality only but in total consummation.[28]

Further, the *al-muta'a* and the *amr* concepts might be astutely related to the familiar *khilafah* doctrine—the bestowal on the human creature of 'trust' of the external world. This 'viceregency' could be understood as a quite different sort of 'on-behalf-of-ness', namely the

---

[26] See Alfred Guillaume, *Life of Muhammad*, trans. of Ibn Ishaq, *Sirat Rasul Allah*, Oxford, 1955, p. 690.

[27] The eloquence almost defies translation into English but the reading of the imagery of nature in its ardour as suggesting the afflatus of the prophets seems confirmed by the clause (v. 4-5) 'By all that deciphers and discerns,' i.e., heeds 'the Reminder'. Muhammad compared to a rain-bearing cloud comes in Anne-Marie Schimmel, *As Through a Veil, Mystical Poetry in Islam*, New York, 1962, pp. l71-211. See also her reference to Surah 33.21 speaking of Muhammad as *Uswah hasanah*, 'a good example' linked with *habib Allah*, 'beloved of God'.

[28] See Nicholson, *op. cit.* (note 24) p. 61 and also W H T Gairdner's translation of Al-Ghazali's *Mishkat al-Anwar*, in *Der Islam*, Vol. 5 1914, pp. 121-53 and the published pamphlet.

vehicle of the divine glory with Muhammad as its ideality in time and place,[29] like elemental fire in a glowing coal.

There was perhaps also a curious potential case from an allusion in Surah 46.28 to pagan 'invention' of 'gods'—always sorry, fallible illusion—*qurbanan ilahitan*, 'as a way of divine approach', or 'as mediators'.[30] These 'gods apart from God' profited their devotees nothing. They were only a snare and a delusion, fit to be the butt of prophetic ridicule, as often also in the Hebrew tradition. Yet they told of a vacancy that—not pathetically from the human end, but authentically from the divine—had been veritably filled in the mediating role Muhammad, on this reading, fulfilled. The query: 'Why did those (deities) not help or avail?' could argue, not against the role they wanted to fulfil, but against their entire failure to do so. The very pagan futility could point to where, in Muhammad's persona, the real 'being brought nigh to Allah' could be ensured.

Many would feel that there was an altogether false logic in this case-making and that pagan efforts to 'bridge distance from God' might never prefigure what the persona of Muhammad effectuated in Allah's own way. Even so, there was a perennial issue present in whether Allah had done so in the enscribed text of a Book only, or also in the mysterious significance that a human figure had been as that Book's instrument. Had he, therefore, a larger ontological role which only these venturesome concepts of logos, *amr*, *khuluq*, *ruh* and *haqiqah* could fully convey?

But, for all these potential Quranic citations about 'those brought near to God', or one such supremely, the Qur'an elsewhere would seem firmly to veto the bold readings we have summarised as legitimately fulfilling *Tasliyah*, with the popular ceremonies which gave them ritual form.[31] One such passage would surely be Surah 3.79-80:

---

[29] Nicholson, *ibid.*, pp. 90f.

[30] The term *qurban* is familiar in Semitic religion as 'that which is devoted to God,' and which, therefore, could be exempted from its human functions (cf. Mark 7.11 of 'consecrated things' not available for moral duties to parents. Cf. also Surah 5.27 and 3.183). The sense in 46.28 may be 'beings placed, as it were, close to God' or 'in Allah's entourage', just as a 'divine *qurban*' could be pleaded in moral matters. But this reading of Surah 46.28 has to be conjectural.

[31] As in *mawlids*, festivals on the Prophet's birthday; rhythmic recitals of the Prophet's name as in the *awrad* and *ahzab*, the prayer-manuals of Sufi orders; use of the name as a charm; his invocation at tombs; and private devotions or *du'a* after ritual prayer and during pilgrimage; on occasions of birth and funeral rites.

'It is not right for any man to whom Allah has brought *Al-Kitab* (the Book') and the *Hukm* (Judgement or Rule)and the Prophethood then to say to the people: "Be servants to me" so excluding Allah. On the contrary, you are to be *rabbaniyyin*—those over whom God alone is Lord, by dint of (or in terms of) your active learning of the Book and your study in it. He has not ordered you to take the angels or the prophets as lords. Has He ever commanded you to go in for *kufr* (the wilful denial of God) from the first moment you became Muslims?'

Clearly, then, emulation of the divine *Tasliyah* by the faithful Muslim must exclude any trace of a diverted, or even a somehow shared exaltation, veneration or devotion.

The theorists and popular practitioners of the 'reality of Muhammad' in the terms foregoing could well insist that they were indeed *rabbaniyyun*, 'Allah's willing slaves', but that He had warranted this concurrent spiritual 'association', taught in the *Shahadah* and hallowed in the *Tasliyah*. Was it not only because of these together that they ever knew authentically of Allah as 'Lord'? Therefore there could be no trace of deadly *Kufr* in their 'obedience' to the Prophet—an 'obedience' that could not fully stay in the sphere of the state, of politics, of legal discipline, but had to enthrone itself within the heart.

So the whole soul of Sufism believed, in a conviction in no way reproached or vetoed by a right reading of Surah 3.79 and similar warnings about mistaking prophets for 'lords'. Yet that soul of Sufism and the esotericism which accompanied it through the long Muslim centuries in such figures as Ibn al-'Arabi, Jalal al-Din Rumi, or the great founder-masters, the *aqtab*, of the Sufi Orders, steadily encountered the stubborn disavowal of zealous *mutawahhidin*, guarding their understanding of the Unity of God.

Clearly there was an issue urgently at stake. In some form all Semitic religions incur it. It is inseparable from their faith in divine action in history, in 'privileged events', be they of Torah (written or oral), of Messiah, or Qur'an, by which that which mediates the divine to the human, summons, invites or draws the human to the divine, constitutes an 'agency', a 'vehicle' that mysteriously partakes of the Sender in being the sent. When Paul writes to his Corinthians (Letter 1, 3.23): 'Christ is God's', he tells the whole New Testament faith. Muhammad, in and for

135

Islam, has a like apostrophe: 'Muhammad is God's.' It was so with the Torah whether of Moses or of Judaism.[32] The *Tasliyah*, enjoined in the Qur'an, holds that possessive in its ritual trust. Our concern throughout has been to study how awareness of its being so came into the soul of Muhammad, lived, grew and fulfilled itself there. What that conviction within him came to mean for the community of Islam when it passed into their loyalty, possessing it in the different idiom of discipleship to him and submission to Allah, requires what three following chapters attempt.

---

[32] Though Muslims never came to resembling that intriguing plea ascribed to Yahweh: 'Would that they would forsake Me but observe My Torah.'

THE INCIDENCE OF
THE PRE-EXISTENT

i

It is plain that religious truth is not placarded on the skies and yet, on all fronts, there is an instinct to feel that it should be. The burden as to the authority by which faith holds itself authentic has always weighed heavily on perceptive minds as the crux of any honesty about belief. The frequent recourse to obscurantism, or to dogmas unaccountable, is negative proof of how hauntingly urgent the issue presses, precisely in thus being shunned as passing beyond any personal management. What is evasive or negligent in sheer assertions in religion is only a failure in integrity as being also a plea for exoneration. Timidity or anxiety can offload due responsibility by pleading: 'Who am I to decide what should decide me?' Religious faith is about ultimates which, in the last analysis, require to be enthroned. The private self can hardly credibly be the king-maker. I need to be mandated and commanded by what is above my personal will or option if I am to be the subject and the servant of the truth of my *confessio*. The familiar *teneo et teneor* ('I hold and I am held') only means well if reversed to read: *teneor ergo teneo* ('I am held and, therefore, I hold').

Thus a religion that does not somehow address me from beyond my own surmisings, wishes, fears, options and demands, has to be suspect as lacking what it needs to have if it is to merit my allegiance. Precisely because its authority requires my recognition—it cannot well turn on my invention, my contriving or discovery. It must be 'the master to which I am subject,' the truth to which I am a party only in the sense—as Muslims would phrase it—that 'I have surrendered.'

The other side of this coin, however, is that authority needs to be worthy of the 'surrender' I bring. Unless it addresses me in my freedom it does not deserve to have my response. Otherwise it is not response which it seeks but only capitulation. It takes a consciously free agent to 'surrender'. Thus authority disqualifies itself if it is doctrinaire, coercive or adamant in its temper or its content. Authority ceases to be religious if it opts to be tyrannical. If, as John's Gospel has it, 'the truth makes free' it cannot begin to do so by bringing only bondage as its claim, the bondage of an uncontested absolute. I may come to find myself optionless in my ultimate conviction—'I can do no other: so help me God'—but I can only rightly arrive there by an option I have willed.

The paradox is everywhere inherent in the nature of authority and the nature of faith. Each has need to be deferential to the other. Both are disqualified if they are not in mutual liability—truth in its presentation and truth in its recognition.

That is precisely why—on both counts—truth, religious truth, is *not* placarded on the heavens. It is also why, strongly why, its credentials have been wanted there—wanted as of an authority to short-circuit and simplify the real task, wanted there by believers to circumvent or demobilise their essential role. To have, by some celestial *imprimatur*, the *ipsissima verba* of heaven is to have religious authority disencumbered of its proper obligations towards our freedom, while faith enjoys the wrong sort of *nihil obstat*, being divested of the dignity of genuine scrutiny and intelligent response.

ii

It follows from these initial reflections that faiths, both in their presentation as from authority and their recognition as from free conviction, set great store by the form of their credentials. In the case of Semitic faiths, they will be credentials God-derived and human-intended, from heaven to earth, the eternal in temporal expression, or in more technical language 'the incidence of the pre-existent'.

The 'eternal whence and human whither' is for Islam the 'uncreated Qur'an' as the eternal Speech, or Word, of Allah. For Christians through the New Testament it is 'the light of the knowledge of the glory of God in the face of Christ'—'the Word made flesh and dwelling among us', the Incarnation. Sharply contrasted as these are in the two faiths, it is well to see how, distinctively, they answer the same need, the need of credentials indubitably God's and ours at same time, from God and to us humans, the 'incidence, in time of what belongs with, and comes from, the eternity of God.'

This situation is enshrined in the Qur'an in the concept (Surah 85.21-22) of 'a well-guarded tablet *(lawh mahfuz)* on which 'the glorious

Qur'an' is inscribed.[1] This is corroborated by the concept of *Umm al-Kitab*, 'the Mother of the Book', in 13.39 and 43.4, the heavenly prototype of what 'became'[2] the Arabic text on earth. There was an 'incidence', a coming-to-pass historically to which, as we have seen, Muhammad was the human party chronologically over twenty-three years. But that *Tanzil*, or 'eventing' of the Arabic Qur'an on the part of Allah was not 'innovative'. It was not a Book which thereby Allah 'acquired' as something having no prior being with Him. For temporal 'acquisition' in no way belongs with the Eternal. What is 'His' must share in His eternity. Hence the need to think and find the Qur'an 'uncreated', not a 'creature' of time but vouchsafed into time by the event of periodic *Tanzil*. It was exactly the same logic, in the different idiom of personhood, that led Christian theology—as we must see and further explore in Chapter 8—to affirm 'the pre-existence of Christ'.

If, in either case, we want to ask whether an 'event' can 'happen' to God any more than a 'Book can be acquired,' so that eternity must rule out 'happening' (whether *Tanzil* or 'incarnation') no less than 'possessing'—if either means or implies 'acquiring'—the answer has to be that such 'eventuating' is implicit in entry into, or at, a time. Such 'entry' is precisely what any 'revelation' from God to humankind requires, since He is 'of eternity' and we are creatures of time. The perplexity has to be contained, not explained, in the conviction as to any actual 'revelation', whether it be via Book or via person. Time is not precluded from being the realm and sphere of eternal action, if the will and the capacity to reveal are understood to belong to the eternal order. To think the Eternal somehow excluded from the time-realm, i.e. self-imprisoned, would—given any creation—be an impossible contradiction. Thus an initiative to reveal is inseparable from the will to create creaturehood and that is where—in the factuality of an earth with us as earthbound—the 'eventing' of revelation belongs. The form it will take, its timing, its scripturaing, will be within the divine counsel.

---

[1] Sayyid Qutb comments: '... a well-guarded tablet the nature of which we cannot comprehend because it is part of the knowledge Allah has reserved for Himself. We benefit however, from the connotations of the statement and the impression that it leaves that the Qur'an ... is the final word in every matter it deals with. In *The Shade of the Qur'an*, Vol. 30, trans. by M A Salahi and A A Shamis, 1979, p. 119.

[2] 'Became' is a hazardous word here. It can only be used as saying: 'Came into being in time as what it eternally was.' The whole problem is explored below—a duty the caveat here anticipates.

Before taking further the implications of 'the pre-existent Qur'an', it is well to note how the theme of a divine Book tallies with the dual aspects of authority-for-faith and a faith-with-authority as initially discussed. The 'pre-existence' constitutes a reassuring 'from-beyond-ness', a revelatory initiative in a 'text' from heaven. Books, however, intend readers and readers participate inevitably in what they convey. No literature can be immune from its literati. As we have seen from the implications of the *ummi* word in Chapter 4, the Qur'an, like any sacred— or other—text is wide open to the readership it addresses. To be sure, a text may have ascribed to it some mysterious aura, making readers diffident or deferential in their postures, but it can never be as if it were not for 'reading'. Precisely in adopting language, words, vocabulary, analogies, rhetoric and all the other devices entailed in being textual, it entrusts itself to minds and spirits. To these it must appeal, as the Qur'an does, for a ready 'unlocking' of the heart, in what it calls *tadabbur*, or reflective scrutiny.

Any scripture, in that way, just by being such invites co-operation, risks its readers and waits on comprehension. It cannot act like some slide-rule in geometry or a template in engineering. Apart from all we reviewed concerning prophetic recipience of its textuality in Chapter 3, the nature of the Qur'an as 'pre-existent' has that other 'incidence' which. all 'occasions of revelation' apart, transpires in day to day, century to century, readership. Recitation, indeed, may be rightly 'word-perfect' and calligraphy also immaculate, but these due proprieties of tongue and pen cannot be likewise achieved in commentary and translation where the Book has its different 'occasions' in the wills and the setting of those who read and interpret. One might almost say that an Allah who scripturises His Word is essentially non-coercive but solicitous, identifying but not imposing His revelation. *Iqra' bi-smi Rabbika*—'Recite in thy Lord's Name,' tells a situation exactly as a warrant awaiting an audience with 'the messenger' mediating between them, secure in the one and seeking the other.

The same point is implicit in the Arabicity of the Book as earlier underlined. The Book, thereby, was 'native' to its first hearers, intelligible in their own speech, a truly 'vernacular' revelation. How the empirical fact of its Arabic in that 'eventing' related to its eternal presence on 'a well-guarded tablet' had to remain mysterious. The rendition from the one to the other lay within the assurance of revelation. The point lay in the fact that the eternal took over the temporal in a language comprehensible and in a quality of language accessible to recognition as superlatively adequate.

The challenge it could make to 'bring a surah—bring ten surahs like it,' as noted in Chapter 3, only further emphasised that it was entrusting itself to lively recognition in terms congenial to local human mind. Literary authority could merit literary admiration and transact what duly obtains between the given and the received, between authority and faith. The quality of the Qur'an's Arabic was always understood as an element in its credentials as 'the speech of God'. For outsiders to Islam, a language only its immediate speakers could adequately appreciate seems a strange commendatory asset for a world-intending revelation. The present point, however, is that it brought the authority of the Scripture into a human category, or criterion, of judgement. It must follow that other human categories of judgement, like conscience, truth-intuition, or soul-yearning, might also have their place in an assessing reception of the text. The divinely pre-existent thus had dealings with a humanly implied competence to evaluate.

The 'bring a surah comparable' call to Muhammad's audience can well be linked with the *Umm al-Kitab* concept as in 43.4 where it follows *Qur'anan 'arabiyyan*, 'a recital that is Arabic,' For both terms are arguably comment on the mystical letters (in this case *ha mim*) which precede a number of Surahs.[3] Whatever be the ultimate explanation of their presence, they are the raw material of Arabic language, the counters in the textualising of the Book, the items conveying intelligibility which the verb in the verse (*ta'qilun*—'perhaps you may give your mind') intends and offers. *Umm al-Kitab* is variously rendered as the Book's 'origin', 'essence', source', all being 'with Him', or 'in His presence'. When the term occurs in 13.39 the context relates to all 'previous revelations' and the divine capacity to annul or confirm their contents, seeing that the irrefragable text from which they all derived is inviolate in Allah's keeping.

---

[3] This rather prosaic explanation of the letters can be taken further into conjectures that intrigue scholars and fascinate mystics. They occur fivefold in Surahs 19 and 42, though differently; twice fourfold; twelve threefold; nine in pairs; and three singly. The most frequent pairing is *ha mim* and the most frequent treble, are *alif, lam, mim* or *alif, lam, ra*. They may well have to do as crucial—not initial—letters identifying key words or terms in the Surah. They give their Surah its title in 38 and 50, while *nun* stands at the head of 68 without doing so. In any event, poetry and prose employ *huruf*, 'letters' and without these nothing.

iii

That eternal 'referent' of all its 'coming downs' in the vocal ministry of prophets and messengers inhabits—we might say—the word-bearing of all these, and the Qur'an superlatively so. Because it 'utters' itself in their speaking, it thereby also fuses with their *Sitz im Leben*. For envoys—if we use that word—are always *to* as well as *from*. They are human to humans. We have seen this in respect of Muhammad, both in the significance of the word *ummi* and through all the vicissitudes of Chapter 1. In respect of what is 'inscribed' on 'a well-guarded tablet', the messenger is only, severely only, a 'reciter'. Nevertheless the themes he finds himself 'reciting' signify by reference to the scene in which he does so. Context is the human side of intelligibility.

The point had its relevance earlier. Here it has place as recruiting history, time and setting, to supply the actual 'co-incidence'[4] of each and every 'saying'. For there is no 'word' in the speaking or the hearing or the reading that is not, by each of these, contexted in a situation to which it is addressed and within which it is understood. In this sense the Qur'an is as 'historical' as any other Scripture though it partakes of scene and setting in its own way. The point is important inasmuch as Islamic Scripture, by dint of its being 'recital', has often been taken as uncomplicated, pure 'utterance'. Thus, for example, a recent writer contrasts what he calls 'Quranic discourse' with Biblical revelation, the latter being made to hinge on historical particularity having to do with events in the 'election' of Israel (Old Testament) and with the person of Christ (Christology in the New Testament).[5] While it is true that Biblical Scriptures are largely event-related, via exodus and exile, Jesus in his ministry and Passion, and differ thereby sharply from the Qur'an, the latter's form of 'word bearing meaning' is no less historicized. For history is a condition of anything—even preaching or declamation—happening at all.[6]

It is this fact which takes us squarely into the psychic dimension involved in all word-bearing believed to have its source in divine

---

[4] Using the word in a pure sense and in no way as popularised into 'chance.'

[5] Mohammed Abu-Hamdiyyah, *The Qur'an: An Introduction*, London, 2000, pp. 38–41.

[6] The difference Abu-Hamdiyyah stresses is right, as also is the point that the Hebraic 'events' are sharply ethnic in land and liberation terms, whereas what he dubs 'Arabic' is not ethnic in those terms while the central language dimension claims to bear, as the Judaic does not, an inclusive reach of peoples. As for historicity in New Testament terms, we must await Chapter 8.

inspiration. The prophetic psyche is peculiarly so in respect of the Qur'an. Hebrew spokesmen for heaven, reading memory of exodus and land-tenancy, or brooding in pain on the puzzle of exile, had these events in their ken as themes around which their 'inspiration' could communicate. Even 'proverb-minters' like the legendary Solomon, or a Qoheleth musing in Ecclesiastes, found their voices from what the world registered within their souls. For Muhammad uttering the Qur'an, however, there is believed to have been a word-bestowal that had no memory-ground, no muse-source on his part, so that his psyche experienced a kind of immediacy between heavenly word and earthly speech.

What could this have meant to him undergoing it, is the question that arises for all Muslim loyalty to Islamic Scripture. For, as *wahy*, or 'inspired recital', was happening through those unique years of its singular incidence, at its centre was a personhood, a citizen, a preacher, a tactician, a sufferer, a military leader, a victor, a hero—human, Arab, Quraishi, Yathribi—one of such stature that his believing contemporaries needed to be warned that he was not immortal. The question, in its full reach, is the measure of the Qur'an-in-the-psyche, in the instrumental human consciousness inside a verbal revelation. That, as orthodoxy holds, there was no mental authorship, no deliberating role in the text, only makes the psychic *viaticum* the more central to what is believed in Islam.[7] Hence the desire to make it so in the several angles studied in the six foregoing chapters.

The centrality could be phrased in another way by saying that Muhammad, being the envoy with the Qur'an, was thereby also the envoy in the Qur'an. He is repeatedly indispensable not only to what the text needs to say but to how it can be said—not how in respect of phrasing (of which word-mediation takes care) but how in respect of pivot, substance, theme and process, culminating via dialogue and decision in dicta like: 'Obey God and obey the *Rasul*,' when the dual demand tells of one régime.

For Islam, it must follow that what is 'with Allah' on 'a well-guarded tablet' is 'preserved' in the Prophet's uttering from slips of the tongue or malicious interjections of Satanic guile?[8] Given a 'literal'

---

[7] *Viaticum* in the old sense of 'the provision by which the journey is made possible.'

[8] As, for example, Surah 22.52, with Satan maliciously seeking to throw into recital what Allah will abrogate in due protection of its meaning. Cf. the issue of the so-called 'Satanic verses' alleging that Muhammad was tempted to use false words in compromise with the Quraish (17.74). Depending on how *idha tamanna* is read there, the insinuation may be into Muhammad's mind—or 'longing', rather than into his text. Temptation including both would rather confirm the entailing of things psychic in words spoken.

understanding of how Scriptures arrive from their celestial derivation, it must be that the messenger's 'preservation' from these hazards will be of the same order. For the Satan who has disputed and defied the whole divine conferment of creaturely 'dominion' on humans, and knows that prophets with scriptures are the crucial factor in that conferment's wisdom being vindicated through their tuition of the human trustees, will naturally target scripture texts and will do so as a prompter might in having errors happen. The 'preservation' in either case will be of that textual order. The imagery of the 'tablet' and the 'text' holds them both immaculate.

Correspondingly, the question is still there for reverent reflection—how does this 'well-guardedness' transpire in the psyche of Muhammad? What did it inwardly mean for him to be aware of factors malign seeking to distort a flow of words? Did the 'preservation' enable or only override an inner disposition 'guarding' or not guarding itself? Either way, thought on a Qur'an, inviolate in its earthly words no less than in its divine origin, cannot well refuse the question of Muhammad's inwardness as where all transpired.

iv

Everything thus far requires the conclusion that the Qur'an is a very programmatic way for revelation and faith through all the aspects we have reviewed. *Tanzil*, or 'the sending down' of divine Scripture, ensures an inviolate text. Calligraphy as its due reception ensures its sound perpetuation by the art of the pen. Recital, syllabically loyal and ever exact, will do for its security in community what 'a preserved tablet' has done eternally. Its having the *hifz* of believers will be the sure *hifz* of their belief. Prophetic instrumentality is immune from incurring the kind of time-long interrogation to which other patterns of scripture-bearing are readily liable. Even the recension of the Qur'an's 'gathering' from fragments into textual 'finality' under 'Uthman, the third caliph, excludes —for all practical purposes—the variant readings that might elsewhere fuel conjecture or require enquiry. Has not the Qur'an, by its very doctrine of itself, made it ideally what any Scriptured revelation needs to be? May not 'the seal of the prophets' epithet about Muhammad be read in this further sense, beyond chronology, as the perfectedness of the prophetic idiom itself and the form of Allah's perfecting of religion? If so, is not the Qur'an the ultimate document of religion as being, on all these counts,

Allah's *imprimatur* in very fact of textual fact? If so, perhaps the study of Muhammad's psyche need go no further, content to be hidden in this 'miracle' of the Qur'an.

Yet is the Qur'an's doctrine or concept of itself as clear and definitive as this supposes? 'The Qur'an on itself' has long been a familiar formula but is it unambiguous to the degree we are suggesting? When we enter the world of the Qur'an we meet the status it commands but we also enter an active arena. Its later heirs may worry and debate concerning its 'uncreated' status as 'the very words of God', but the 'creature' situation with which it engages is not in doubt. Being where and what Allah speaks, it moves and belongs within a human scene it must 'warn, exhort, admonish, remind and arraign.' Its entire thrust is manward where its inviolate origin in *Umm al-Kitab* has a bitterly violating reception. The very excellence of its status is brought into odds with the heinous ill-will of a reception it must threaten, condemn, accuse and disown.

There is, then, a supreme contention at its heart. No sane reader can ignore the urgency of the Book's indictment of human wrong, its pained awareness of the lengths of *zulm* and *kufr*, of *kidhb* and *fisq*, in the social scene. *Écrase l'infâme* is the other part in the voice that cries *Subhan Allah*. The Qur'an is far from having a 'doctrine of itself' that proposes an amenable world for its audition. On the contrary, it carries as its watershed an enterprise of studied, if still tactical, repudiation of the world it first addressed. It is not essentially a stranger to the logic that led Jesus in his preaching experience to the parable of the usurping tenants of a Lord's vineyard, or that led His disciples to find their Christology in His Gethsemane.

It would be idle to 'read the Qur'an' without 'reading the Hijrah' as its witness to the obduracy with which divine speech is greeted in the human world, and even when in Medinan terms that condition is politically retrieved, there remains the pointed warning of Surah 110.

> 'When God's help comes about and conquest, and you have
> seen people come crowding into the religion of God, then
> sing the praise of your Lord and seek His forgiveness. To be
> merciful was ever His wont.'

A 'seeking of forgiveness' about success itself could only mean that what 'conquest' had resoundingly achieved was not the whole end for which the Qur'an was meant. The aftermath in the Islamic story all too soon disproved any such illusion. For it was humanity, in its generous 'createdness' in relation to the words of the 'uncreated Qur'an' that was critically at issue in the Book's 'doctrine of itself', rather than what became the burden of discursive theologians in the middle centuries, busy with case-making and schism on the 'created/uncreated' theme about the Book itself.[9] For their intellectual concerns around a Scripture which theological security required to be eternal could, nevertheless, be so obviously immersed in temporal, mundane circumstance. Their legitimate mental anxiety had to be left for the paradox it was, inside their acceptance of the whole given-ness of revelation which inevitably incurred it. So much we have seen.

If we are engaged in knowing 'the Qur'an by the Qur'an', in fully ascertaining its own doctrine of itself, there is a far more realist study waiting on us as between eternity and time, as between uncreated origin and created handiwork. It locates in the divine enterprise of humankind with their creaturehood set over the material order as custodians on behalf of Allah. To this end they are endowed with the autonomy proper to this vocation—an autonomy they are called to bring into *islam*, into a responsible and perceptive conformity to the divine design intended in their dignity, so that, effectively, they will as God wills, inasmuch as God has willed to have His will through theirs.

Prophet messengers to interpret, commend and in detailed law and guidance lay down this destiny with a view to the vital human conformity, both willed and done, are the clear corollary of this creaturehood. Everything Adamic, because it is so focal in Allah's world-concept, turns on the tutelary summons of the prophets of whom Muhammad is the climax.

However, the wisdom and propriety of this divine-human scenario—if we may use so late a word—have been relentlessly challenged, disavowed, as the whole scene in Surah 2.30 explains, by 'the accursed Satan' who—as it were in Allah's own better interests in creating at all—

---

[9] Those discourses developed in the context of the increasing sophistication of the Muslim mind from the 9th/10th centuries (CE) over the moral problem of 'free-will' in view of divine 'destining', and the role of reason in the play of religious authority. The Qur'an was so manifestly involved in things in times and places. How could these be eternally pre-inscribed in heaven. Mu'atizilite intellectualism busied itself with that issue and 'uncreated'/ 'created' was the terminology it adopted. Inevitably, with doctrinal debate, politics entangled itself therewith and the 'Abbasid caliphs patronised one side or the other.

thinks the human custodial privilege no less than divine folly to be eternally rued and abandoned. The very sovereignty of Allah, thinks Satan, is at odds with itself in thus having humankind so far 'deputies' for Himself in the good earth.[10]

Given this radical Satanic dispute with Allah concerning humankind, there ensues a perpetual crisis in the earthly realm. For Satan's quarrel with God because of His dispute about man is no academic matter. Satan means to press the point, to elicit the evidence of human frailty by which Allah may be dissuaded about what in His 'uncreatedness' He fondly and madly 'created.' This eliciting of the evidence means the steady, relentless temptation of humans, ensnaring and plotting to have them begin to argue that a given autonomy meant for *islam*, powers granted to be only ordered to conform, were all a sort of fraud calling for the suspicion that said: 'Has God said …?' Why not stretch that freedom to obey into a license to rebel?

Thus Satan cultivates a psychology of distrust of God, a culture of forgetfulness that worsens into wilfulness, in a word a *Jahiliyyah* that wills to be ignorant and ignores what should be willed.[11] It follows, then, that there is perennial crisis in human society, a demonic conspiracy against our highest good which we have to detect, identify for what it is and steadfastly repudiate, so that—if only via this travail—Allah is vindicated in the thwarting of 'the accuser'. We humans are beset by 'a liar' of our humanness to whom we have to give the lie, accusing the accuser, denying the denier. In this vital task, messengers and their 'book.' are at once our light, our spur, our mentor and our well-being.

Here, finally, is 'the Qur'an on itself', its inclusive philosophy of history and, indeed, of sociology, through a superb mythology explicit in the figure of Satan as the arch-adversary of Allah in being the arch-antagonist of man. The Qur'an is extremely alert to the threat from *Al-Shaitan*, indeed pluralises the word into *shayatin*. For his wiles belong with collectives no less than with private selves, in the machinations of bodies politic, structures of power and vested interests, all of which are wide

---

[10] 'Deputise' is no idle term here. It holds the sense of the verb *khalafa*—'to fill the room (or role) of'; from 'to follow' or 'succeed' another. Hence *khalifah*, 'one doing so', and *khilafah* ('dominion'), the act itself. It is intriguing that *khilafah* is only one diacritical point different from *khaliqah*, 'creature'.

[11] Borrowing the term used to describe the pre-Islamic world of Mecca and its condition of 'barbarity' stemming from 'unenlightenedness'.

open to corrupting insinuation and greed of every kind. *Al-Shaitan* has the descriptive *al-rajim*, an intriguing reflexive adjective meaning 'stoned' as the most fierce form of repudiation. The 'stoning' that has a vivid role in the Meccan pilgrimage symbolises what a right *muslim* mind must do with each and every Satanic wile, namely resist and deny.[12]

If, then, we may think of the Qur'an by the analogy of a panorama or, better, a drama, Muhammad as the prophet messenger might be thought on in something of the role of 'the chorus' in a Greek tragedy, as if appealing to readers: 'Admit me chorus to this history.'[13] For the stage was set in the culmination, as the Qur'an sees it, of the final summons—through the climax of prophethood—to recognise the divine stake in the human realm. We might think of it as 'the artifice of worship',[14] the shaping of the rule of God in the overcoming of that *shirk*, or human deviation away from 'Godwardness', which is the ultimate expression of Satan's success and the constant burden of prophetic charge.

Thus the cry *Allahu akbar* tells a truth only also in the form of a claim. Uncreated sovereignty is not in doubt but has willed to obtain within created consent. That drama has been joined; messengers are the 'tutelary spirits' through whom humans learn their part as cast into an action where their *taqwa*, their 'God-submission', is artfully countered, deterred, reversed, by a principle of evil they must steadily resist and defeat under the urgent tuition of those prophetic presences that share the stage, and in whose scriptures the whole is told—told for warning, told for prompting, told for achieving. The finality of Muhammad in this divine-human scenario would make him the last 'presenter' and the Qur'an the inclusive stage.[15]

---

[12] See any alert exposition of the ritual of *Hajj* and the casting of 'stones' (pebbles) against the *jamarat* at Mina on the tenth day of Pilgrimage when, also, the *Hajjis* conclude the sacral state of *ihram*. The cry *Allah akbar* accompanies the hurling of each stone. There are few gestures more energetically repudiatory. Satan must have no place or quarter in the retaken 'profane' state.

[13] William Shakespeare, Prologue to *Henry V*. In Greek drama, as recurring in John Milton, *Samson Agonistes*, the Chorus is half outside the action in articulate commentary and half inside in pained sympathy and a register of grief. T S Eliot's *Murder in the Cathedral* used 'women of Canterbury' as a chorus both ways, as did also Salah 'Abd al-Sabur of Cairo with merchants of Baghdad in his *Ma'sat al-Hallaj*, consciously modelled on Eliot's drama.

[14] Meaning 'artifice' in the strict sense as 'means shaped to achieve an end in view'.

[15] In hope that the analogy is seen to be fitting. In which case 'stage' has the double sense of 'place where' and 'time-point' of, 'inclusive' making it also 'final'.

v

There are issues for a mutual theology between this measure of 'the Qu'ran on itself' and the 'God-in-Christ' theme of Chapter 8. These must come in the closing Chapter 9. Meanwhile our thought of Muhammad in the role of 'chorus to this human history', the history of the 'uncreated Allah's' way to acknowledged sovereignty in the due *islam* of created humankind, bears powerfully on themes relayed from Chapters 3 and 6 and, perhaps differently, from Chapter 5.

These all had to do with the stature of Muhammad, the meaning of his 'sentness' as 'enmantled' and how in *Tasliyah* that agency was associated with the divine approbation. Chapter 5 was occupied with the legitimation of power in the Hijrah to Medina. Our analogy of 'chorus to this history' has to be kept consistent with all these dimensions.

The 'uncreated/created' discourse we have borrowed from the theologians, exploring the Qur'an's dual quality as Islam finds it, and applied to the drama of human creaturehood called to *islam* as disputed by a principle of evil bent on the success of *shirk*, may also be applied by biographers of the Prophet. It belongs with Muhammad's *Sirah* or life-story, no less than with the human drama. Creaturely, severely human, as he was, Muhammad's role somehow entailed an 'uncreated' dimension, sometimes taken over by theosophical conjecture, but firmly—if mysteriously—located in the Qur'an itself.

Crucial to that dimension are the famous 'Night Journey' and the heavenly *Mi'raj*, already relevant in Chapter 3 above.

> 'Glory to Him who by night took His servant journeying from the sacred mosque to the distant mosque, al-Aqsa, whose precincts We have blessed, in order to show him Our revelations. He is the One who hears and sees all.' (Surah 17.1)

The echoes of this passage reverberate through the entire history and the devotion of Muslims. The three following verses at once link the meaning with revelation via Moses to the people of Israel, suggesting the immediate significance of Jerusalem—'the distant sanctuary' far beyond Medina, if that city was already the focus of Muhammad's mind, For it is generally held that Surah 17 belongs shortly prior to the Hijrah.

'To show him Our revelations' are the words that tell of Muhammad's *Mi'raj*, or 'Ascension' into heaven, whereby after meeting earlier messengers in Jerusalem, he and they were carried up to the divine realm with the Prophet carried furthest thitherwards. Not defined in the Qur'an but copiously traced in Tradition, this heavenly disclosure of truth and light happened by what, elsewhere in relation to ordinary believers is known as *sharh al-sadr*, 'the opening of the heart, or bosom', for the evacuation of all self-falsity and the bestowal of pure truth.[16] Muhammad's being 'shown Our revelations' was supremely unique, as befitted the final envoy of divine meaning. It would seem that the *Mi'raj*, as the prompt sequel to the journey and in the context of antecedent prophethood, must be read as one mystical event, at once a geographical and a mythic symbol.

For some in Islam, both journey and ascension are to be understood as literally happening, even to the point of naming the steed on which Muhammad rode as far as Jerusalem. For many others, however, both are essentially conveying the clue to Muhammad's recipience of the whole Qur'an, namely an initiation, sustained through over two decades but here mysteriously intensified, whereby he was possessed of 'the very words (or light) of God', and that, not by proxy, but in his own authentic person. What may at other times have been mediated by 'the angel', was now 'face to face'.

Thus the whole significance of Surah 17.1 is the counterpart, in prophetic experience, of the 'created/uncreated' paradox of the Qur'an to which, as a divine Book, he was humanly instrumental. Surah 17.1—we may say—possesses Muslims biographically in the Prophet thus authenticated, with what they cherish scripturally as authentically the Qur'an. The two validations belong together. He is thus dramatically attested as the prophetic means for the *Tanzil* of the Book: the Qur'an has

---

[16] The concept of *Sharh al-sadr* has to do with the 'enabling' by which 'revelation' is imparted—an 'expanding of the bosom' (*sharh* used of texts is 'exegesis'). In Surah 94.1 Muhammad is asked—as from Allah—'Did We not enlarge your heart?' the question supplying the Surah's title: *Al-Inshirah*. In 39.22 the phrase is used in respect of a 'heart opened to *islam*' by Allah as being thereby 'on a light from his Lord', as contrasted with the unbelievers who have hardened hearts (Cf. 6.125). In 20.25, Moses prays: 'O my Lord, enlarge my heart.' It is often assumed that the occasion of Surah 94 belongs with a point in Muhammad's *Sirah* earlier than the *Mi'raj* when he needed re-assurance in face of of ridicule and calumny. Tradition, however, can well link 94.4 about 'raising high his repute' with the later theme of 'ascension'. See p. 64 above.

the tribute of what has always been necessary to it, namely a human voice lifted to where *Tanzil* derives.

If so, then 'comprehension'—if we seek it—of Night Journey and *Mi'raj* has to be contained, like the paradox of the Qur'an itself, in the double phenomenon that revelation has always been, namely a divine initiative and a human reception, an eternal deriving and an historical arriving. Those so minded may visualise a physical journey, a literal ascension, taking up the liability for heaven also as a 'place' in both senses. Others understand a mystical symbolism where journey and rapture are alike a metaphor of intercourse with light celestial.

The word *'abdi*, 'My servant', used in 17.1, rather than *Al-Rasul*, would seem to commend the case we are arguing, a recruitment of what is human in respect of what is divine. Often the Qur'an stresses that Muhammad is man and mortal, perhaps in studied distinction from what Christians—on Muslim ground erroneously—hold about Jesus in their Christology. Yet, crucial as that distinction is, there is inevitably in the concept of *Mi'raj* something about Muhammad in his personhood which, coupled with what belongs with Allah's 'greeting' of him in *Tasliyah,* involves a 'word-bearing' that is more than merely verbal and oral. Implanting in the *sadr* implies something made to be inherent in his persona whereby he speaks, yet also symbolises, message and meaning. Certainly the vast array of Islamic tradition seized on this clue and drew from his human 'perfection' the guidance that enlarged upon the verbal Qur'an.

So to appreciate only returns us to the central theme, namely how this intensely subjective experience is stated as if by a third party. It tells of how his Lord 'took His servant by night ...' Yet the speaker in the context of preachment in Mecca is the one of whom the third person narrative speaks. We might think of those 'women of Canterbury' in T S Eliot's Cathedral play presenting what is happening, or about to happen, to the central figure who is not themselves as 'margin-parties' in the drama, or the 'merchants' in Salah 'Abd al-Sabur's parallel 'Tragedy of Al-Hallaj' who comment tellingly on the periphery of the action.

Given that the whole Qur'an is uttered by Muhammad alone, what must this passage about him in third party terms, yet also on his own lips, have meant inwardly for him as a reality which he both experiences and narrates? Surah 17.1 only posits for us readers in a hyper-charged form a situation comparatively present throughout, whether in the context of a preached message or a presiding leadership. Muhammad is at one and the same time the theme and its bringer, the third party and the first, subject in, as well as subject with, this Qur'an. How should religious study do right by what, in this way, must be called 'the psychic Qur'an'?

The question is in no way raised out of perversity or depreciation. On the contrary, it only arises if the Qur'an—as the phrase goes—is 'taken seriously'. In some measure it must be seen as variously attaching to the phenomenon of scripture-bearing everywhere among the faiths. The mystery of the self-consciousness of Jesus will concern us in Chapter 8 in an effort to align with the faith of the mosque what has been a crucial responsibility for the faith of the Church. As we must then see, there are very different pre-suppositions involved. But in the New Testament, and in the Fourth Gospel supremely, there is this 'chorus' like situation where Jesus is at once both object and subject in his discourses. In Buddhism, is it not broadly said that the Buddha does not 'teach' the Dharma, he epitomises what each 'reader' must find it to be?

Yet, Surahs 17.1 and 53.1-18 being as they are, Islam in its perception of the Qur'an and, indeed, the Qur'an in its conveyance of Islam, have always insisted on the 'recital' clue, have always held revelation to be constrained to words alone, so that 'Book' is its vehicle, writing its text, and recitation its education. Its defining vocation against Arabian paganism and pluralism required it to exclude all thinking that was incarnational, lest such beguiled it again into flouting criminously the uncompromised Unity of Allah.

Even so, the question stays whether revelation can suffice itself in words, whether even a given Scripture that wills to have it do so in fact moves beyond, and always with, the verbal into where the voice becomes more than an echo and the envoy is seen to be sign behind all words. 'Glory be to Him who carried His servant by night ... to illumine him from Our signs ...'[17] could be so understood if the second clause, as tradition holds, truly means rapture to the divine presence. That reading is certainly in line with the way the *Shahadah* so uninhibitedly inter-associates Allah's being as One and Muhammad being His *Rasul*.[18]

---

[17] Rendering *li yunirahu min ayatina*, sometimes also 'to show him Our signs' if the preposition *min* does not reserve what remains ineffable. The formula of doxology lays an aura of hallowing around the whole.

[18] That bonding sequence: 'Allah One, Muhammad His envoy'—often set in large equal medallions in the mosque—holds in the utmost brevity the most profound of theological issues, as embracing—in different terms—as any Christology.

As categorically indicating more than pure, uncomplicated verbalism, Muslim orthodoxy has taken: 'show him Our signs' or 'illumine him with Our signs' as the meaning of 17.1 and of the *Mi'raj*, in more than verbal initiation. Then his 'ascension to the presence' means what faith has always held it to mean, making the 'messenger' in such wise 'intimate' with God. There is, doubtless, the matter of *ayatina*, 'Our signs', having, elsewhere, the double meaning of 'Our mysteries' and 'the verses of Our Book'. But it would be odd to take the *Mi'raj* as Muhammad reading the script on 'a preserved tablet'. It was a supremely transcendent occasion in which 'Our servant' is far more than the 'reciter' he had been enabled to be, all heavenward rapture apart, in the more mundane sequence of the Qur'an's *Tanzil*. In one sense, *Mi'raj* dispenses with *Tanzil* in lifting the Prophet to sublime rendezvous itself.

Whatever, for Quranic exegesis around Surah 17.1, may finally be the meaning we should find, there abides our central question as to 'incidence of the pre-existent' in the inward self-awareness of Muhammad. Perhaps the question cannot be answered. Perhaps it should never be raised. Either way, it will always be latent both for the sincerity of piety and the integrity of scholarship. However it be resolved, or rested, it still enquires whether revelation can ever be wholly and only verbal, a thing of words as sufficing it, and therefore whether their bearing messenger bears *more* than them alone—the *more* of a persona and a sign. The Qur'an—as grammar would state it—is so much a 'first person' event ('Muhammad, Allah's messenger) so far told in a 'third person' pattern.

In due course in Muslim history the philosophers sought their own response.

vi

It is by Islam's fourth century that we meet them in working towards a prophetology that draws on Greek concepts of 'genius' and 'wisdom'. Study of how they reasoned about the gift of revelation and the persona of Muhammad could well begin from Surah 17.93 with the same initial doxology: 'Glory to my Lord! Am I other than a human, an apostle?' The 'glory' formula is often used as a kind of protective against false imputation such as idolaters make. Muhammad's entire human-ness has to be in no doubt. But should the two nouns, *basharan rasulan*, by which he is denoted, 'a human, an apostle', be read as virtually synonymous? Muhammad is, indeed (for example) 'mortal', as all humans are. Yet he is no ordinary human by virtue of being also *rasulan*. Apostolate is not a calling inclusive of all mortals. If a translator joins them with 'and' to read: 'a man and a messenger', should the 'and' carry no significance beyond mere addition of terms or is there also 'addition' of status, making for some sort of 'humanity-plus'? Clearly the latter is the case. Yet what is the 'plus' that 'being *rasulan*' imparts to the 'human' bearing it? Here, it might be said, we have our whole problem captured in two words.

It has to be noted that Surah 17.93 returns to 17.1 in responding to challenges from incredulous Meccans among which (the seventh) is: 'Were you to ascend into heaven never would we believe your ascension, unless (or until) you bring down upon us a book which we can read.' Their scepticism tallies with his presentation but does so only by literalising both his alleged 'book-bringing' (by stages to which they also allude) and his *Mi'raj*. His Lord is invoked to protect him from the wilful calumny that maliciously took his scripturing and his ascension as a kind of 'errand-boy' affair. If that is ruled out on the ground of his being truly 'human', it also rules *in* an apostolate that, on every count, is no crude literalism but in some sense a transcendent encounter.

That 'apposition' of 'human' with 'apostle' (or that 'and' if, translating, we insert it) was what philosophers explored, if they did not explain, in terms of 'divine wisdom' with which, in being *Rasul*, Muhammad was superlatively endowed. Their theory developed from Greek ideas of an immanent principle of truth and knowledge by which the active intellect in the human mind related innately to the active intellect emanating from the transcendent/real. Muhammad's encounter with 'the angel' of 'revelation' could be read as symbolic of this capacity of the (or his) human soul as ever potentially—and there *qua* Qur'an comprehensively—inter-associating with the wisdom that was ever divine. It might be possible in this way to understand the experience in which 'the Book' was vouchsafed to him as an intellectualist grace bestowed and in that 'bestowal' *wahy* transpired.

This sense of the Qur'an seemed totally at odds with the traditional portrayal of an entirely 'illiterate' messenger who owed his destiny completely to the 'miracle' of his utterance of sublime words to which his mental processes made absolutely no contribution, and which, therefore, was the more credibly and authentically 'given' precisely by fact of his being personally in 'abeyance' while the 'deliverances' were received and uttered.

It was not, however, only in order to salvage something more intellectually satisfactory to them that the philosophers speculated as they did about capacities in the human soul. It could genuinely be pleaded, on their part, that the traditional *ummi* version simplified the same reality for which they contended in sophisticated terms. They did so without radically changing the 'event' the Qur'an had been. They merely revised, or re-conceived, what in its first time and place had needed to be couched the initial way to underwrite, for that society, the essential truth of divine revelation. It had been a sort of *argumentum ad homines* in a community long alert to the inspirations' of poets, seers and verbal celebrants. The fact that Muhammad in the Qur'an had repeatedly to dissociate his deliverances from such kinships only demonstrated how prone his people were to that assumption. His being—there and then—'de-personalised' in Qur'an recipience was an urgent present token of precisely that divine bestowal of the text which a later philosophy could more aptly—and congenially— explain in different terms, retaining, by so doing, the essential claim of the Book to be 'God-given'.

Though in one sense such philosophy, in making the Qur'an 'non-miraculous' in the old form, in no way disengaged it from a 'preserved tablet' that was co-relative to human capacity, it did present a radical challenge to orthodoxy in its implications. It could be seen to forfeit, or at least jeopardise, the imperative and categorical quality of the traditional view and, with it, the absolute authority of the *Shari'ah*. The Prophet, thanks utterly to God, was subtly different from the Prophet thanks somewhat to himself, or—rather—to capacities he humanly possessed. To be sure, these capacities were only his by gift, but the 'gifting' was seen as responsive to 'excellences', moral and spiritual, that he possessed, and thus, in some sense, merited on his part. Such innate merit, making Muhammad the very exemplification of *islam*, had its massive place in the elaboration of tradition. But, classically, tradition was almost always firmly distinguished from the Qu'ran.[19] In effect, the philosophers, in their subtle way, incorporated the person of Muhammad into the Qur'an by reading the role he already played in tradition as that of heir to transcendent wisdom or the light-bearer of divine illumination.

---

[19] With the exception of so-called *Hadith Qudsi*, where a 'saying' of the Prophet was held by some to have a legal or a moral status and to be virtually equivalent to a Quranic text. What came to be gathered into the Book, however, was habitually distinguished from *obiter dicta* that did not have the *imprimatur* of the Quranic state.

Intricate and scholastic as the long debates became, philosophers and savants from Ibn Sina to Ibn Khaldun across four centuries of Islamic Qur'an-evaluation were searching for a prophetology that could interpret their Muhammad and underwrite their allegiance to Islam. There were mediating positions between absolute 'illiterate miracle' and 'soul-worth' in divine wisdom. The exceptionality of Muhammad was never in question, nor the ultimate faith in the finality of the resulting text. 'Revelation', in any event, is a taxing concept that must somehow incorporate a giving and a receiving, an imparting and a participating. Seemingly contrary positions could be reconciled in 'the angel' through whose proximity in a divine-whence and a human-whither everything transpired.

Issues of faith are sometimes best left where alone finally they belong, namely in the will to faith by which believers are moved and in the readiness of the will faithfully to undertake the duties it incurs as being what it may not faithfully ignore. It might be fascinating for speculating minds to locate the ultimate 'mystery' of Muhammad's Prophethood in a supreme instance of human register in the personal soul of that 'active intelligence' which creatively sustained and moved the whole intelligible world. The analogy of light from that supreme source kindling an answering illumination in the receptive soul could bring together the central significance of the Qur'an and the ideal epistemology of the Greek thinkers.

Yet, if it satisfied the speculative bent of an Al-Farabi, it still left the riddle unresolved of how and why this intellectual account of the Qur'an had contrived the sort of historical incidence that Book had undergone, why it had located in the years before and after Hijrah and shaped itself in the highly particularised immediacies that constituted the *asbab al-nuzul* critical for all exegesis. For these, with their specifics of city and camp, of tent and trail, seemed far removed from the forms and themes of universal intellect. Orthodoxy, prejudice or passion apart, had reason to suspect that the Qur'an would cease to be the magisterial imperative 'speech of God' if it allowed its traditional doctrine of itself the compromise of philosophical accommodation.

Perhaps all that is at stake here is in the realm of the old defiant question: 'What has Athens to do with Jerusalem?' Ought religion to philosophise? The classic view of Muhammad's prophethood as a wholly religious recipience of divinely-given truth exemplifies the need for religious faith to enjoy, for authority, what is intrinsic to itself, and therefore admits no further negotiation. Or, conversely, philosophy only becomes religious when it finally leaves philosophy behind.

When, in wrestling with the meaning of the Christ-event, the Fourth Gospel and other sources reached for the Logos concept they were, in measure, comparable to the philosophers of Islam's middle centuries. For they sought to identify the person of Christ with the 'Word' of creative and upholding reason that Greek thought made central to philosophy in perception of the natural order. So doing, they were certainly religiously philosophical and philosophically religious or, *pace* Tertullian, 'Athens had much to do with Jerusalem,' as they believed. Despite minds like Tertullian's, the will to have it so persisted all through the story of credalising the faith up to, and beyond, the Council of Chalcedon. And the New Testament Canon had things Johannine in its embrace.

This Logos theme in Christianity had its warrant on two grounds—the first being the centrality of the person and work of Jesus as the Christ, the second a concept of 'the Holy Spirit'. It was the latter that allowed Christian faith to think its finalities akin to philosophical obligation. It was the former that could welcome elucidation by means of the Logos concept in a way that the Qur'an could not, by virtue of its defining character as 'the Book' of Allah.

By its being 'the Book' the Qur'an's revelatory status turned on the recipience that was personal to Muhammad, whereas for Christianity the revelatory status was in Jesus himself being the Christ in a history only later inscribed because it had that status.[20] Thus it would be one thing to think philosophically around Muhammad as 'text-receiver' and another around Jesus as 'text-personifier'. Or, put differently, what Christians meant by 'the Incarnation' could welcome the Greek Logos theme in terms that heirs to the Qur'an could not.

It may be illuminating in the next Chapter to study—as far as wisdom and reverence may—the self-consciousness of Jesus in the Gospel story, not as a mere comparative exercise, but to see what light the study affords for prophetology in Islam. So long as the venture is patiently academic we may hope to avoid the tangle of prejudice or the veto that would otherwise attend it. If it appears that by their handling of Muhammad's prophethood the Muslim philosophers were reaching towards

---

[20] The 'history having that status, pre-supposes large questions—in which Muslims are involved—around the New Testament record. Some of these will be faced in Chapter 8, not exhaustively in their full right, but for the purpose of the elucidation proposed.

something like a logos concept, it must seem clear that they were also reaching for something like a concept of 'the Holy Spirit'. For only via 'Holy Spirit' can faith and philosophy combine. Insofar as they are doing so, either prophethood or Incarnation will be their territory, common in profound contrast.

Chapter 8
THE FOREGOING AND
NEW TESTAMENT CHRISTOLOGY

i

'Christianity itself is just the intellectual colony of Arabia.' Even in his younger, novel-writing years the romantic imagination of Benjamin Disraeli reached for imperial analogy. In his novel *Tancred* the hero had a dream, or vision, in which he encountered Solomon on Mount Sinai. The royal paragon of all wisdom informed him that Christianity, Judaism and Islam were simply alternative versions of a 'theocratic equality' which had been granted to the world at large through the intellect of Arabia.[1]

That an imperial statesman in the making should be fascinated with his Jewish antecedents was natural enough. The sense of three related but contrasting theisms was widely shared by his contemporaries. That he should see them all as 'colonies of Arabia', of Arabia as 'intellect', was more surprising. What underlay his reasoning, if we can be sure of reaching it, can serve well the purpose of this present chapter which is to relate the role of Muhammad in the Qur'an to those perceptions of the role of Jesus which took New Testament shape in what is known as Christology.

At first sight, it may seem an odd proceeding. Why any study of something Islam so rigorously discounts in a book primarily liable for 'Muhammad-in-the-Qur'an'? The answer has to lie in the fact that Christology belongs squarely with the same theism that Islam comprehends as entailing the Islamic dogma of the Qur'an as reviewed in Chapter 7.[2] Fusing the eternal and the temporal, in the status of a heavenly Book mediated in time and place via *Tanzil*, is what Christology does in the different idiom of the person of Jesus understood in Christhood through time and place as 'the Word made flesh'. It can be illuminating both ways to bring them reverently together as contrasting economies of divine revelation and so, in turn, differing dimensions of confessed theism.

---

[1] Benjamin Disraeli: *Tancred*, London, 1847, iv-vii.
[2] 'The same theism' here, not ignoring disparities but affirming the common dimensions, since it is only out of these that the divergent elements arise.

Disraeli's romance with an 'intellectual Arabia' affords an intriguing inspiration for doing so.

For ' dreamer as he was ' he was not alone in praise of Arabia as the matrix of everything Semitic, the singular cradle of theism. In his pioneer work on Jerusalem the historical geographer, George Adam Smith, describing 'the essential city', noted how its 'eastern tilt' 'bound over the city to eastern interests and eastern sympathies.'

> 'Hidden from the west and the north, Jerusalem, through all her centuries, has sat facing the austere scenery of the orient and the horizon of those vast deserts out of which her people came to her ... the Greeks were not at home in Jerusalem. Hellenism though not forty miles from the Levant, never made her its own.'[3]

Less poetically, Muslim sentiment, too, has wanted to derive all things Judaic from Arabian roots, stressing how Hebrew and Arabic share the same consonants, merely in different order—'A/B/R and 'A/R/B. A recent writer wants to coin the term 'Arabaic' to tell this commonalty. Palestine. Judea, Syria, Iraq are all 'the fertile peripheries' of the Arabian peninsula.[4] Earlier the Muslim thinker and polemicist, Isma'il al-Faruqi, argued that 'Arabism' was the great original that engendered everything Semitic and preserved the definitive norm of theism against which Jewry rebelled with their 'special, ethnic privilege' and from which Christianity strayed by its 'pagan divinisation', allegedly, of Jesus.[5] It is precisely the confusion in that allegation that requires this present chapter's alignment of a study in the self-consciousness of Jesus with the entire prophetology of Islam.

There can be nothing incongruous in that intention. Islam has always been at odds with Christian Christology for reasons rooted in

---

[3] George Adam Smith, *Jerusalem The Topography, Economics and History from the Earliest Times to A.D.*, London, 1907, Vol. 1, pp. 11-12.

[4] Mohammed Abu-Hamdiyyah, *The Qur'an: An Introduction*, London, 2000, p. 28. The 'peripheries' phrase is clearly much loved for it recurs again, e.g. p. 12. Arabia is more usually thought of as the 'hinterland' to 'the fertile crescent' and the Roman Province of 'Arabia'.

[5] Isma'il al-Faruqi, *'Urubah-and Religion, on Arabism*, Amsterdam, 1962, and with Lois Lamya' al-Faruqi, *The Cultural Atlas of Islam*, New York, 1986, Part 1, pp. 1-70.

theistic faith, while—in Christian perception—it is precisely theistic faith that sustains the Christology it has required. To bring this conundrum to reckoning can only be a mutually urgent exercise in the sincerity of either theism.

It proves, further, to be an intention made urgent by the Qur'an itself. Whatever, following Chapter 6, we may finally hold about *Tasliyah*, the pre-Hijrah Qur'an was always solicitous for Christian audition and, in its veneration for a virgin-born 'messenger', was eager to retrieve him from what it saw as the vagaries of divine 'Sonship'. Was there a deep wistfulness for Quranic credence on the part of previous Scriptuaries and were Christians meant when Surah 17.109 has them 'falling prostrate and weeping' at some hearing of Muhammad's words? As so often, and tantalisingly, with the Qur'an, there is no local detail or scene-sketching but the sense is vivid. The note that by hearkening they grow more humble may refer to the ethnic pride of Jewry or to Christian 'pretension' in misreading Jesus but, either way, it is eloquent of the Prophet's solicitude around what, in other terms, is the central issue of the New Testament, namely: 'What think ye of the Christ?' The tears of humility are always fitting in theology.

It follows that, whether they like it or not, Muslims with their Qur'an are duty-bound to assess Christology no less than Christians with their New Testament, are duty-bound to address the Quranic Jesus, or 'Isa. For neither can pretend to integrity if they refuse. That reckoning, either way, must include the reality of his Passion, if not as an event, certainly as an event that was intended.[6]

There is one Quranic passage where this double duty comes together, namely in Surah 4.172 where Christology is held to be excluded—indeed repudiated—on precisely the grounds on which Christology rests.

It is well known that the Qur'an always refers to 'Isa with the matronymic 'Son of Mary' with the added term *Al-Masih*. The word, however, carries no 'Messianic' sense in the New Testament way. 'Isa, the

---

[6] The New Testament can speak of the Cross of Jesus as an 'event'. It is one, however, whose 'eventfulness' the Qur'an (in Surah 4.157-58) denies. It does not deny that there was an intention that it should happen on the part of the society in which Jesus moved. The notion of its being thwarted by divine action requires that. This 'will to crucify' irrespective of its being—according to the Qur'an—aborted by the 'rapture' of Jesus is a vital part of its being an 'event'. See below and Christology.

'messenger', is 'anointed' to that preaching role without the highly-charged theme of 'salvation-hope', or divine 'saviourhood'. Yet, strangely echoing a central term of Paul's Christology, 4.172 says: 'Messiah will never disdain to be servant to Allah.' The verb with the 'never'—'scorn', 'find beneath him,' disallow himself to undergo'—is precisely the *huparkhon ouk harpagmon* of Philippians 2.6: 'He did not read his Sonship as a prize (a status, a dignity) to be clutched, retained, asserted at all costs, but rather a quality to be foregone, laid aside, emptied out *(kenosis)* as its very nature's meaning.' The parallel is exact and unmistakeable. Clearly no claim can be made for its being conscious or deliberate—manifestly not—yet the entire affinity is arresting.

Surah 4.172 is saying that because 'Messiah' is wholly 'servant', he would never refuse—as 'Son' surely would—to be wholly ready for the divine will. In Phil. 2.5-9, it is this very readiness that makes 'Isa both 'Son' and 'Messiah'. In the former a Christian 'Messiah' is being denied as one needing to be dispossessed of the pretentious pride that disqualifies him. In the latter, it is exactly a self-foregoing servanthood which constitutes the Son and the Messiah he truly is. The theological astigmatism—if we may so speak—could not be more complete.[7]

In the forming of Christian faith around the significance of Jesus the two terms 'Son' and 'servant' define and include each other. The Quranic verb *yastankif* in 4.172 holds exactly the sense of *harpagmos* in Philippians 2, that of a precious perquisite to be clutched as a trophy and never to be forfeited since doing so would be to forego one's very identity. The English term 'status' corresponds, or 'face', loss of which—either by one's own default, or by letting others filch it—would be intolerable.

It is just such a tenacity about 'status' which Muslims, by analogy from social norms of hierarchy, associate with 'sonship' and since Jesus is so entirely 'a servant' (as in the Gospels) any 'sonship' in him is unthinkable. Yet such ready foregoing of 'status' is precisely what, in the Gospels, 'sonship' does and brings, seeing that it takes 'the Son' to do so. The word is totally performative before ever it is indicative.[8]

---

[7] 'Astigmatism' is defined as when 'light rays (the same ones) are prevented from meeting at a common focus.'

[8] Borrowing the familiar distinction between language that does things, like the cry; 'Fire!' rather than words that merely state, as in 'Fire burns'.

ii

It is this sorry incidence of theological misreading of the identity of 'servant' and 'son' that makes the self-consciousness of Jesus in the Gospels so relevant to the Qur'an's indications—as we have studied them—as to the inner consciousness of the Prophet. We need, then, to see why Christian theology needed to capitalise the word 'son' into 'Son of God'. The reasons were deeply Islamic, taking us to the core of religious authority and integrity. But first, the Qur'an's concern about not 'letting Jesus be crucified' presents a useful clue to these tasks ahead.

It has often been noted that the words *shubbiha lahum* in Surah 4.157, having to do with the 'apparentness' of the crucifying of Jesus, have a striking association with the Greek verb *dokeo*, 'to seem so'—the verb which gave name to Docetism, the 2nd-century Christian heresy which denied the actuality of the Cross as happening to Jesus. The Docetics wanted Jesus 'uncrucified' because they believed Him 'divine'. The 'divine' could not suffer. Jesus' 'divinity' must at all costs be secure. Therefore his alleged crucifixion must have been in some way 'fantastical', 'only in the realm of seeming'.

The Quranic parallel is clear—however obscure the historical factors involved. The Muslim mind needed Jesus 'rescued', not allowed to suffer, because he was a 'messenger' from God and virgin-born. Though, to be sure, the threat or the fact of suffering (cf. Surah 2.87) always waited on prophetic ministry, the ignominy of crucifixion, the explicit triumph of evil perpetrators, would be something outrageous in the case of Jesus, an unthinkable compromise of the sovereignty of Allah.

The Docetics, in this context, were thus, arguably, precursors of Islam. But there was a fundamental contrast in the logic, namely as to the 'status' that was being safeguarded by having the Cross circumvented—in the one case Jesus' being 'divine', in the other his being 'a prophet'.

It is more than merely interesting that differing logics could lead to the same need for an inviolate 'servant' or 'son.' But classic Christianity overturns both logics out of one and the same conviction, namely that neither of the two categories can truly be inviolate. Given the identity of 'sonship' and 'service', the tribulation that is endemic for the latter is apposite in the former. Such is the case made in Philippians 2.5-9. The human evidence on all hands, including the Quranic scene, as to the experience of the prophets, presents a pattern of resistance and ill-will, of hostility and distraint.[9] These enmities against them are meant for their 'sentness', and—since their 'sentness' is from God—are meant for God in the sending. They become part of God's 'experience' inasmuch as the 'sending' was within His purpose. Thus they—the prophets *and* the enmities—bear marks divine.[10]

It was characteristic of nascent Christian faith to move from within the identity of 'service' and 'sonship', and from the divine 'experience' these expressed, to the conviction of 'God in Christ', so that what happened in the ministry of Jesus and came to a climax in his being crucified belonged squarely with the Lord who sent him. This was both the ground and the meaning of his 'Sonship'. In becoming persuaded of his 'Incarnation' that faith was interpreting a 'prophetology' and doing so inside a realism about humankind that all prophethood underlined by the travail it underwent.

There is a graphic way of grasping how and why a human realism leads to that quality of divine involvement in the sending of prophets which Christian faith comprehends in the mission of one who is 'the Son'. It comes in the Parable Jesus told of the tenants of the vineyard, which is 'the good earth' entrusted to managerial custody. It occurs in all three Synoptic Gospels and—as we must see later—marks a crucial point in Jesus' ministry. After the hostile reception of the 'servants' requiring what is due to their lord, it seems utter folly for him to say: 'I will send to them my son.' Why risk the beloved heir himself and put the whole enterprise at stake? For the dusty answer, cumulatively mounted, to the 'servants' means that the tenants are conspiring to possess themselves of the vineyard, repudiating the absent owner by steadily throwing into doubt his nexus with the land. Such conspiracies were familiar enough to hearers in the Palestine of Jesus' day. There is a descending spiral of mischief, of miscreance, in which the issue of dues merges into the issue of lordship.

Such are the ways of human perversity *vis-à-vis* the lordship of God.[11] In this situation, only the mission of 'the son' can assert the

---

[9] 'Distraint', for the most part, has a legal sense, but fits here as pressing an obligation to desist from an action, or compelling against the will.

[10] Using 'become' here within the incidence of human time, not as divine 'acquisition'. Cf. point made in Chapter 7.

[11] The vineyard analogy was familiar enough from, e.g. Isaiah 5.1-7, as a figure of covenant and human (Hebrew) liability for the rights of God. It is evident that Jesus' hearers recognised the force of the Parable as an implied judgement on them and their nation's history. It is important to note how it depicts the cumulative nature of evil. The first 'beating' of the messenger made more likely the second.

fundamental ownership. No 'servant' as simply a 'bidder' to 'doing the right' could fulfil that meaning or symbolise that final issue. Only 'the son' could meet and fit the ultimate challenge made, not merely against the year's yield but against the owning lord.

By that telling analogy Jesus made articulate the meaning of what the Christian faith came to identify as the divine 'Sonship' in culmination to the long Hebraic tale in prophethood of divine appeal to entrusted creaturehood. 'Servants' and 'son' were in a continuity arriving to a climax. It was a climax which answered to the full measure of human perversity and so, in turn, to the full obligation of divine sovereignty, as both were the dual theme of all prophethood. In these terms the Sonship of Jesus is one with the Self-consistency of God.

This Parable with its twin clues of the seriousness of humans in the wrong and of responding divine Lordship is a proven point of departure for a study of Jesus in his ministry and mission. But first it is well to ask why the 'son' who 'serves' becomes 'the Son' in the theme of Christian theology? The capital letter is a device which Arabic, and so the Islamic mind, does not utilise.[12] The question, bearing on: 'I will send to them my Son,' is really asking: 'What can be meant by a "pre-existent Christ?"' A full answer can only emerge out of a study of Jesus in his story. If suffices here, to note how close the reason is to the concern of Muslims about 'the pre-existent Book' which we carry over from the previous chapter.

Christians—and Muslims no more no less—need to be assured that whatever, like 'Son' or 'Word' or 'Speech', they associate with God they properly and truly do so. For, otherwise, they are liable to *shirk* in ascribing to God that which does not belong. They are heading into idolatry. In Islam, this does not mean that they have to think of a 'pre-existent Muhammad' (unless a certain deviance attracts them). It does mean, as we have seen, that they need 'a pre-existent Book'. For it is in the 'Book' category that their faith engages with the problem of the eternal in the temporal.

What is at stake here is captured in Christian credal terms in the words 'Very God of very God'.[13] It is a striking turn of phrase, inasmuch

---

[12] The device in English (and theology) has great point in making possible when a common noun becomes a proper noun, i.e. has ultimate or definitive expression.

[13] The phrase is in the Nicene Creed preceding 'begotten not made', 'truly divine and truly human'. It is anticipating the impulse to think the former could never be the latter and so precluding it. It wants to be in good faith with the hesitant by showing that their hesitancy has no grounds. It is rather like Isaiah 53.1, asking: 'Who has believed our report?' puzzling but true, nevertheless.

as 'very' is usually an adverb qualifying action, not an adjective intensifying a noun, as one might refer to 'my very eyes' (seeing an event) or 'those were his very words' (affirming a statement). Faith, when theological, is exactly in such situations where veracity is crucial and can be surely attested. The prophethood that subserves the Qur'an claims this verity as from 'a well-guarded tablet'. The Sonship of Jesus affirms, by being such, the divine authenticity Christology needs and confesses. It might even be possible to express the Qur'an's doctrine of itself by a like phrase: 'Very Qur'an of very Qur'an.'

The reason why a religious integrity requires for itself this kind of intrinsic warrant has been well expressed by the celebrated Baron Von Hügel.

> 'Religion is ever *qua* religion authoritative ... (It) is not simply to hold a view and to try and live a life ... but the holding this view and this life to proceed somehow from God himself ... The distinctive religious act is ... an unconditional surrender ... Not simply that I think it, but that I feel bound to think it, transforms a thought about God into a religious act.'[14]

Islam could hardly quarrel with that sense of things. Faith has to command me when also inviting me. If surrender to its truth is what it seeks, its invitation needs imperative grounds for addressing me. It is to deploy these that Islam has always needed, and affirmed, its Qur'an as the eternally 'well-guarded' Book. Christian faith in the Incarnate Sonship of Jesus to God is the Christian satisfaction of the same necessity.

Doubtless, it is always possible, in either case, for the sceptical outsider to say, or suspect, that the intrinsic quality of the veracious thing is no more than what the believers affirm for their own re-assurance, so that the issue of authority is still self-enclosed. Faith provides for its own requisites. Its assurance is a self-persuasion.

Let us defer answer to this charge and meanwhile take up thought on the self-consciousness of Jesus in the Gospel and how 'very God of very God' became the faith resulting communally from it.

---

[14] Baron Von Hügel, *The Mystical Element of Religion*, 2 Vols., London, 1908, pp. 46 and 72.

iii

It is a study of deep relevance to Islam, though—for the most part—Muslim scholarship has neglected it or dismissed it with a bland remark, as for example:

> 'Christianity, as it is known today is based on the Christ of faith and not on the Jesus of history. The shift from following the teachings of Jesus as an inspired person to that of the mythological Christ ...'[15]

At least, it is agreed that the crux of the matter is a person in a role and not, first, in a Book, and, further, that this role, as with Muhammad, involved oral preaching, a figure with a mission to an audience.

However, what supremely distinguishes the preaching situation in the Gospels, from a counterpart in the Qur'an at Mecca and Medina, is the crucial presence in the former and crucial absence in the latter, of the Messianic dimension. The Messianic theme in the Jesus context, from which in every sense Christology derives, reflects—as noted earlier re the Parable of the Vineyard—the deeper seriousness there of the human condition as something not radically met by hortatory guidance and ethical teaching. Whereas the Qur'an resolves the human situation by the mission of the 'messenger', the Gospel meets it in the ministry of the 'saviour'.[16]

It is a sense of things which reaches back into the Messianic hope as the emergent logic of the Hebrew story. It is this dimension which explains why revelation, for Christianity, is personal and performative, that is, in a Person and a Passion, rather than in a text and instructional.

There was, as alert Muslims know well, an intense focus on tribal identity in the Jewish tradition and in the Scriptures to which it gave rise. For the Qur'an sharply rebukes it as an unwarranted corporate egoism that made exclusive to itself the covenant of Yahweh, while

---

[15] Mohammed Abu-Hamdiyyah, *op. cit.*, note 4, p. 19. Though incidental to his main case-making, the remark does no justice to a large and scholarship-testing subject. The Christology that stems from 'the Jesus of history' is no 'mythology'.

[16] Unwarranted 'saviourism' is what Isma'il al-Faruqi alleges in '*Urubah* (note 5) and also in his *Christian Ethics*, Montreal, 1967, where, correspondingly, he belabours Christian 'peccatism', i.e., pre-occupation with 'sin'.

Christianity tried at length to persuade it to accept to be universalised in grace, though without success.[17] Nevertheless, that intense privatisation of divine calling meant that it took its own history with an ardent seriousness which, in turn, meant that it deeply registered the pain and mystery of evil. If its exodus from Egypt and its land-entry into Canaan told divine destiny, its long exile signified the burden of requital for wrong and demanded some righteous agency of correction and redemption. For, otherwise, Yahweh and covenant alike had failed. In this reading of history the great Hebrew prophets were unparalleled in a moral perception of theism and time. The excellence of their vision drew its fervour from the conviction—in one—of ethical and ethnic peoplehood.

If we comprehend that quality in Biblical story as deriving from initiating concepts of creation and human dominion—and these made special in the 'pilot' scheme they thought Israel to be—we have the inclusive hinterland of 'Messiah', the need and task of human hope. For, in that concept the 'natural history' of humankind on earth merges with the 'political history' of a 'covenant people'. Both are seen to yearn for that which will redeem their tragedy and fulfil their true destiny.

Through all its mutations, it was this 'Messianic hope' that waited in the context in which Jesus pursued his ministry. To do right by the accounts of his Gospel which the Gospels present, there is one prime consideration to keep in mind. It is that as documents in time, those Gospels are preceded by the Epistles in the New Testament, despite the fact that most readers meet them in the reverse order. It was to a community of faith, already shaped by a perceived Christhood in Jesus, that the Gospels as texts owed their existence altogether. They were both possible and necessary only because a community existed, as their *raison d'être* which, by its extension in place and time and no longer contemporary with, or local to, its origins, needed these in narrative.

It is this fact which illuminates what has so often been obscured by casual contrasting between a Jesus and the Christ of faith. The Gospels, being written from inside the Christology of those prior Epistles, could

---

[17] 'Without success' in respect of Jewry at large which after the Fall of Jerusalem and the lapse of Temple worship, fell back on to insistent Judaic identity—despite all Hellenisation—through Torah, tabernacle, Talmud and Mishnah, reinforcing ethnic and religious community. But the almost wholly Jewish apostolate that pioneered the open Jewish/Christian unison in the New Testament, was far from 'without success'. It is important to stress that it was an inner Jewish decision to belong in Christ with 'Gentiles' who, thereby, ceased to be such in any sense that mattered.

not have been written in neglect of their retrospective stance. Nor could the writers have been unaware that they would be writing about what, in its primary character with Jesus, had been—as it were—pregnant with the Christology they had come to find. They would be telling it as it was, as being 'on the way to' what only their awareness of 'the Word made flesh' would at length comprehend.

Thus the Gospel writers, while deeply affected by their Christology, told of its antecedence in Jesus in the simple, synoptic terms of its narrative inauguration. They, and their readers, were already in the world of the Epistles—the world that all would pre-suppose, the world that had moved them to learn their Jesus roots. Thus, in the New Testament, the historical priority of 'the Jesus of history' is reversed in the documentary priority of 'the Christ of faith'. The Epistles, we might say, 'write' the Gospels by way of understanding themselves.

With this in mind, we can more readily ponder the differences in the self-conscious Jesus of that story and the self-conscious Muhammad in the Qur'an. The latter—as the Qur'an itself proclaims—moves, speaks and acts as being recipient of a sequence of pre-inscribed divine texts whose mouthpiece, in parallel with them, he becomes. The former moves, lives and preaches out of an existential sense of a context which takes in the good earth as Galilee knows it, the covenant of creation universal and of the Hebraic in particular, the political environment of Roman rule and Graeco-Roman culture, and—with these—the several logics of Messianic hope. The Quranic scene, as earlier argued, is also existential (how could it fail to be?) but subject to the less than spontaneous factors present in *Tanzil*.[18]

If 'spontaneous' is the right word we need about the teaching ministry of Jesus, referring it back to the sense of a context just listed, then we trace it in the appeal to nature that controls the parables. 'Consider the lilies ...' in their silent, careless beauty; the joys and hazards of human husbandry; the country wisdom that can read the weather in the skies; and through all these in the panorama of the seasons and the face of the earth the steady sense that Jesus knew of a presiding Fatherhood. 'One there is ...' he would say 'who forgives all your sins,' 'One there is who numbers your hairs,' 'One there is who feeds the ravens' and 'you are more than they.'

---

[18] In order to do justly by Muslim conviction as to Muhammad's entire passivity in the reception of the Qur'an but also to have in view the aspects studied in Chapter 1 above.

This sense of the immediacy, the intimacy, of divine grace, central in the teaching ministry also steadily characterised the daily habits of Jesus in his living and conduct. There was a 'sonship' quality around his practice of prayer. Indeed, it was this practical 'sonship' to a 'Father in heaven' that first prompted the 'Son' language in the doctrine of the Church and undergirded it thereafter. A 'communion' with 'the Father' was the prime lesson for the disciples in their following of Jesus' active travels around Galilee. It seems to have been his example that prompted their plea: 'Lord, teach us to pray' and drew in response from him the ever familiar words of 'the Lord's Prayer'.

Its opening in 'Our Father in heaven ...' exactly breathed what he had exemplified, with that (surely) inclusive pronoun, 'our', which could be employed—as he said elsewhere—by 'whoso-ever would ...', none being barred by accident of race or place or exclusive privilege within a closed covenant that held the 'Fatherhood' somehow private to themselves.

Only so, could the triple prayer concerning 'the Name', 'the Kingdom' and 'the will' intelligibly follow, seeing that the 'hallowing', the 'eventuating' and 'the fulfilling' of these interlocking themes could only happen 'on earth'. Qualified by 'as in heaven', that theatre of their meaning could only be universal, where—as Raleigh's poem had it—'no corrupted Voices brawl, no conscience molten into gold.'[19]

The forgiveness for which we pray argues the forgiveness we are ready to offer. For, clearly, as in the Parable of 'the unforgiving servant', if we cannot answer another's penitence we have disqualified our own. If, as we well may, we take the words: 'Give us this day our daily bread'[20] in their usual sense, they breathe the same air of quiet dependence on God.

There is, however, another dimension in the Lord's Prayer to which all the foregoing has been leading, namely the often unsuspected Messianic significance of that clause as to 'daily bread' and to those other clauses about 'trial' and 'deliverance from evil'. In coming to 'the Messiah' implicit in the Lord's Prayer, it is well to let all the foregoing, as to the 'Father/Son' significance in the practice of Jesus, in his teaching and his education of the disciples, be—as it was in fact—the prelude to things

---

[19] Walter Raleigh's poem 'The Passionate Man's Pilgrimage,' cited from *The Oxford Book of 16th Century Verse*, ed. E K Chambers, 1961, p. 498.

[20] Matthew 6.11. So taken by innumerable expositors, among them the ever redoubtable John Wesley.

Messianic. It was all these factors that tended to make the person of Jesus in himself the focus of all else—the self-consciousness we set ourselves to study.

iv

Recital of the Lord's Prayer has long been either negligent or puzzled over what can be meant by 'Deliver us from evil' and 'lead us not into temptation.' The latter phrase rides oddly with the former and is 'temptation' where God needs dissuading from 'leading us'? Unease about its intelligibility should have led us to think further and suspect we have misread. Examining the clause about 'daily bread' can yield us the clue we seek.

'This day' is plain enough and has kindled many homilies about 'the day sufficing' for our cares and needs. But then why the adjective 'daily'? The repetition seems superfluous. But is 'daily' what *epiousios* means? It is so rare a word that it occurs no where else in the Greek New Testament nor, apparently, in the Greek language. 'The bread of the coming' would translate literally. Hence some have wanted to read: 'tomorrow's bread' (i.e. of 'the coming day').[21] But that would contradict its necessary 'dailiness'. 'Our future bread' would do the same.

Could it then be that 'the coming one' is the Messiah, the expected redeemer? What then could it mean to pray daily to 'have his bread'? Surely, it must mean, in paraphrase: 'Let us be eating day by day Messiah's bread whose "bread" is to do the will of Him who sent him.'[22] Were there such Messianic overtones in the task—preaching and healing—which Jesus had set himself? There is every reason to think so.

First among them is the clause about 'temptation' or, better, 'trial' in the same prayer. Popular thinking about 'Messiah' in that first century world harboured the idea that his 'coming' would be preceded by maximised evil and wrong. The logic was simple. For if 'Messiah' came and dealt with less than climactic evil, his work, being premature, would

---

[21] The sense of 'that which is ahead' is there but has to be reconciled with 'this day'. Efforts to link the words with 'manna' in Jewish tradition 'gathered at evening' are ingenious but 'off the track'.

[22] There is ambiguity here in that the prayer might be read as an impatient interest in having 'everything Messianic'—especially 'the banquet'—right now. That James and John (or was it their ambitious mother?) had this in mind is clear from Matthew 20.20-23.

lack its necessary finality. Evil would have outlived him—assuming we think of evil quantitatively.[23] Hence the expectation of 'times of woe' preceding his appearing, times, that is, of grievous 'trial', from which people might well pray to be 'delivered'.

'Do not bring us to the time of trial' (undoubtedly the right English for Matthew 6.13), read closely with: 'Give us today Messiah's bread,' would at once echo the popular fear but link it firmly with a present task. Both should be tied closely with 'Deliver us from evil.' The meaning—in one—would then be: 'Partnering Messiah's task, we are to pray against our fears of what could overwhelm us in its climax and so come into our deliverance from evil.' Read that way, the closing petitions of the Lord's Prayer are intimately one with the triple invocation that begins it.

New Testament scholarship has long known that it must live with loose ends and that 'findings' stay open to query. Such is the nature of honest faith. Some would contest reading the Lord's Prayer in the way we have but doing so will not rid them of the issues. Moreover, if it is asked how the foregoing about 'the time of trial' fits what actually transpired in Jesus' story, one point is vital. It is that we distinguish between evil, in a quantitative sense—as used earlier—and evil that is qualitative. Ideas of Messianic 'woe' had to do with what accumulated in time sequence. Hence *peirasmos* (the word in question) was translated as 'time of trial', with ages of wrong 'quantified' at last. But what of the word used of Gethsemane and Jesus' Passion—where evil is at its climax as a quality, as, in John's term, 'the sin of the world'? If so, does it not belong with Jesus praying: 'Father, let this cup pass from me, nevertheless not as I will but ...' (Matthew 26.39)? What was ultimate and climactic in the Cross of Jesus was not quantity of human wrong coming to a stop like the last stone piled on a cairn. It was the representative quality of human wrong, at work in the will to crucify via a conspiracy of forces corrupting in politics, society and religion.

It is noteworthy how this word *peirasmos* recurs in Jesus discourse in the closing weeks. 'You have been with me in my *peirasmous* (pl.)' he told his disciples (Luke 22.28). 'Pray that you enter not into temptation' he said (Luke 22.40 and 46. Cf. Mark 14.38 and Matthew 26.41) in the immediate prospect of suffering, as if underlying the meaning of what

---

[23] The point of 'quantitatively' will be clear below. The human 'evil' that culminates in the time of trial' not at a date, *when*, but in an event, *how* is qualitative.

they had always been taught to pray. The Messianic 'woes' were being cancelled as a fiction about 'the end of the age' and identified in the precincts of an agony, his and theirs. He and they were, indeed, 'brought to it' but only in the realism of a destiny that had known how urgently it prayed to have it otherwise.[24] The quality of 'the sin of the world' that it measured had the making of the travail it would be. 'Your will be done' in the prayer in the Garden was the inner logic of the invocation of 'the Father' taught in Galilee.[25]

Ought we, then, to think of the disciples praying in these terms through all the time of their following Jesus, as being the form of prayer that he himself had taught them? Was anticipation of what, in the event, his Cross proved to be, somehow with him as what a Messianic vocation would come to mean? If so, we are close to realising that about him which we seek, namely his inner self-awareness.

There are other evidences that it could well be so, beyond these clauses in the Lord's Prayer. There were those careful echoes of the image of 'the suffering servant' in Isaiah—words like 'a ransom', 'his soul an offering', 'being despised and rejected' and 'set at naught'. Scholars have suggested that such sayings register what the apostles believed, adapting a Scripture to sustain their own memory, rather than predictions Jesus ever actually made. That, however, would leave us clueless as to where their conviction came from. Searching for it, in turn, would only lead us back to the sayings as authentic. Faith has to make its judgement.

But, further, there is that pointed Parable about the husbandmen, earlier studied. It is clear that the Jewish authorities understood its import well. Prior to it, there had been a kind of watershed in the ministry at which the theme of Messiahship was central. Breaking off his itineraries in the Galilee region, Jesus withdrew with the disciples far north into Banias, or Caesarea Philippi, in what seems to have been a retrospective retreat.[26] There he enquired of the disciples what the popular verdict was.

---

[24] Jesus and the disciples were 'brought to it' differently—he in the climax of a sustained obedience, they in the bewilderment of a pained perplexity that seemed to leave them no option but 'desertion'.

[25] In both places, 'your will be done' meant action and decision, not passive acquiescence as the words so often are taken as meaning.

[26] The fullest narrative is in Matthew 16.13-23; Banias nestles under Mount Hermon at the head waters of the River Jordan—'Caesarea' in honour of the Temple Herod built for Augustus, 'Philippi' to distinguish it from the other Caesarea on the coast. The 'rock' imagery was poetically tuned to the natural feature there.

'Whom do men say that I am?', followed by the intimate question: 'And what of you?' 'What is your verdict?' When Peter volunteered the blundering reply 'The Messiah-Christ', Jesus renewed the anticipation of suffering.

This questioning can only mean that the issue was deeply present as implicit in the public ministry—brooding in hearer reaction and relevant, however confusedly, to the disciples' allegiance. Rather than mirroring a quest for prestige, still less for adulation, it reflects a genuine sounding, in perplexity, of all the implications of the preaching/healing action from which the group had purposely withdrawn, in order to return to it with clearer forward sights.

It is here, though in the differing idiom of time and place, that we encounter a feature we found so conspicuous in the *Sirah* of Muhammad, namely that the central role of message-bringing, inevitably kindles enquiry as to the 'message-bringer's' identity. The sequence from 'What is he saying?' to 'Who is he anyway?' is both natural and insistent. It was so—witness the steady altercation around it on the part of the Meccans—in Muhammad's Meccan years. In its own terms, the situation in the Gospels tallies closely.

The difference arises from the fact that Muhammad's role had to do expressly with a prophet's text, whereas that of Jesus, inside its verbal relevance, carried the Messianic overtones abiding in the Jewish milieu, so that public attention to his presence merged into communal speculation about a destiny. Nevertheless, the parallel is illuminating, insofar as we are ready to perceive it in two situations rarely or patiently compared.

For, plainly, what contributed to public posing of the question as to who Jesus was were those several features to which the Gospels witness. There was the quality of his sense of 'the Father' already noted. There was the authority with which he preached, contrasting the book citation of the learned Scribes with his: 'But I say to you ...' It is clear from how, later, Matthew's Gospel presented his teaching, that hearers saw him as somehow 'a new Moses',[27] just as Paul later found 'in Christ' a sort of 'new Torah'. The sense of liberty from dusty tomes, of spontaneous confidence with truth, and the charisma of his works of compassion all combined to focus on an identity quite inseparable from their verbal impact or their 'sign'

---

[27] Given that the evangelist is in editorial control of his presentation, there is no mistaking what he means to indicate, in chapters 5 to 7, by assembling Jesus' teaching (on many occasions and doubtless often renewed) into one whole corpus, prefaced by 'when he was seated ...' as with a gathered 'Israel', he gave them 'the new law'. The parallel with Sinai is clear.

quality. If, as was said 'The common people heard him gladly' there was more to their gladness than what hummed in their ears.

It was precisely here that great danger lay. Since—if we may phrase it so—all the foregoing was Messianically potential, how urgently it needed to be held liable for the right Messianic policy. Hence the retreat for urgent reflection in Caesarea-Philippi. What fiery material for insurrection could have been kindled out of the personality of Jesus had he been minded to release it to satisfy the ardent souls who thought their Messiah a political liberator! Yet how distant the Jesus of this teaching ministry among the common crowd stood from Essenes cloistered in the wilderness, awaiting a Messiah for the pious.

How far, too, from either sense of things was the universal note in Jesus' stance and language—those parables about 'a certain man', where the 'Jew or 'non-Jew' query was irrelevant, that anger about a Temple impeded from being 'a house of prayer for all nations'.

On every count the Messianic question was not only 'When Messiah?' nor 'Who Messiah?' but rather 'How Messiah?' where, effectively all other questions turned. The world, Jewry, the Romans, all would know the 'person' only when they saw the 'policy'. For these would define each other.

It is evident that ambiguity in the public mind beset the whole course of Jesus' career from the great Synagogue Sermon in Nazareth to the Last Supper in Jerusalem. It was one the disciples also shared. Jesus, accordingly, could only *be* 'Messiah' by simultaneously defining how Messiah should be. Did this urgent and hazardous issue explain his relative reluctance about the word itself?[28] There seems to have been a clear preference for the—still enigmatic—phrase 'the son of man.'[29] It was—so

---

[28] That the 'Messiah' term is so seldom found has led to scholarly speculation about some 'Messianic secret', namely that the seeming 'hiddeness' of the 'Messiah theme' indicates that it only came to prominence when the disciples, later, used it to identify Jesus and his meaning for them. The simple explanation suffices, namely that it was wisdom not to obtrude a term, so liable to confusion—even dangerous incitement of mob-passion—while its 'definition' in actual fulfilment was so hedged with perplexity and passion.

[29] There have been volumes of discussion as to this 'son of man' which Jesus favoured over all other terms of self-description. In simplest form it was synonymous with being 'human', as 'The son of man has nowhere to lay his head' meaning 'humanity is ever restless, not at home until ...' yet could more subtly mean that 'Messiah could never take refuge in the panaceas and politics of worldly kind' (cf. Paul in 2 Corinthians 5.16 about worldly notions of the Christ). For our present purpose, we need not linger over all the complexities of 'the son of man' attributions since the Book of Daniel.

Christian faith came to understand—out of this context of popular perplexity and of inward decision that Jesus read, in the very text and texture of his ministry, the guiding clue afforded by 'the suffering servant', namely that Messiahship could only be achieved, without 'remainders' of evil unredeemed, by the fidelity to truth and to forgiveness which suffering love fulfils.

That clue was provided by the evidence accruing from his ministry as Jesus experienced it. Its course was increasingly characterised by what a later Christian writer aptly described as 'the contradiction of sinners' (Hebrews 12. 3). Such *antilogia* (his Greek word) was, quite literally, 'against-his-word-ness', i.e. a bitter disputing of Jesus' mission and message. The religious custodians were angered by the personal authority with which he preached. They were at bitter odds with his attitude towards the 'Gentiles' and the Temple. What his followers saw as his intimacy with 'his Father', in reliance, prayer and perception of his role, was to hostile minds dangerous pretension or near blasphemy. If, as at Caesarea Philippi, Jesus had enquired about popular opinions about him, there was little need to enquire about how the 'holyminded' saw him. The 'murmuring' word Luke later used of them (Luke 15.2) suggests either the rumbling of approaching thunder or the growling of gathering conspiracy, 'seeking opportunity to destroy him' (Mark 3.9, Luke 19.47).

Keen awareness of this situation and of its accentuating menace occupied the mind of Jesus, shaping his self-consciousness and compelling the decisions required in facing it. What were those to be? There was always the option of abandoning the task, breaking off engagement with the issues and surrendering his Father's mandate. Such was the one option every fibre of loyalty and honesty dismissed. Or the structured antagonism of religious power might be answered in its own coin of institutional rivalry welding his followers into a school of insurrection, whether against the priesthood or against Rome. Or, with ardent memories of John the Baptiser still devoted to his cause, Jesus might have withdrawn to the wilderness and baptisms of personal repentance that left the city in its sins.

Any of these options could arguably have tallied with readings, or notions, of who and how Messiah would come to proof. If the actual sequel in the Gospel is the surest clue to the mind of Jesus, it must also be the final proof both of that mind and of the Messiahlship it accomplished, and so again, in turn, proof of the economy in the will of God. For it was to that economy, that arbiter in heaven, that Jesus had steadily appealed.

Everything is there in the gentle analogy by which he told it: 'The cup my Father has given me, shall I not drink it?' (John 18.11).

If we borrow from the philosophers the word existential, as describing what selves are, and do, in situations out of their own entire volition,[30] then it exactly fits the choice of Jesus that was the making of the Gospel. The situation was the patently human one of society, religion, politics, underscoring the human paradox of hope and despair, yearning and guilt—the situation his ministry brought compellingly to light. The volition, responding to what the situation presented, came from his 'sonship', his reading of his Father's mind—a reading prompted also (New Testament study would have right to say) by the haunting precedent of that strange figure of 'the suffering servant'.

For that experience of *antilogia* and the travail it brought had been reproduced in the things that befell Jesus, and—for the most part—for the same reasons, namely the unwantedness of an upstart, the disturber of a *status quo*, the pretender to divine friendship, the servant of a divine wisdom. Nor was the Isaiah writer alone in perceiving what Messianic dimensions of mission would come to undergo. There was that discerning passage in *The Wisdom of Solomon* (2.10-22) of one 'made to reprove (men's) thoughts', whom they found 'grievous to behold', and of whom they said:

> 'Let us prove what shall happen in the end of him ... let us examine him with spitefulness and torture ... let us condemn him to a shameful death ... (he) who makes his boast that God is his Father.'

Even 'Solomon', unknowingly, might have foreseen the ministry of Jesus and its culmination in the Cross. Ensuing Christian conviction about these took them for authentic and, so doing, set the clearest witness to their veracity.

But why should that clue as to the self-giving into suffering being the necessary condition of Messiahship avail either to motivate Jesus or to vindicate the ensuing Christianity? The answer begins to be formed in the climax of Biblical prophethood. Fidelity to truth is the only thing that saves society from the bane and blight of truth-suppression.

---

[30] The New *OED* has: '... a free and responsible agent determining each their own development through acts of will.'

Such fidelity is always costly. By the paying of it society is redeemed from its damnation. Truth survives, its challenged benediction preserved. Its sufferers have been its saviours. The 'faith' of 'the just' is vindicated and evil is denied its triumph.

Such the narrative of the likes of Jeremiah and that 'goodly fellowship'. The Cross fits into their pattern, but apostolic Christian faith carries the logic onward. 'The faith (fidelity)' by which 'the just live' is ripened into a larger dimension so that 'faith' (trust in) this vicarious suffering can make 'all just' through an acceptance of forgiveness—of forgiveness seen to be there for the grasping in the quality of the suffering that had borne (and so 'borne away') the wrong that made the suffering. What lends to such suffering this saving capacity belongs wholly in the forgiving patience, the gentle hope, in which it was endured. So ran, so for ever runs, the 'persuasion' of the Christian Gospel. Or, in more formal words, 'God was in Christ reconciling the world.' Theology, using them, has only formalised what Jesus had known in saying, concerning what lay before him because of the things through which he had passed: 'The cup my Father has given me.'

v

The purpose of the foregoing was not, primarily. to reach a Christian *confessio*, but rather to cast what light a Christology might throw on the selfhood of Muhammad in the conscious reception of the Qur'an.[31]

The light that is thrown has to do with the absence from the Quranic scene of the Messianism so formative for New Testament Christology, and the presence in its place of the verbal Scripture, formative, in whatever terms, for a Quranic prophetology. The 'Messiah' term comes in the Qur'an only in respect of 'Isa's title, following the matronymic *Ibn*

---

[31] All readers of the Gospels (and the rest of the New Testament) in quest of the self-consciousness of Jesus, need to be alert to what is happening in the Fourth Gospel. It is, indeed, a Gospel and is telling the Jesus-story but it is doing so in a perspective differing—for the most part—from that of the other three Gospels, called 'Synoptic'. It depicts Jesus' personality and activity from inside the standpoint of the developed faith about his identity, which it holds teaching and career destined into. This 'proleptic' standpoint makes for 'the truth of meaning' beyond, yet through, 'the gist of action'. We are given the Jesus of the story moving and speaking as 'the Christ of faith', as 'the Word made flesh.' This does not make for 'untruth' (unless the situation is misread): it offers the 'truth of the actual' when it was fully comprehended. This explains the Fourth Gospel's marked contrast with the others—though these, at rare points, have a Johannine mind-view.

Maryam. The 'office' Muhammad fills, that of *Rasul Ullah*, has its sufficient precedent in the *rusul* and *anbiya'* of long generations. He is not 'anticipated' in any other terms.[32] His ministry is 'message-bearing'. When 'message-bearing' comes steadily to mean 'adversity-bearing', intensifying through the Meccan period, it issues into necessary Medinan campaigning that counters *antilogia* by the prowess-quality of physical success. Islam holds itself rightly vindicated in those Medinan terms.

Thus two potentially comparable situations of painful malignity to divine errands on the part of human societies taught by 'word of servant' are brought to climax by contrasted patterns. What distinguishes prophetology in Islam from Christology in Christianity derives from the underlying faith-premiss concerning the economy of God and the measure of humanity in need. Islam's steady adherence to 'divine speech' as all-sufficing divine ends in human means is, therefore, entirely consistent in its disavowal of 'the Word flesh' and of the Christology which thinks and tells it otherwise.

Likewise, Christian faith is wholly consistent in taking hold of old Messianic hope and finding it realised in the Christ that Jesus became—given its more radical measure of human waywardness, a measure to which the Jesus story through his ministry brought ample evidence. In terms of contemporary faith-relations the task, surely, is to appreciate the contrasted resolutions of two situations that had the one thing in common and all else in contrast.

The one common thing was an issue waiting for its answer. Muhammad's thirteen years of Meccan adversity held in a tense ambiguity how prophetic mission would or should reckon with the heavy odds it faced. Ambiguity waited on every feature of Jesus' ministry in the tortured environment of Messianic hope. There the comparability of the inner self-consciousness ends in either case. The contrast in what, respectively, ensued dramatised the contrasting theologies of humankind and God.

---

[32] Muslim readers may expect note to be taken here of the 'foretelling' of Muhammad in Surah 61.6, where Jesus is said to have 'brought tidings of a messenger coming after' him, 'whose name is Ahmad.' Reading 'Ahmad' as 'Muhammad', the prediction is seen fulfilled in him as one whose 'coming' was 'promised', as of 'a messenger'. The passage is not, therefore, 'Messianic'. It is generally understood as echoing what Jesus, according to John 14.16, said concerning 'the Paraclete', the 'Holy Spirit' of the Christian tradition. (See fuller discussion in my: *Jesus and the Muslim.* London, 1984, Oxford, 1996, pp. 262f.

Chapter 9
THE *SIRAH* IN OUR
CONTEMPORARY SCENE

i

'It falls on deaf ears. It is as though it were offered to blind eyes. They are like people being called to from a long way off.'

The comment of Surah 41.44 on Muhammad's immediate audience in Mecca would be fitting enough for the experience of the theologian of the present century. 'There is a deafness in the ears' for many when the name of God is invoked or divine Scriptures are cited. Distances of indifference or boredom or indolence or suspicion yawn between witness and awareness, or negligence promptly silences the sound of urgent meanings. Whatever may be the popular assurances or illusions of world religions at large, theology for heart and mind is in a Meccan situation.

Knowing it so, the purpose of this final chapter is to face the vocation this imposes. The two previous chapters have shown how two theologies doing so are one in the duty but clearly not one in the criteria by which to measure what the task demands. There is point in being concerned for theology as *one* enterprise and much to be gained among us for proceeding that way. Only so, in any event, can either Muslim or Christian faiths be loyal to the unity of God. Yet distinctive theologies we certainly possess—the one turning on an 'eternal Scripture' sufficiently educating humankind into a moral régime via a structured discipline for which they may become amenable, the other turning on an eternal Christology as to 'God in Christ' inaugurating a moral régime of redemption and grace in the fellowship of a 'new people of God' to serve humankind in that Messianic meaning.

The two distinctive themes were explored in Chapters 7 and 8. That they radically diverge is the onus we have to carry forward, but only because they purport to disclose what either mean, by affirming the unity of God. When, in that same passage, Surah 41 visualises a Qur'an sent in some 'alien' language (whereas in fact it is in 'luminous Arabic'), it

180

might be thought to anticipate our current problem. 'What!'—as the Meccans would have said—'what foreign, non-Arabic, and you (s.) an Arab! ... Why were its revelations not made intelligible?' (v. 44)[1] Scriptures have always been awaiting, requiring, exegesis but exegesis usually assumes that there is a will to listen to it and that a common language readily admits of it. It is precisely these that too often our contemporary situation casually lacks or deliberately withholds.

If this is so around us—mosque and church alike—it is also massively so between us, in that Christians at large have been prejudicially related to the Qur'an and accustomed to phobias or anxieties about the Islam they perceive, while Muslims have long been largely at unstudious odds with the core meanings around 'the Christ of God'. For these reasons it is the more necessary to insist on a 'theology despite disparate theologies'. This, in turn, means wisely appreciating the mediating conception of 'divine agency' present, albeit contrastedly, in the convictions we severally hold as to the Quranic role of Muhammad and the Christ role of Jesus.

If, despite all the tensions of mind or soul, we can—for relational purposes—take up this 'agency' theme, it will at once be clear how it both embraces and bridges our disparities. So doing, it can engage us together without compromising our loyalties, assuming that these are ready to relate. It may help us into the language world of secularity.

By 'divine agency' is meant a state and vocation of 'being on behalf of God' and that, not presumptuously, but at divine behest.[2] The theme is deep in all Semitic tradition. Israel thought of itself as 'chosen people' on behalf of Yahweh in the world. They were to be 'a people dwelling alone', in the sure capacity of 'witness' to the nations, the *ethnoi* whose very exclusion from that dignity made them the more urgently in need of what Jewry had in trust.

It was from within that self-awareness, via the vicissitudes of their own historical reproach, that the Messianic concept derived, the mysterious taking-on, perhaps by a remnant, perhaps by a singular figure, of the corporately thwarted destiny. 'Messiah' would somehow retrieve and make good the vocation of the whole and so fulfil the hope in the

---

[1] Here, the literal question around a native, as against a foreign, language symbolises the much more vexing issue around how commentary by 'readers' (official or lay) registers the meaning meant, the 'intelligible' always at risk there.

[2] The two words 'behalf' and 'behest' have an intriguing relation—being 'for the sake of' and being 'at the desire of,' a 'capacity' serving the other.

'promise' to Israel. The Christian faith is so evidently heir to that 'agent' ancestry. Its very name 'Christianity' denotes it. Something of its outworking in the logic of the New Testament and the Church was traced in Chapter 8. It was a fulfilment which believed itself implementing the heritage that had formed it, precisely in freeing that heritage from its central limitation in a private ethnicism and thus extending the range of divine servanthood to 'whoso-ever willed' from all nationhoods. It became necessary to hold, and to say, that 'God had only chosen peoples,' all potentially 'bringing their glory and honour into the kingdom'.

At the centre of that ongoing 'agency'—the Christian Church in ideal self-definition—stood the 'sentness' *qua* the person of Jesus as the Christ, that we have studied in Chapter 8 and for which the terms 'Son' and 'Sonship' were required. These, sadly, have long and unnecessarily offended and alienated Muslims. We all now need a longer patience about the intention they expressed, the logic that required them.

It was not that 'agency', servanthood, a mission of 'on-behalf-ness', were falsely told or perverted into deification. It was that 'sentness', without ceasing to be such, had in Jesus become also a 'coming'—a 'coming' apt, right and necessary by the very dimensions of what 'divine agency' had in hand. (The adjectives fit both in respect of the divine nature and of the measure of the human task.) Each and every 'sentness', if we truly hold it such, argues a 'coming' on the part of God into our ken insofar as there is a rendezvous between His revealing cognisance of us and our cognisance of what and whom He 'sends'. So much is explicit in our being the Muslims or Christians that we are. God's relatedness to us and ours to God are not in doubt. Nor are they at issue whether we do, or do not, allow ourselves to hold that the themes between God and ourselves might be as critically intimate as the Gospel perceives them to be in its confession of 'the God who was in Christ.'

For the 'agency' in all revelation has to do with the vocation all humanity possesses in the common creaturehood all three Semitic faiths affirm. The 'sending' of that revelation passes, by its very mission, into a 'coming'. The Qur'an accumulates and, in its earthly comprehension, arrives to be uttered by the Prophet, in turn recited by believers and at length a complete volume ready for perpetuating calligraphy and audition. What is understood to be 'eternal' in its 'uncreated' status with God has 'arrived' in the Meccan and Medinan scene and has 'come' to be what with God it ever was. The 'agency' of Muhammad—for urgent reasons associated with Arabian paganism—needs to be confessed and recognised in patently human terms but that it has 'come' from God is insistently how it tells itself.

Despite the mystical uses of *Tasliyah*, the role of Muhammad in this 'coming' from God of the Scripture to which he is 'partnering party' precludes all divinisation of that instrumentality. There is, emphatically, no deification. Nor is there in the Christian comprehending of Jesus as God's Christ, though it has long been an Islamic misreading to think it so. The New Testament nowhere deifies Jesus.

Its logic is all the other way. It identifies in a 'sent one' what calls to be recognised as 'self-expression', a giving of meaning through a divine participating inside human experience, so that the contour of what is in and with God could be intimately with us and operatively for us in the measures of the teaching, serving, caring and suffering Christ. Islam may not yet, even never, allow that conviction to be for Muslims a criterion for those very qualities of power and majesty which its theology makes central in its piety. Or perhaps only certain Muslims may allow that it is 'truth for Christians'.[3] At all events, it is surely right to expect its being understood as a theology that, far from violating the divine unity, may be treasured as the veritable tribute to it.

There is perhaps a clue in the intriguing Quranic twin descriptives of Allah as *Al-Zahir wa-l-Batin*, 'the evident and the hidden' (Surah 57.3). Though the reality of God transcends all *idrak*, or 'conception', His 'evidences' are on every hand. 'He is closer to everything than anything else could be.'[4] Given the centrality of our human creaturehood to His earthly enterprise, that *khuluq 'azim* of Muhammad's mission, it is conceivable that the sort of 'agency' long Messianic hope awaited and which the Gospel saw realised in Jesus as the Christ, could be the human realm of His proper evidences—proper in their fitness to our human tragedy and to His divine response. If so, then 'God manifest in the flesh' (1 Timothy 3.16) could be the very 'mystery of godliness', 'closer to everything', that way, 'than anything else could be.'

---

[3] 'Dialogue' sometimes leads to acknowledgement of 'truth for' the other party—the honest conviction with which a meaning is affirmed, while still exempting that recognition from any personal assent. See, for example: ed. A H Green, *In Quest of an Islamic Humanism: Studies in Memory of Mohammed al-Nuwaihi*, Cairo, 1984, pp. 181-95.

[4] Cited from Al-Tabari by Muhammad Asad in his *The Message of the Qur'an*, Gibraltar, 1980, p. 856.

ii

But does it matter that two theologies, having so much in common in creation, creaturehood and 'messages via messengers' should want to mediate between themselves this contrast between God's agencies and evidences, Qur'an-wise and Christ-wise? Does the dubious world around attend at all to the discourse of theology, having more urgent or more entertaining things in hand? Can the differing concepts of how Allah relates to us humans, to our competences and our disenchantments, enter far into the preoccupations of the modern world with where and how we are? Theology belongs only with the punditry of those who want to indulge in empty discourse.

To be marginalized or dismissed in those terms is the first reason for refusing that fate. To be sure, the quarrels have dissuaded many and discredited the witness, but only to increase the urgency and enlarge the scope of duty. The two theisms that believe themselves in trust with 'the very language of God'—albeit, as we have seen, in their contrasted idioms of Book and person—face a variously sceptical world. It is a different scepticism from that which greeted the first Christians from a scandalised Judaic kinship of privilege or the philosophical paganism of Graeco-Roman society. It is also a different cynical 'distance' (41.44) to that so sharply contesting Muhammad's Meccan preaching.

It, therefore, needs a more subtle register than the original confident response brought by witness that felt its truth intrinsic to its identity as being in trust with 'the divine language'. For some it may still persuade and suffice, if they are still secured by an allegiance they do not interrogate. For many more such confidence belongs to a mind or a mood that do not know how lost they are. Faiths that hold they 'have God for their author'[5] are presently the victims of His 'disappearance.'

One contemporary poet assessing another of a previous generation offers a random case in point. Writing in 1994 in *Winter Pollen*, Ted Hughes saw in T S Eliot a burdened fear that 'religious institutions and rituals had ceased to be real in the old sense,' that is, the sense of being and reality as centred on God. 'They continued to exist only as forms of

---

[5] A phrase often used in Roman Catholic thinking about the Bible and very much how classical Islam thinks of the Qur'an. It must be clear, from the whole thrust of this book, that 'God as author' is a profoundly rich and laden term, not to be minted with such reductionist simplicity.

make-belief, ways of behaviour ... Man had lost the supernatural world and the meaningless had replaced its infinite consolation.'[6] Works like *The Wasteland* and *The Four Quartets*, despite their reaching towards Asian, Buddhist answers, told this 'evaporation' of old faiths' meanings. 'God in His own language' could no longer deserve serious heeding in the human world or, at best, only dubiously console it.[7] For, in Jonathan Swift's definition, 'happiness is the art of being well deceived.'

How, then, is 'There is no deity but Allah' to affirm itself in this context where its task is not the old Meccan, plural diversity of worships but the vacuity of worship itself? The burden is no longer the divinisation of nature in its sundry phenomena as haunting a superstitions mind-set. It is its desacrilisation in a mood of human loneliness or pride. To read the situation in these more than Meccan terms has also to enlist the Christian mind in the urgent, necessary response of theism, duly alert to the full measure of its current duty, How are the scruples or misgivings of contemporary agnosticism to be properly faced? How should the answer inter-associate differing, and long contending, theologies?

This is far other than the crude notion some might have of fronting up to a common enemy. For the situation is unknown if only known in those terms. Believers and theologians need a gentle solicitude for the emotional and mental distance others are from their havens, how unsure about the credentials that could satisfy.

Perhaps we could usefully begin from the human 'world of all of us' and note how we could only be present in a universe that happened to

---

[6] Ted Hughes, *Winter Pollen: Occasional Prose*, ed. W Scammell, London, 1994, p. 269. Characteristic as such moods are in 20th century writing, there is nothing exceptional about them. Cf. William Wordsworth's perception of a church-going piety anticipating Thomas Hardy's well known 'Cathedral Evensong' poem in which he sees himself an excluded 'impercipient'. Wordsworth wrote

'They came
But with one fervour of devotion meek,
I see the places where they once were known
And ask, surrounded even by kneeling crowds:
Is ancient piety for ever flown?
Alas! Even then they seemed like fleecy clouds
That, struggling through the western sky, have won
Their pensive light from a departed sun.'

Poetical Works, Oxford, 1905, ed. T Hutchinson, Miscellaneous Sonnet xxii, 'Decay of Piety', p. 256.

[7] This recurrent theme of the bankruptcy of religious faith as being merely—and deceptively—'consoling' is frequent, for example, in the writing of Iris Murdoch. See my *Islam among the Spires: An Oxford Reverie*, London, 2000, pp. 150-53.

supply our needs. We could take that obvious truism further by querying that 'happened' word—not returning to any crude 'case from design' but simply pondering the fact of a strange and wondrous tenancy in a setting so incredibly amenable to human capacities we freely bring to it. By measuring and cherishing the mystery of experienced human-ness we might turn the case for the 'absence of God' totally on its head.

Doing so this way would be a deeply Quranic and Biblical thing, a strategy outflanking alleged divine elision by the evident dependence and dependability of the human entrustment on a benign planet and a mother earth. That was always the *khilafah*/dominion perception of what humanity occupies in terrestrial domain. It has been told in earlier chapters.

What then is wrong with the much indicted notion of 'the consolation of religion'? Maybe the sense of deep significance from which it derives, as humanly known both in delight and despair, is reciprocal to a divine reality kindling its quest and answering its conviction. Have the sceptics only argued an 'absence' by first arbitrarily disqualifying the crucial tokens of a presence? We are not here tediously labouring the case for the existence of God: we are taking the measure of the God of existence. We echo the psalmist crying: 'O God Thou art my God, early (i.e., in the springs of my being) will I seek thee' (Psalm 63.1). The Qur'an is liable, to be more impersonal in the cry: 'There is none but He,' yet will also cry: 'There is none but Thou.'[8]

To be sure, our potentialities are circumscribed and the world of human history is full of daunting inequalities and gnawing questions. But there can be no sane mistaking the waiting privilege of existence in the mysterious whence and whither of our mortal span. It could be in fact only a craven cowardice that double-crosses itself by reading a sorry turpitude at the heart of reality, so that we must perpetually suspect the springs of gladness and the invitation to significance. A sense of a lively guesthood in all the guises of the world, to be greeted as the hospitality it spells, is the founding confidence of open theism. It needs to take the note and joy of it into sure conflict with the baneful and blighting counsels of secular ingratitudes. These are no more provable than spiritual intimations of existential meaning that belong with the worship of 'the God of hope'.

---

[8] In the Qur'an the formula 'He' occurs from 2.163 to 73.9—some twenty-nine times: 'there is none but Thou' is found at Surah 21.87 on the lips of Yunis (Jonah): 'there is none but I' at Surahs 16.2, 20.14, and 21.25.

Nor are they wisely argued by invoking a duty to exclude from our souls what most fitly belongs in them. To prefer to be adamantly inconsolable is to misread our very selfhood.

Samuel Taylor Coleridge was no stranger to being disconsolate and could well describe 'the poor, loveless ever-anxious crowd', repelled and wearied by nature seen as 'that inanimate cold world'. But he knew also how inward springs in the ever running theatre of the mind could transform that desolate mood.

> 'Ah! from the soul itself must issue forth
> A light, a glory, a fair luminous cloud
> Enveloping the earth—
> And from the soul itself must there be sent
> A sweet and potent voice, of its own birth,
> Of all sweet sounds the life and element.'[9]

'From the soul itself' comes the responding register of the countering reality that has evoked its birth and done so all the more surely for that will to incredulity which is always the mark of love in its awakening— whether love to God or human kin. Then the very will to find it so is the more aware of its own surprise. To talk here of suspecting bare consolation in the will to belief is to be like an artist setting up his easel for the enchantment of the landscape and brusquely deciding that his brush would be wasted on its beauty. The anti-consolationists are a sort of secular hermits dispossessing themselves of a proper heritage.

To see positive human vocation in a lively awareness of God and deliberative custody of the natural order is the deepest theme of the Meccan Qur'an. It is at the heart of its steady catechism of humanity in its grateful reading of landscape and husbandry, of precarious fertility in the ever vulnerable, ever resilient, good face of the earth.

> 'It is God who made the earth for you as an abode and the heaven for a building. He fashioned you—and how admirably!—and with good things did He provide you.' (Surah 40.64)

---

[9] S T Coleridge, *Poetical Works*, ed. E H Coleridge, Oxford, 1912, 'Dejection!'

'With truth We created the heavens and the earth, He fashioned you: well He made your frame. To Him is your destiny.' (Surah 64.2)

'People! Have in mind God's grace towards you. Is there any creator other than God who provides for you from the heaven and from the earth? There is no God but He. How then are you so prone to deception.' (Surah 35.3)

'To Him all belongs in the heavens and in the earth. Those who abide in His presence allow no pride to hold them from His worship, in which they are unwearied, praising Him night and day in praise unfailing.' (Surah 21.19-20)

'God it is who created the heavens and the earth and gives the rain that comes down from heaven, bringing forth fruits in provision for you. His ordering makes possible the ships that at His command traverse the sea. He makes the rivers also to serve you. Sun and moon, likewise in their constant orbits He recruits to your service, night and day as well. Everything you desired of Him He has brought you. If you were to add up all God's grace you would not reach the sum of it. Man is perverse and thankless.' (Surah 14.32-34)

'Have they not beheld the heavens above them, how We established and adorned it in its unbroken reach?
And the earth also We stretched out, setting thereon the mighty hills, where We made every kind of joyous thing to grow for insight and for token to every penitent servant.' (Surah 50.6-8)

Such panegyrics celebrating humankind in nature and nature for humankind are a steady refrain in the Qur'an.[10] Always there is the cry for cognisance, the fear that gracelessness may forestall it and pride or sloth break the intended communion of true guesthood with the divine

---

[10] The many celebrations of nature in the human order are brought together conveniently in my *Readings in the Qur'an*, London, 1988, and Brighton, 2000, pp. 86-117.

hospitality, or, in the earlier analogy, the ready canvas of the cherishing converse between artist and scene. The Qur'an was never in the business of depreciating the human dignity, nor of suspecting the impulse to greet the 'good faith in things' with the 'good faith of worship' born of instinctive wonder at hallowed mysteries. Modernity may think the examples of tillage and navigation, of rains and rivers, primitive and barely scientific but the principle of reverence abides when saluting nuclear fission or keyhole surgery or the webs electronic.

These, to be sure, have to do something to our simplicity of perspective but they must do nothing to diminish the subtlety of our self-awareness. 'From the soul itself must issue forth' a deeper impulse towards worship, worship in its abiding sense of liability for grateful wonder and serious devotion. Let agnostics understand that such worship is not because we are limping cripples needing it for crutch but because we are handlers of more than, otherwise, we can safely or sanely undertake. Then the plea of frailty that so often dismays the proud is known to be the human realism of the people of faith.

Nowhere is that sense of things more simply said than by 'Abd al-'Aziz al-Dirini in his *Taharat al-Qulub wa-l-Khudu'a li 'allami-l-Ghayub.*

> 'O God, my plea is my need (*hujjati hajati*—play on words, 'my argument is what is lacking in me'). All I have to offer is what is wanting in me. My intercessor is my tears, my treasure my weakness. O God, a drop of the ocean of your glory will suffice me. So have mercy on me, provide for me. Pardon me and it will be pardoned me. Breathe on my sorrow and make glad my stress and strain, by Thy mercy, O Thou most merciful of all.'[11]

It is evident enough that these are not prayers said by a technician at a laboratory bench. But they could well be. The attainments of human sciences in no way lessen the summons to the human heart. On the contrary, the business of lowliness is ever more tensely enlarged. So an alert theism, Muslim, Christian or other, must always be at pains to disabuse a self-

---

[11] 'Abd al-'Aziz al-Dirini, *Taharat al-Qulub*, Cairo, undated edition, p. 177. Al-Dirini (died c. 697 AH) was a much read Egyptian poet and Qur'an exegete, in the Sufi tradition. This work was very widely disseminated and loved.

sufficing prayerlessness of its illusion of superior mind-set, in hope of its learning 'something not yet understood'.[12]

Or to cite again 'Abd al-'Aziz al-Dirini, saying in his worship:

'O Lord, it is enough for me of honour
That I should be Your servant.
It is enough for me of grace
That You should be my Lord.[13]

So the patient war must be pursued against those whose bald measure of their own humanity leaves no room for the befriending sovereignty of God.

iii

If, in this way of *hujjati hajati* ('The case I argue is the case I am needily in'), we are rooting the claim of divine worship in the human identity told in our experience, it must mean a careful sifting of our theologies. For some of their accents and emphases have been less than honest with our human-ness, too elusively cerebral, too heavily dogmatic, too sharply assertive. While there is no dismissing the intellectual task, the greater stress must be on the impulses of heart. This is not to have thinking wishful but to have it soulful, as claim to rational provings often failed to be or which claims to revelation were prone to browbeat and subdue. The very capacity of Islamic doctrine to permit, if not often also to foster, the rich emergence of Sufism inside its revelatory assurance, is proof enough of how theology in its keenest reach is taken into 'the love of God'.

This perception of how faith responds to agnosticism in today's world wants to intensify human humility precisely in tribute to human competence—a competence in the sciences that argues an ever deeper need to forestall all self-idolatry and to 'let God be God.'

'And if our hands are glad, O God
To cast them down like flowers,

---

[12] Echoing George Herbert's 'Something understood' among his several definitions of prayer. *The English Poems*, ed. C A Patrides, London, 1974, p. 71.

[13] As note 11, p. 177.

'Tis not that we enrich Thy hands
But they are saved from ours.'[14]

Such, surely, is a present meaning of Islam. It is at the heart of the Quranic counsel of unfailing 'praise' in the several formulae of *Al-Hamdu li-Llah* or *Subhan Allah*. It has this sustained instinct to relate all things to the inclusive reference-realm of divine sovereignty. There are, to be sure, aspects of this 'submission' that have been overly craven or subdued, so condoning if not often generating attitudes of apathy and negligence or the crudities of the superstitious. Intelligent praise of divine ordering is no party to these subversions of the mandates to autonomy such praise both salutes and pursues. Advancing technology and the mind-sets it educates can be left to overtake these unhappy vagaries of the religious mind.

Seeking to turn the flank of a wonderless secularity by lively commendation of discerning theological confidence, told in gratitude, means no depreciation of present measures of sheer human competence— to which, in the middle centuries Muslim scholars and scientists massively contributed. On the contrary, it is urgent precisely because these are so monumental. The very concentration of scientific techniques, in their ever more confining specialisations, tends to have them perceived as immune from criteria external to their professional conquests. What is isolated in order to be attained can also isolate its own legitimacy from the wider obligations stemming from its fruits. Sciences physical, biological, chemical, can be so gloriously magisterial in their operations as to admit no hesitancy about their over-all social role—far from the modesty a right theology would commend.[15]

Thus, for example, a recent *Literary Companion to Science* observes:

'Science ... is free—the tribulations of technology always excepted—from the crises of purpose and identity that have

---

[14] G K Chesterton, *Collected Poems*, London, 1932, 'A Song of Gifts to God,' p. 143.

[15] This is not to obscure the deeply sensitive approach of many scientists and technicians to their impact on society. It is only to say that the concentration of expertise, its focus on necessary discipline about the exercise in hand inside the laboratory (or its equivalent) *can* be an exclusion also of vital factors properly held scientifically irrelevant. Or the social factors that have stimulated the scientific pursuit (war, armaments, sexual appetite, national will, pride, or utility) determine, if they do not control, the direction the science takes and what finance exacts its returns. That way, too, science *can* abjure being 'religious' in the sense being argued.

afflicted Western music, literature, architecture and painting.'[16]

Hardly so: for its 'freedom' is only in its methodology. It is in no way innocent of those 'crises'. It has rather sharply contributed to them, while its processes are chronically exposed to what those 'crises' portend around the destinies it steadily shapes. The social realism that should properly result should be its school of humble self-interrogation precisely because its freedom to pursue its proper goals, by its own proper liberties, is fraught with heavy consequence. Rightly seen, it becomes a deeply religious enterprise and has need to be consciously so.

If, however, theologies, Islamic, Christian or other, are to serve that fact of things truly, they need to rely more on habits of intelligent reverence than on prescripts of exhortation. To address society in neglect of the degree to which human autonomy, in and through nature, has too often *seemed* to prove the 'disappearance' of God, is to play into the hands of those who blindly or loftily think so. The claim of the law and love of God never addressed us as other than parties to a 'dominion' and, thus, partners in the enterprise creation had in view.

Still less did it proceed by threats and dire requitals inconsistent with the *khilafah* once for all granted to human status in an ordered creation, fitted into creaturehood and piloted by prophethoods reinforcing all that status meant.[17] 'Am I not your Lord?' (Surah 7.172) has always been the way God, in a right theology, waits on our surrender and summons us to gratitude. The reach of current technology, far from outdating its appeal, only demonstrates how for ever apposite is the answering cry of the human cosmos: 'Yes! We so acknowledge.'

---

[16] Walter Gratzer, ed., *Literary Companion to Science*, (Longman) London, 1989, p. xv.

[17] Such is the clear 'mind' about humankind of both Biblical and Quranic theism; Awe at awareness of privilege and entrustment in the meaning of 'the fear of the Lord'. It was in clear contrast to classic Graeco-Roman notions of 'gods' of fickleness and—sometime— malice, who begrudged what humans attained or played havoc with their options. However, there have been factors in both Biblical and Islamic theology that ill-suited the *khilafah*/dominion and fell back on tyranny, dark force, inhibiting domination and harsh threat. This is present, for example, in the Qur'an's frequent stress on retributive themes in the Qur'an. See, for example, David E Marshall, *God, Muhammad and the Unbelievers*, Richmond, 1999.

iv

If the crudities of secularity are to be out-thought and its inroads reversed, its tragedy retrieved, theology and theologians must take due knowledge of its sources. One—as we have now seen—is the stance of a self-sufficient science purporting to conclude that humans are 'on their own' and can well comport with being so, with the divine seen as an antiquated and dispensable hypothesis. The way back must be for that very 'self-sufficiency' to learn itself as still a truly religious experience of awesome liability thrown back onto a necessary humility in the presence of a large destiny in trust.

But theology, too, needs a humility of its own, refining aspects of ancient case-making and aligning its witness to the reality of God with a sharpened perception—as secularity must surely have taught it—of the right place of the human dimension in the economy of the divine. That the human role is inherently within the divine reign is central to true theism. That fact is crucial both for the secular recovery of worship and the theological devotion to that hope as its present task. It is the scene of Muhammad's *Sirah* today.

Before we go further, it will be useful in parenthesis to note how far the political realm knows, or needs to learn, the truth of 'the human role inherently set within the divine'. Ever since the Hijrah Islam has been a highly politicised religion, convinced of the due role of power in the success of faith. Yet that sense of things had its *raison d'être*, its origination, in the prior shape of a non-political preaching entirely innocent of power.[18] From Medina onwards the concept of 'theocracy'—the very rule of God obtaining in *Dawlah* ensuring *Din*—has characterised Islamic thinking, to be markedly renewed in the option for Pakistan in the predominantly Muslim areas of India at the demise of the British Raj.

Yet wherever theocracy is invoked it transpires that some human means, or organ, or agent, is always its requisite instrument. The divine rule must perforce recruit for itself some human exercise of its writ and power. Such necessary recruiting will become the sphere of human competition in a claim to divine sanction staking its right. The criteria of where and how such sanction falls will be in human debate, seeing that all eternal mandates are time-wise contestable.

---

[18] See citations from Syed Valiuddin and Abu-l-Hasan Ali Nadwi on this theme in my *Islam among the Spires: An Oxford Reverie*, London, 2000, pp. 181-83.

Recent history holds a very evident case of this tangle, the Holy Places in Jerusalem being so thorny an issue in any purpose of genuine peace between Israeli Zionism and Palestinian claims to statehood. The state-creating Resolution (for both parties in 1947) laid down internationalisation for Jerusalem as a pre-condition of all else. Though steadily ignored, even sharply denounced by Israel, the idea was revived in the autumn of 2000. The further suggestion was that the Holy Places might be 'entrusted to God'. But how? Who would 'acknowledge receipt' or play the necessary role of custody and verification?

The point of the parenthesis is clear. It is not to decry or disparage the desire to have 'all things under God', nor to ridicule the ideal that hope of theocracy enshrines. It is only that, even in its most operative realm of power and politics, it always returns back to some human 'on-behalf-ness' where divine rule and right are served or disserved. This being so politically and state-wise, it is plainly more exactingly so doctrinally and faith-wise.

Sobered by this realisation, how ought faith-custodians who think their worship and interrogate their theism tell what they have in trust, in lively awareness of how the world is, in the climate of their present heritage? For 'a trust' is how they must always understand the givens of their witness, whether 'this Qur'an—God's Speech' or 'this Christ—God's Word'. The things confessed, as what God has given us to make our reliance, are the things commended. They only belong to their faithful as being that wherein those faithful must belong with the world—the world where their faiths are called to be inclusive. What credits them is that they are witnesses. To privatise truth is to disown it.

Muslims and Christians alike are separately gathering around a formative event, the character and content of which identifies them for who they are. They hold to the act of God's initiative, whether the 'sending' of 'the glorious Qur'an' or the 'coming' of the Christ. These are, we might say, 'privileged moments' of divine giving, of divine shaping of meaning (using 'moment' as is in 'momentous' not 'momentary'). They have their antecedents without which they could not be intelligible. In the one case the long sequence of prophet-messengers, in the other the Judaic matrix of Messianic hope. Both these reach back into an understanding of the created order and human occupancy of an intelligible earth as the intention of the God of their existence.

These prefatory antecedents, however, are seen as slanted towards, and waiting for, the 'moment' that is read as their culmination and their clue. What they awaited they received. The definitive thing that fulfilled and crowned them was a manifestly different clue in either case. To call either a 'privileged act' of God is to mean—not that it is exempt from scrutiny or query (for that would be inconsistent with divine honesty)— but that it addresses responsible faith as a powerful concentration of significance, where scrutiny is brought closest to the index it needs, where both mind and heart can sense they are coming home to truth. So much at least is implied by the evidence that characterises orthodoxy in either case— not forgetting how much allegiance escapes that kind of discerning responsibility.

What is thus seen to be '*the* privileged act of God' towards our humanity and meant to denote what we should think to believe calls both for intelligent minding and heart-feeling. The situation is well expressed by the writer in Ecclesiasticus 15.14.

'He (God) Himself made man in the beginning,
And then left him free to make his own decisions.'

A footnote points out that while the Septuagint reads: '… in the hand of his own counsel', the Hebrew has: '… in the hand of his own inclination'— i.e. 'his own impulse'.[19] The true believer will be consulting both intelligence and emotion, will feel meaning as well as assess it. We will return to this unity later.

It would seem fair to see this double inner grounding of faith, as the duty both of thought and desire, coming within that *khilafah* by which in Islam humans are endowed. It certainly coincides with a Biblical 'loving of the Lord with all one's mind and soul'. This is the more so in that the Hebrew of Ecclesiasticus 15.14 adds that man was 'left open to (or handed over to) the power of his enemy.' The decisions that move towards faith and read its signposts are attended by the wiles of Satan, making them the more seriously personal.[20] The trust of creaturehood, our immediate

---

[19] *The Jerusalem Bible*, London, Standard Ed. 1966, p. 1055.

[20] The Qur'an (Surah 2.30 *et al.*) sees human creaturehood as at test in the divine conferment of *khilafah*, or rulership over the natural order because of the machinations of Satan, designed to ensnare and beguile the human 'trustee' and thus demonstrate the divine unwisdom in bestowing that dignity on so fickle a creature. Satan disavowed Allah's mandate to mankind in refusing to 'worship' Adam and that enmity 'mythologises' the principle of evil in history as an inclusive 'crisis' over humans and their amenability to 'side with Allah'. See above pp. 35-37, 146-48.

possession of it in personhood—these are the living arena of a faith's encounter with its proper credentials.

It follows that there is this double liability in the art of believing, of responding to where we are disposed to find its evidences. In being responsive to doctrine we have to be responsible for it.[21] Just as there is no political theocracy without a human means within it, so there is no revelatory authorship from God without a human readership. Just as theocracy must recruit its humans before it can exist, so the 'privileged event' of the divine-in-revelation requires human perception of its character.

v

It was certainly in this co-operative way that the first Muslims felt themselves being Allah's earthly 'theocrats', both in their believing at Mecca and in their obeying at Medina. They and their successors responded to the *Sirah* of the Prophet both in their awed reception of the Qur'an and their steady use of the *Sirah* as the quarry for tradition and so, in turn, of *Shari'ah*. Such was the extent to which they were responsible *for* as well as *to* all that the *Sirah* held for them. The question now is how Muslims emulate them and fulfil that liability in the climate now so largely indifferent—if not inimical—to that first assurance around the *Sirah*, the divinely granted locale, the Qur'an via Muhammad and Muhammad with the Qur'an.

The times being rarely serious about theology and mental habits distractedly preoccupied elsewhere, Islamic faith in sacred trust with itself needs—as Christians too have learned—to concentrate its witness around the vital essentials and, in its presentation, let incidentals be such.

To be sure, at once comes the question: How do we apply that distinction? To whom is it assigned? One believer's precious emphasis may be another's dispensable feature. Even so, that a governing focus is proper is implicit in the entire conviction about a defining event. There has to be what might be called 'the principle of inclusive simplicity'. This means letting the 'supernatural' (if we want to indulge in that highly dubious term) be located where it belongs, namely with the divine initiative—apart from which nothing—as that initiative is congruent with all that we ought to believe about the nature of God. Then we are not—

---

[21] Echoing Dag Hammarskjöld, *Markings*, trans. and ed. Leif Sjoberg and W H Auden, London, 1964, p. 156.

as a sceptical world would think—in potentially superstitious fee to bare 'miracle' but in intelligent surrender to honest meaning.

This does not imply some idea of being disembarrassed concerning elements—or participants—in our religion. There will always be need for communal inter-liability of each for all. Nor does it mean that faith is equating itself with sophistication. It means that its defining 'original' was never something fortuitous, sheer 'miracle', making consequent faith right to be credulous, and not intelligently discerning. In respect of the privileged event of the Qur'an's *Tanzil* to Muhammad must not this imply for Muslims—as previous chapters have tried to indicate—a reception of him as existentially involved and of the Book as contingent (in its temporal order) upon his active persona? For otherwise, Islamic fidelities will not be truly vested in the actualities of Mecca/ Medina, but in a subtle depreciation of the phenomenon of the Qur'an. They will also be the more prone to the rigorism or fanaticism that are born of wilfulness. The wilfulness of credulous belief will pass into that of likely bigotry. These will not be possessing the faith by its own lights and its true measure.

There is a comparable situation in what Christians hold as the Incarnation, the confession of 'God in Christ'. It was always vital that this *not* be confessed in terms that could confusedly mean that the Incarnation had never really happened, with the manhood of Jesus no more than a pretence or a charade. The occasions in the ministry of Jesus that elicited the disciples' faith are not well seen as 'miracles' for sheer astonishment but rather as 'signs', intimations of the incidence of divine love, a making 'concrete' of 'the kingdom in the midst'. It falsifies the meaning if we tend to think of 'omniscient omnipotence' walking around, dispensing largesse and sometimes seeming to ask to be informed about his 'standing'. That, apart from conjuring up crude credulity, could be no 'incarnate lover of the human soul.'

Such hollow inducements to pseudo-faith were, in any event, ruled out by the significance of' the 'overture' to Messiahship recorded of Jesus by three Gospels telling of a sojourn in the desert. For those 'temptations' had to do precisely with the rejection of sheer miracle.[22] It

---

[22] Though shared provender could 'signify' the Messianic kingdom sheer economic plenty would in no way constitute it, leaving humans—as it would—unaccused in their sins, and unforgiven of them. Nor would descending unscathed from the high pinnacle of the Temple into an astonished crowd of awe-struck spectators have any Messianic relevance or redeeming power.

was a rejection which in no way precluded the proper evidences of an active compassion, fit to convey what 'the Incarnate Word' was bringing, always on condition that men did not 'seek him because of the loaves'. That was a condition loyally applied and reinforced by the avoidance of popularity and the admonitions against publicity because 'he could not be hid'—revelation alert to its own proprieties of integrity and grace. The Incarnation could never be understood, or believed in, as 'a roadshow'. That way no 'grace and truth' could 'have come by Jesus Christ.'

There are numerous ways, whether for Muslims or Christians, whereby the principle of simplicity avails as mentor and guide. It means realising the shaping theme which then has to be understood as 'containing' all else in contributory significance and 'all else' held as 'counter-signing' that defining theme, not displacing it or being trusted in its stead.

Thus Islam turns centrally on Allah in the final 'making-His-messenger' of Muhammad—as the *Shahadah* holds, so that the Qur'an is received as 'His Book'. That is the meaning which constitutes it. Its being 'uncreated' is, for Muslim faith, the corollary by which that central thing is 'signed' as being equally of eternity and time, that is, of God and to humankind. The 'Night Journey' and the *Mi'raj* do not constitute that meaning by right of 'miracle': they corroborate and illuminate it in the role of 'sign'. Muslim faith, as the *Shahadah* tells it, stands not in linking credulity with 'miracle' but in trusting the substantial thing that stood behind the 'sign'.

Similarly, the oft-remarked 'illiteracy' of Muhammad is more religiously understood, not as some incapacity to compose, miraculously achieving superb insight and eloquence, but as a receptivity made the vehicle of a world-scripture. Then the challenge to 'produce a Surah like it' was not to argue from predictable failure but to identify what signified for faith. The 'sign' had a view, not to competition, but to comprehension. The eloquence was not in itself, what mattered, except for what it served and, serving, conveyed—which was the 'language of Allah', thus commended to receiving faith.

It is important to have the centre of gravity of a faith where we can intelligently see it belongs, rather than in ancillary features which tend to attract credulity rather than 'signify' the central reality. To believe with a ripe discernment does better justice to the sense of God over all and makes for a deeper ministry to the human spirit. It also bears fruitfully on how theology responds to secular agnostics who, all too often, are dissuaded from what they suspect is superstition or make-belief, as if faith consisted in a capacity to be self-deceived.

vi

It has to be acknowledged, however, that this 'principle of simplicity' has not always obtained in the history of religions. Indeed, all too often the grounds of popular allegiance have all been of the other kind with an instinctive trust in, if not sheer yearning for, what would not only override intelligence but positively invite credulity. There has always been a fascination for arbitrary interventions, mind-baffling phenomena with the imprint of stupendous miracle, whereby credence would be caught in magnetic fields of mystery. 'Come down from the cross and we will believe!' 'Let us see whether ...'—these have always been the patterns of impulsive belief, of desire to be forced into credence.

Such fascination was never part of any *mysterium tremendum*.[23] For it exonerated the mind from any necessary reflection and drew the will into a false surrender. 'Do they not reflect on the Qur'an?' (Surahs 4.82 and 47.24). Such reflection must clearly include all the factors we have reviewed through Chapters 1 to 5. Muhammad's *Ummi* role in the Qur'an could well be held 'miraculous' around it but not, surely, to the displacement of its contents. The Arabic and its quality were certainly its 'signs' but their role as such had to do with the Book's intelligibility to Arabs.[24] It would be odd to think that the 'signs' displaced the substance when their presence was on its behalf.

Yet conceded it must be that much faith—everywhere—has historically been near to superstition, if by superstition we mean an instinctive presumption of 'miracle' as the hallmark of religion or the acceptance of its tokens, not as directed to mind and conscience but, instead, to curiosity and the thrill of being dumbfounded.[25] For many, faith is still enjoyed or coveted in these irresponsible terms. That it should be so is a major deterrent to the secular mind which is, to be sure, prone

---

[23] The sense of 'the numinous' which Rudolf Otto identified as the deep human source of 'holy reality' in the register of the human soul, in his *The Idea of the Holy*, Eng. trans. J W Hardie, Oxford, 1923.

[24] It has to be noted that where the Qur'an speaks of 'an Arabic Qur'an' the context has to do with Arabs being in mind. Even Muhammad's detractors scoffed that it would be odd for him to bring his message in any alien tongue.

[25] The word is suggestive—'made speechless', 'confounded'.

to superstitions of its own, but for ever dismissive of those it detects in the sanctuaries of religion.

What then for contemporary custodians inside these, the people of faith and their guardian mentors and, here explicitly, the scholars and preceptors of Islam? It would seem that the *Sirah* of Muhammad, with its weight of significance carried in the Qur'an and tradition and thus into *Shari'ah*, requires to be present in the contemporary scene worthily of its long relevance. Worthily must mean the centralising of what is central so that meaning and import are possessed, less through a need to marvel, more in a will to comprehend. 'The principle of simplicity' goes back to the 'privileged event' with faith in its time-long relevance and translates and applies it now, still historically possessed of the 'dimensions of marvel' that first accompanied it, but commended now for its content's sake alone.

That intrinsic content has to be—in some measure—subject to mental/spiritual assessment in relation to how worthily it presents the divine and how realistically it deals with the human. Indeed, in the Qur'an and in the New Testament such assessment is part of the very act of 'submission' or of faith. 'Do they not reflect ...?': 'God commends His love.' What controls in its centrality must be allowed to do so: what 'signifies' on its behalf belongs in doing so, whether finding Muhammad 'illiterate' to make the Qur'an more God-bestowed, or understanding the *Mi'raj* as a physical ascent.

The point—quite outside any Islamic context—was well made by Dag Hammarsjköld in his private reverie.

> 'We act in faith—and miracles occur. In consequence we are tempted to make the miracles the ground of our faith. (Then) ... we lose the confidence of faith ... It is not derived from, nor created, nor carried by anything except its own reality.'[26]

Its 'reality' for Islam, surely, has to be the vocation, *Sirah*-given message and significant persona of Muhammad, believed on as *Rasul-Allah*. It was this that acquired—as the condition of being a viable religion—all the

---

[26] *Loc. cit.*, note 21, p. 145. As often in Hammarskjöld there may be a double meaning in this passage, so that sense here drawn from it, is not what he had in mind. But the citation certainly fits the case being made here. All turns on the words 'its own reality', whether (as here) the theme of faith, or perhaps with D H its exercise in some crisis.

other features that belief clusters around it. So to conclude is certainly part of what is necessary in facing the secular agnostic, but the reason belongs only in the integrity of a right faith.

Understood for its great positives, there need be no doubt about the bearing of what the *Sirah* 'said' to human history via the Qur'an. It had to do with human dignity as commissioned to undertake all that earth affords to mind and sense, to science and art and economy and human community, and to do so in glad response to a destiny, willed by Allah and meant for consecration. It meant taking up and taking on a sustained *khilafah* or 'dominion' in order to vindicate the divine bestowal which first put at human risk the entire enterprise of a created order. Such is the Quranic reading of our 'here-and-now-ness' as humans and such the whole concept of an accountability to God, worked out in the web of being human, and educated by the agency of prophethood perpetuated in reminder and a structured pattern of *Shari'ah*.

In their broadest terms, these elements of what Islam prescribes and enjoins can fitly commend and apply themselves in active relation to other religious faiths sharing the urgency of their vision. Doing so, however, like all else about self-confident religion, they need humility of mind and gentleness of will. There is, in all the foregoing around Muhammad's *Sirah*, no proper call for 'a globalisation of Islam and an Islamisation of the globe.'[27] Such unilateral ambition has no place if it pretends to an exclusive proprietorship of the world's sanity or of the secret of its need.

That *might* be potentially true of *islam* (small *i*—with the distinction in mind made earlier) in the sense of a human realisation of the divine Lordship through due loyalty—as we have argued—to the given trust of the earth. But it could not be true of a capitalised Islam, with its distinctive, often combative tradition, its legacies of aberration and the compromises within its retrospect. All faiths are similarly disqualified from unilateral solutions proposed for the human world. All have prior vocation to the urgent correction of themselves, as history tells them.

It is well to realise how that *islam*/Islam distinction takes us back to the most radical dichotomy inside the *Sirah* of Muhammad, namely the Hijrah from Mecca to Medina. For what *islam* holds for all— preachment, awe, summons to trust, the word in innocence, the travail in

---

[27] As, for example, in the words of 'Ali Mazrui, writing in the London-based journal *Discourse*, No. 3, Oct. 2000, on 'the receptive and the penetrative sides of Islam', p. 11.

witness—were the realities of its Meccan story. What, via Medina, became Islam was then in its sincerest[28] religious shape. It moved only in the strength of its authentic call to the reality and rule of Allah. The exclusively *religious* theme of *islam* lived in and moved from the Meccan *Sirah*.

To be sure, the migration to Medina was on behalf of that Meccan meaning, the preached *balagh* or 'message'. Yet was there not also a sense in which it was a move out of it? In Mecca, in its innocence of any sanction but its truth, it had been solely 'religious'. Its appeal was to the evidences of nature about which Muhammad was eloquent and insistent. Its case stood in the retrospect of history, the relics of long-gone tribes whose unheeding perversities had been manifestly requited. The minatory element in the preaching, the warnings that gave it urgency, could be seen to be within a deeply-felt conviction that had no other thrust but its own content. Then the *Sirah* was a monumental story of religious fervour at odds with entrenched paganism. It needed the deeply religious instincts of perseverance under adversity and sustained devotion to a given destiny.

Those qualities underwent a subtle transformation when the Medinan scene unfolded. *Balagh* in measure continued but the *Sirah* moved into another key, as explored in Chapter 5. What ensued, in being for the sake of the message, proved a pained interrogation of its nature. The wholeness of the *Sirah*—as the Mecca/Medina listing of the Surahs tells— was drawn across a Rubicon. For whole it always remained, yet now always astride a watershed after which its Meccan message found itself told in the different language of Medina. The consequences have been radical ever since. Initially the appeal of *islam* had been to a recognition of the human dignity rooted in the sovereignty of 'the magnanimous Lord', over against the wilfulness of a graceless pagan order. As gathered into the militant Islam of post-Hijrah provenance, it became a strife against treachery, a 'cause' to be 'established' against conspiracy that, of necessity, ceased to be persuasive in the first moral and hortatory terms.

Thus the *Sirah* and its role in contexting the Scripture were involved in the hardest of all religious issues, namely how truth reads— and answers—its own rejection, how it undertakes what disputes it. The path it takes reflects back on what it has in trust to say and so conditions,

---

[28] The noun *ikhlas* and the descriptive *mukhlis* are frequent in the Qur'an. The origins of the English 'sincere' are uncannily close, meaning 'unadulterated', 'unmixed with falsity', 'uncontaminated'.

for good or ill, the form of its success. Such was the decisive quality of the Hijrah, both for the *islam* that was antecedent and the Islam that ensued. The latter (Islam) would surely always account itself liable to, and for, the former *(islam)*. Indeed, it was after the Hijrah that it became thoroughly an institution with the coming of Ramadan, the emergence of a Muslim pilgrimage,[29] and the steady development of Muhammad's political stature and command-control with the imprint of successful combat. Yet, in that very process, *islam* became a different entity.

This is not to say that a religious faith, via a preaching mission, can only be true to itself under duress, in powerlessness or persecution. It is to say that when it acquires political and military sanctions—especially when these are deliberately sought and applied rather than willed on to it from outside[30]—those new factors enter into the nature and the quality of its appeal to heart and conscience. They also bring new factors of vested interest and ambition, so that these, in their institutional form, take over from the faith itself and pursue their ends by means that quickly compromise the meanings from God they had in trust.

It was, to be sure, in the post-Hijrah period that the Qur'an declared: 'There is no compulsion in religion'(2.256). What, however, should the dating signify if not that a growing empowerment was making it a necessary caveat about what was happening? There would have been no point to it in the Meccan adversity. And what were the stated grounds for disavowing all 'compulsion'? 'The right has been clearly distinguished from the false.' 'Who affirms his belief in God has laid hold on the most sure hand-hold which will never break ... God is the befriending guardian of believers.' In other words, the sufficient security of belief is in its own integrity which needs no other constraining factor and will be marred if any other is invoked or wielded.

Further, those other interests that structures of religious power come to prize in their enshrining of faith will not only jeopardise its spiritual theme. They will always fail its inner mission. There will always

---

[29] These features of institutional Islam came to the fore in the Medinan sojourn. As a focus of pagan pilgrimage Mecca enjoyed the status of a sacred *Haram*. The significance of Muhammad's 'return pilgrimage' several years after the Hijrah out of Mecca symbolised the intention to retrieve pilgrimage itself from pagan distortion and restore to Mecca its prior status as sacred to Allah alone. This could only be initiated from outside Mecca, once he had secured his alternative base.

[30] As by Constantine in the second decade of the third Christian century after original Christianity had been a harassed, powerless minority gathered communally around faith and sacrament only. The distinction has definitive meaning either way.

be reaches of inner evil which systems of power, or régimes of authority, do not avail to redeem—perhaps even fail to identify. There are burdens of human wrong, accumulations of enmity or workings of malice which only a suffering patience can reverse or overcome. Law, as 'powers', can ensure and enforce it in its proper role in society (which no sane religion would dispute), properly incriminates but cannot of itself redeem. If it remains only hortatory and admonitory it discovers its own frustration.

So it is that religious faith—to be adequate to the reality of the human situation—must have at its heart a capacity to redeem, 'to overcome evil with good', to read the world as only answered in its deepest need in terms of the love that suffers and forgives.

It was that feature which underlay the Hebraic theme of 'Messiah' when that theme found its fullest expression in 'the suffering servant', stemming from prophetic experience of how obdurate our human perversity could be. For it was the experience of a suffering vulnerability that became the supreme evidence, on the one hand of the world's wrongness, and on the other, the inescapable burden that this laid on the bearers of the divine word. Nascent Christian faith learned to recognise that central Messianic clue made vivid in the ministry of Jesus and finally confirmed in the event of his crucifixion. Then the perception of 'the suffering Messiah', achieved in the Christ-event, became the sufficient clue to the nature of God. For it was God who, all the time, had been present in that experience of His servants because of the agency they had fulfilled in His name.

May it be that the ultimate significance of the Hijrah lies in its contrast to this Biblical/New Testament 'Messiah' as the divine 'answer,' or, in Paul's language 'Christ is God's'?[31] The antecedents of that 'answer' were wholly 'Meccan' in their character, their demand on patience and tenacity, the perplexity they aroused about what ultimate upshot there could be. Muhammad's *Sirah* in Mecca had a comparable anguish of heart in the situation which had its physical resolution in the Hijrah. Its results, in turn, might be understood as a different sort of 'Messiahship' in Medinan terms—terms of 'manifest victory' and a purposive acquisition of power by which to make real 'the prosperity of His servant'.[32]

---

[31] 1 Corinthians 3.23. It is intriguing to speculate what noun the possessive waits for—'answer' fits well, 'Messiah' being how God responds to the wrongness of His human world, terms suitably realised in Jesus and the Cross.

[32] Psalm 35.27. The phrase was hauntingly used in a study of Zionism by Christopher Sykes in his *Two Studies in Virtue*, London, 1953.

It follows that the *Sirah*, in both its parts and in the sequence between them, becomes—as did the Cross in Christianity—the defining point of theological reference concerning a faith to fit the human situation.

vii

It remains to ask how this contrast can be mutually received among us in open perception, laying upon us the onus of patient theology and the task of mental and spiritual ministry to the bewilderments and anxieties in the contemporary scene. The single relevance of either faith to the matter of technology, its fruits and duties, is clear from all the foregoing. How to mediate all else sets a caring theology at the heart of inter-faith, a theology undertaken by a gentle mind-set, a leadership of patient concern for what unites and what distinguishes in our vision of God and our versions of His human world.

There is, for many Muslims, the problem of what they see as 'a Western agenda' from which they demand to be free. But we have seen how far the 'agenda' has become 'human' so that what might have been suspect as only one hemisphere's has become truly global. There is now no adequate 'frame of reference' that does not belong to us all, nor any distinctive method of solving world problems. The supreme lesson of pluralism is the summons to inter-action.

Too often the response of either to other is merely reactive. We assume what we are thereby liable to perpetuate, namely something impervious in the other always inherently unready for more than an incorrigible self. Islam is all too easily demonised by a superficial Western impatience. Muslims aver that 'a Christian perspective could give no validity to the revelation of Islam.'[33] Of that stance our study of the *Sirah* is an exercise in refutation.

For the Muslim mind the *Sirah*, as we have argued, was 'the privileged event' by which divine language addressed the human scene in the terms the Qur'an enshrined and Tradition possessed. Perhaps the most telling link between what was contemporary then and what is

---

[33] Merrill W Davies, *Knowing One Another: Shaping an Islamic Anthropology*, London, 1988, p. 66. Yoakim Moubarac, a disciple of Louis Massignon and a Lebanese Islamic scholar, argued in his *L'Islam*, Paris, 1962, that there was no final Christian position *vis-à-vis* Islam. The Christian 'options' were still very much open.

contemporary now is ours in the theme of *Jahiliyyah*, that condition of 'wilful ignorance' out of which Muhammad's mission came and which its meanings addressed.

There has been an instinct among Muslims, especially those most anxious about the perils they see its orthodoxy running, to regard the *Jahiliyyah* no longer as a period in history but as a present state of affairs—the *Jahiliyyah* of this fifteenth Islamic, this twenty-first Christian, century. Sayyid Qutb in his *Ma'alim fi-l-Tariq* wrote in 1964:

> 'Everything around is *Jahiliyyah*: perceptions, beliefs, manners and morals, culture, art and literature, laws and regulations, including a good part of what we call Islamic culture.'[34]

It would seem a strange commentary on those long centuries, wherever the onus of blame is laid. Given faith in what banishes the plain 'ignorance' element in *Jahiliyyah*, it is the obduracy, the wilfulness, the un-readiness for the claim of Allah which stubbornly abides. So much Sayyid Qutb says, indicting materialism, man-made 'devices', secular humanism, supine Muslim religious leadership and—conspicuously blame-worthy—the machinations of the West. The *hakimiyyah* which alone reverses *Jahiliyyah* is the recovered rulership of Allah.

The core of all we have reviewed of the *islam* in Mecca and the Islam of Medina, in the pivot of Muhammad's *Sirah*, where all began, turns on the amenability of the human scene—then and ever—to its summons and its sanctity. What belongs with divine omnipotence presents itself for human willingness. Faith in the one has wisely to read and faithfully to redeem what lacks in the other.

viii

That conclusion leaves our case-making with one final query. It has to do with the nature of what is now so popularly described—at least in the West—as 'dialogue' and 'inter-religion'. It has urgently to be asked whether

---

[34] *Signposts on the Way*, published in Cairo in 1981. Sayyid Qutb was a noted leader of the Ikhwan al-Muslimun, executed under 'Abd al-Nasir in 1966. See *inter alia* my *The Pen and the Faith*, London, 1985, pp. 53-71 and 174-75.

the usage is not unduly complacent and sanguine and, therefore, dubiously serving its own good intent. To be sure, the diversity of faiths is, and needs to be, deeply disturbing to the doctrinaire, as it seems to defy their assurance and disorient the solace in their unilateral vision.

The contrasted urge to 'be and let be', while happily abating bigotry and strife, must all too easily disserve the genuine responsibilities that belong with differing itself. Sincerity everywhere must share the perplexity that John Milton ascribes to his creature. Adam:

> 'Yet this I apprehend not, why to those
> Among whom God will deign to dwell on earth,
> So many and so various laws are given,
> So many laws argue so many sins
> Among them how can God with such reside?'[35]

His 'God deigning to dwell' has, of course, in mind the Christian faith in the Incarnate Word of 'God in Christ'. It is the very seriousness of that faith of his which sets the problem of plurality in the first place. To hold the latter simply sweetly and congenially tolerable is to let go the former. The dilemma is the same for all heart convictions, however malleable or absolute, pliable or resolute, their disciples conceive and live them.[36]

The issue, then, which 'dialogue' too readily excludes, is to maintain an effort patiently to relate such heart convictions to their heart counterparts in every other faith-system in order, not merely to co-exist, but to keep their contrasts steadily bearing on their mutual cares and hopes. This means keeping ever in view the interior self-debate that is present in all faiths. For none are truly monolithic, none inwardly immune from the interrogation of the agnostic world.

There are genuine ways in which the very contrasts we are sometimes exhorted to neglect belong squarely with such inwardness

---

[35] John Milton, *Paradise Lost*, Book xii, lines 280-84.

[36] Religions are sometimes classified in terms of their rigorist or tolerant attitude, both descriptives being variable, given sects and accents various. Thus Hinduism is often presented as being susceptible of great diversity and, therefore, admirably accommodating. Yet when, for example, Hinduism became identified with Indianism, it proved capable as in the case of Gandhi—of sharp intolerance. See the issues raised in S H Harper, *In the Shadow of the Mahatma: Bishop V S Azariah and the Travails of Christianity in British India*, Grand Rapids, 2000. Contrastedly, Islam is often seen as rigorist *par excellence*.

elsewhere. There is thus no sense of diversity that can be honestly absent from the will to undertake its onus as a task inseparable from faith itself and incumbent precisely where convictions are not shared. We do not relate if we have renounced ourselves on the way. Letting convictions, rather than sentiments, converse we may hopefully reconceive what we tell, to its own pure gain and serve in others reconceptions of their own. Either way the open potential is allowed to be in play, rather than precluded by an inarticulacy that fears to differ.

For, everywhere, there are things to be forsaken, negations that need to be made, in the interest of a truer comprehension. What could T S Eliot have meant by the sigh of a Magus in his *Journey of the Magi*, saying: 'I should be glad of another death'? The old king returns to his kingdom, sensing that his people are still 'clutching their gods'—gods that were once his gods also. Now in the light of Bethlehem they are altogether alien to him. He is impatient that the gods should 'die' there too, in the realm where he returns.[37]

Right 'dialogue' can bring 'clutched' things to riper mind or perceptions it may disclose transform how it once saw itself. That often hidden, always latent, prospect has to be the mediating principle of inter-religion. For

> 'All have secret fears to face
> And minds and motives to amend.'[38]

We may think ourselves invincible in our faiths but to know ourselves vulnerable is the price of integrity.

The foregoing chapters, rightly or wrongly as any reader freely judges, have meant to take this way in the bilateral case of Islam and Christianity. It may seem odd, even disloyal, in the view of some Christian readers, to understand Islam in terms like those Fazlur Rahman captured when he wrote of his faith: 'God is in intimate touch with history.'[39] Too much, such readers will say, has been conceded. The Qur'an has been handled as comprising a 'metahistory', an 'event' in which human faith has found anchorage as intrinsically veracious. The old controversy has

---

[37] T S Eliot, *Collected Poems, 1909-1962*, London, 1963, p. 110. The meaning is elusive but could certainly allow the point being made.

[38] Cyril Taylor, *Hymns for Today*, Norwich, 1983, No. 53.

[39] Fazlur Rahman, *Islamic Methodology in History*, Karachi, 1965, p. l.

been foregone when it should have been vigorously pressed. For this 'metahistory' is at odds with vital affirmations to which intelligent Christian faith is committed—the entire range of 'God in Christ' and of 'the Christ in God'. Without these how can the ensuing relation remain 'Christian'?

But these *are* present. They are not laid aside. They are the very logic in the will to think with the Islamic 'metahistory' that holds Allah 'in intimate touch with history' in terms of moral prophethood and religious polity, if not in terms of redemptive love. The 'intimate touch' is deeply contrasted but the phrase belongs with either. The Qur'an is *not* conceded in its anti- (to the Christian's 'God in Christ') quality: it is acknowledged in its *de facto* place of 'divine intimacy' in Islam's holding it so. The argument throughout has been that faiths have first to be allowed as what and how their faithful have come to receive and conceive them.

The abstract validity of their so doing is not susceptible of proof or disproof—as remains the case for all other patterns and structures of conviction. The beginning of inter-relation has to be where faiths have their origins and with what they and their origins have done with each other. This last is a process that is still continuing and its imponderables may be the liveliest part of the 'dialogue' situation. How do we begin to relate if we disallow the identity we find or *ab initio* will it to be what it would not itself recognise? That this is a reciprocal situation means also better hope that the never abandoned Christian 'divine intimacy with history' may ever be in the frame for Muslim recognition.

'With what measure you meet it will be measured to you,'[40] is reported of Jesus in the Gospel. It has been familiar enough for Christians to relate to Islam only in terms of their own verdicts as to its identity. This has too often stultified their converse. Thus, for example, John Heath-Stubbs:

'Islam may be regarded ... either as an extreme anti-Hellenic Christian heresy or as a militant de-nationalised Judaism.'[41]

Happily there are other alternatives. They have been taken here. To stay with that magisterial 'either/or' would be utterly to circumvent the hope

---

[40] Matthew 7.2, Mark 4.24, Luke 6.38. meaning—not that we should forego all critical judgement and bring naive approval but that a generous foregoing of assumed contradiction or disavowal can engender something reciprocal in others. There is point in 'justification by faith'. Attitudes that are stolidly prejudicial will find themselves reciprocated and no open transactions will ensue.

[41] John Heath-Stubbs, *Literary Essays*, ed. T Tolley, London, 1998, p. 113.

of intelligent appreciation whether of 'the divine intimacy' of the Qur'an or of the Gospel in its New Testament. For the stance sadly circumscribes the terms of reference, alike of careful honesty or a hopeful converse, by imposing their *a priori* prejudice. That there have been many such devices of estrangement in both directions is all too evident. To remove and disown them is a first principle of relation, no less vital than the 'principle of simplicity' argued earlier.

And all between us is under the constraints of current non-theism and urbane—or desperate—secularity. Writing more than a century ago in *The Fortnightly Review*, the architect of the *Dictionary of National Biography* reviewed Henry Buckle's monumental *History of Civilization*. He blamed it for

> '... that curious tone of popular complacency ... when people
> held that the Devil had finally committed suicide upon seeing
> the Great Exhibition of 1851.'[42]

The realism we all need about the hazards of our human arrogance must generate the open frankness with which alone religious diversity can be truly addressed. For when it truly knows itself, being 'religious' is precisely this posture of humility, of wonder and endless liability that belongs with 'divine intimacy' and our confessional trust with its meaning and with the shape by which we know it. Only that posture can truly relate with the shapes that others give to it and the prime task of all of them is with themselves. For religions, in their structures and their pride, have always been their own worst enemy.

---

[42] Quoted in John Kenyon, *The History Men*, London, 1993, p. 118.

NOTES ON QUR'ANIC VERSES

These are intended to indicate the weight of the Prophet's task as it eventuated into the text. They are from *Readings in The Qur'an*, London, 1988, 2nd ed. Brighton, 1999—an edition aiming to find a more contemporary and literary English, faithful to the Arabic but not slavishly so. A few points need justification.

'Recite ...' It is surely well enough known that this means giving voice to text already there in heaven with Allah. 'Read' might mean only 'peruse', and 'utter' what was the speaker's own. Neither serves well. 'Recite', however, must not imply, e.g. a poem that has been memorised. The Prophet is held to be using words, there and then 'inspired' in or to him.

'Sole liability' 'thing preached' translate what, stilted, would read 'There is not upon you except the communication.' Several times repeated, this injunction means that—as his title implies—he only brings 'the word'—*balagh*.

'Your reputation'—*dhikraka* 'how you are talked of'—refutes and dispels the sundry calumnies urged against him in the long Meccan years. In the face of hostility and denigration he needed to be affirmed as 'truly sent'.

'Distressing your very soul with grief'—*balighun nafsaka*—is a very powerful expression indicating deep stress and heaviness of heart ... 'over the way they are' *'ala atharihim*—is, literally, 'their traces'. Some go for 'footsteps', others have it read 'following after them' but that would be wrong if it meant 'going their way', i.e. in error and sin. Can it mean that Muhammad is 'on their heels' in the zeal of his message?

Most problematic among all nine extracts is 68.4—'You are on ...' or 'you are of ...' The phrase is *la 'ala khuluqin 'azim*. Many hold that *khuluq* means 'disposition' or 'character'—the way one is 'given to be'. Many exegetes take the clause to be praise of Muhammad as man and messenger. *'Azim*, however, is more properly applied to Allah. Surah 68 is 'the Surah of the Pen' and the immediate context is about 'the pen and what they write', and about Muhammad being sane and sound. Such vindication against calumny may well support a translation about his 'nature', but it could better be exalting the task in hand as 'tremendous', or 'sublime'. Need we have to choose between the one with the task or the text which the task meant? They inter-define.

QUR'AN CITATIONS
and
Biblical References

Surah	Verse(s)	Page(s)
2.	30	36, 45, 66, 120
2.	41	72
2.	87	163
2.	97	16
2.	124	131
2.	128	81
2.	135	81
2.	144	82
2.	186	23
2.	190–195	97
2.	218	97
2.	248	119
2.	256	18, 100, 115, 203
3.	3	72
3.	7	84
3.	20	71
3.	64–75	71, 80, 81
3.	79–80	134, 135
3.	140–143	98
3.	144	10, 11, 98
4.	47	72, 79
4.	82	105, 199
4.	125	81
4.	157–158	161, 163
4.	171–172	124, 161
5.	17	124
5.	38	19
5.	56	72
6.	16	55
6.	30	24
6.	33	18
6.	35	18
6.	39	43

Surah	Verse(s)	Page(s)
6.	113–115	17, 19
6.	125	64, 150
6.	161	81
7.	2	18
7.	157–158	70, 74, 76, 77
7.	172	35, 36, 41, 77, 192
8.	1	97
8.	41	92
8.	67	94, 95, 100, 105
8.	70–71	42
9.	26	120
9.	40	119
9.	103	116
10.	10	37
10.	66	18
10.	99	100
10.	105	19
11.	12–13	65
13.	37	73, 81
13.	39	139
14.	4	70
14.	32–34	188
15.	27	43
15.	96–99	16, 18, 64, 65
16.	89	40
16.	103	75
16.	123	81
16.	127	18

INDEX OF NAMES AND THEMES